The Life
&
Teachings of Christ

His Early Years and Ministry

Volume 1

Gordon Lindsay

Published by:

CHRIST FOR THE NATIONS INC.
P.O. Box 769000
Dallas, TX 75376-9000

Copyright 2012

ISBN# 978-0-89985-390-1

Cover design by Gustavo Morán

Cover illustrations by Gustave Doré

TABLE OF CONTENTS

Chapter 1
Is Jesus the Son of God? 6

Chapter 2
The Miracle of the Virgin Birth.........................……35

Chapter 3
The Mission of Christ...…43

Chapter 4
Why We Must Accept Christ..............................51

Chapter 5
The Birth of John the Baptist.........................…54

Chapter 6
The Voice Crying in the Wilderness...................63

Chapter 7
John and Jesus...71

Chapter 8
John the Baptist and Herod...............................79

Chapter 9
Death of the Prophet..85

Chapter 10
Josephus' Record of John the Baptist and Herod..............89

Chapter 11
The World When Jesus Was Born…....................101

Chapter 12
Mary, the Mother of Jesus.................................107

Chapter 13
The Birth of Jesus..116

Chapter 14
The Boy Jesus...128

Chapter 15
The Visit to Jerusalem..135

Chapter 16
Return to Nazareth..140

Chapter 17
Jesus and the Scriptures...144

Chapter 18
The Divinity of Christ..165

Chapter 19
Temptations in the Wilderness...............................172

Chapter 20
The Cana Miracle..187

Chapter 21
Cleansing the Temple...193

Chapter 22
The Night Visitor..200

Chapter 23
The Woman of Samaria. 206

Chapter 24
The Visit at Nazareth and Cana 215

Chapter 25
The Demoniac in the Synagogue...........................221

Chapter 26
Healing the Leper..233

Chapter 27
Healing the Centurion's Servant......................................239

Chapter 28
Raising the Son of the Widow of Nain............................246

Chapter 29
Simon, Son of Jona...249

Chapter 30
The Appearance of the Forerunner.............................252

Chapter 31
The Call of the Other Apostles...............................256

Chapter 32
Christ Stills the Storm......................................263

Chapter 33
Legion of the Damned...271

Chapter 34
Raising Jairus' Daughter and Other Miracles..................281

Chapter 35
The Disciples Are Commanded to Heal the Sick.............294

Chapter 36
The Pool of Bethesda...301

Chapter 37
Feeding the Five Thousand....................................314

Chapter 38
The Miracle of Christ's Walking on the Water................320

Chapter 39
Message on the Bread of Life.................................327

Chapter 1

IS JESUS THE SON OF GOD?

In attempting to write the story about the Man of Nazareth, one feels inadequate to do the subject justice. It is so far beyond human understanding—the full measure of the greatness of the God-man—that even the most gifted writer will fall short in accomplishing its purpose.

Indeed, if one had the talents of an archangel, he could hardly hope to portray in human words the full majesty of His unique character, the dignity and grace of His matchless person, and the exquisite beauty and perfection of His words. Truly, Christ stands far above the most noble of our race, for this person is none other than He, "... whose goings forth have been from of old, from everlasting" (Micah 5:2).

"Everlasting" is a word that the human mind can only vaguely grasp. "From everlasting," means Christ has existed from the eternity that is behind us. But who can even partially understand the meaning of eternity? The thought staggers the imagination and baffles the profoundest intellect.

As the inhabitant of eternity, Christ holds the position of Lord of the universe in His own right. First, because He is the Creator. "All things were made through Him, and without Him nothing was made that was made" (John 1:3). But He is Lord of all for another equally believable reason. When sin entered the universe and spoiled God's fair creation, as Paul states, "For we know that the whole creation groans and labors with birth pangs together until now" (Romans 8:22), only one Person, and He, at an extremely high cost, could repair the damage.

In this present century, scientific discovery has enlarged the scope of the known universe by a million-fold. Powerful telescopes have probed the distant galaxies, glimpsing some which lie in the most remote regions of the universe "mere fuzzy points of light." Yet, each galaxy is composed of millions of flaming suns, many perhaps attended by unknown planets, and each of them millions and in some cases billions of light years away.

To the rationalist the universe has become too big for God to have created it! The atheist reduces his philosophy to the absurdity that dead matter created itself! Instead of beginning with God and working down, he begins with dirt and tries to work up. But the honest believer, as he considers the majesty of the heavens and the boundless extent of the universe, can only in bowed reverence exclaim, "Oh God, how great Thou art!"

The Incarnation is another mystery that is beyond the capacity of the natural man to understand. It was and is a miracle. However, is not the universe itself a miracle? How did it come into existence out of nothing? Yet, the universe is here, and we must accept it. The condescension of Deity in the miracle of the Incarnation links God to man by blood. By this Christ became our elder brother. The humility of Him who emptied Himself of His pre-incarnation attributes and became a man is not less awe-inspiring than His infinite exaltation.

God became man that He might save man. Nothing is more obvious than the fact that humanity, in order to survive, must have a Savior. The wise men of this world— the philosophers and intellectuals—are preoccupied in devising ways and means for man to save himself. The utter failure of man's best efforts to become his own savior is reflected in today's appalling breakdown and disintegration of the very foundations of society.

Today, we see law and order and even the basic principles of common decency rapidly giving way to lawlessness, anarchy, crime, immorality, perversion, and wickedness, and in such a revolting nature that it shocks the sensibilities of everyone. This corruption of society proceeds at an ever-accelerating pace, although never before in our history have the masses enjoyed such affluence, or such educational opportunities. The increase of psychiatrists, psychologists, and physicians who study and work with the mind, all appear helpless to stem the tide of social disintegration. The number of emotionally disturbed persons in proportion to the population continues to increase at an alarming rate. Man has indeed proven beyond all doubt that he cannot save himself. Vainly, he tries to lift himself to Heaven on his own.

The only answer to the world's ills is Christ. In Him alone is the secret of redemption; in Him alone is the power to regenerate fallen human nature by healing and restoring the sin-sick soul.

Christ's words are both majestically simple and infinitely profound. They go with startling directness straight to the conscience of the human heart. Colonel Charles W. Lamed in his introduction to Teachings of Jesus in Subjects expresses this thought beautifully in the following words:

"In nothing else have I seen or realized so fully the sublime conciseness of this delivery of truth to man—the holy grandeur of its reticence and completeness. The great silences are no less imposing and overwhelming than the terrible directness and simplicity of its rhetoric. In both, the soul of man stands naked before its maker, abashed and conscience-stricken as in the first day of sin, but to receive instead of a curse the absolution; instead of rejection reconciliation; instead of forfeiture, the promise."

While the finite cannot hope to comprehend fully the infinite, God did not intend the purpose of the Lord's mission to the world to remain a mystery. The beauty of Christ's words is in their simplicity, as well as their profoundness. While His salvation may be hid to "the wise and prudent;" its great truths are fully open to the devout and humble. Jesus clearly brought this out in His words in Matthew 11:25-30.

"At that time Jesus answered and said, "I thank You, Father, Lord of heaven and earth, that You have hidden these things from the wise and prudent and have revealed them to babes. Even so, Father, for so it seemed good in Your sight. All things have been delivered to Me by My Father, and no one knows the Son except the Father. Nor does anyone know the Father except the Son, and the one to whom the Son wills to reveal Him. Come to Me, all you who labor and are heavy laden, and I will give you rest. Take My yoke upon you and learn from Me, for I am gentle and lowly in heart, and you will find rest for your souls. For My yoke is easy and My burden is light."

One thing is essential in understanding the mission and teachings of Christ. The hearer must first settle in his heart the all-important question of whether Jesus is actually Divine or only human, whether He is the Son of God, uniquely the only begotten of the Father, or merely a human. Jesus said, "… I am the Son of God" (John 10:36), but the proud Pharisees could not accept the revelation. On the other hand, He made His Messianic mission known to the Samaritan outcast, and she believed it.

Are Christ's claims true? Was He what He represented of Himself, or was He a pretender? This question must be answered before the study of His life can be of real value.

PROOF 1—JESUS DECLARED HIMSELF TO BE THE SON OF GOD.

"… do you say of Him whom the Father sanctified and sent into the world, 'You are blaspheming,' because I said, 'I am the Son of God?'" (John 10:36).

Through this Scripture we find that Christ Himself claimed He was the Son of God. There are some who say that Jesus was a good man, but that He was not Divine. Yet, if Jesus lied when He said He was the Son of God, He was not actually a good man, but either a deceiver or a man greatly deluded.

Notice what Jesus claimed. He said that He lived before Abraham, the father of the Hebrew and Arab nations.

"Jesus said to them, 'Most assuredly, I say to you, before Abraham was, I AM'" (John 8:58).

He was in Heaven with God before He came into the world. "What then if you should see the Son of Man ascend where He was before?" (John 6:62).

God had given His Son power to give men eternal life with God. Just before Christ was put upon a cross to die, He was praying.

> "Jesus spoke these words, lifted up His eyes to heaven, and said: 'Father, the hour has come. Glorify Your Son, that Your Son also may glorify You, as You have given Him authority over all flesh, that He should give eternal life to as many as You have given Him'" (John 17:1, 2).

PROOF 2—CHRIST'S RISE OUT OF OBSCURITY.

There is nothing in all of history or in the processes of nature to account for this man, Jesus, Who emerged out of total obscurity—this One Who is incomparably the most perfect figure of all time—One so immeasurably superior to all other humans that no comparison is possible.

During the nearly 30 years Jesus was growing up in Nazareth, Israel, there was no striking evidence that an extraordinary person was living there. The remarks of the people who lived in that village and knew Him revealed their amazement at the power displayed in His ministry in the following words:

> "And when the Sabbath had come, He began

to teach in the synagogue. And many hearing Him were astonished, saying, 'Where did this Man get these things? And what wisdom is this which is given to Him, that such mighty works are performed by His hands! Is this not the carpenter, the Son of Mary, and brother of James, Joses, Judas, and Simon? And are not His sisters here with us?' So they were offended at Him" (Mark 6:2, 3).

In other words, although his brothers and sisters had lived in the same house with Jesus for almost 30 years, they apparently had seen nothing unusual or remarkable about Him. To them, and their neighbors, He was probably above average, but that was all. Jesus occupied a position as a humble carpenter of the village Who attracted little notice.

And yet, within a three-year period, the impact of His ministry made Him the hope of not only this life, but the life to come for millions who have accepted Him into their lives. His words were carefully collected and written down to be treasured as the words of more than a man. Even though He was hated by His enemies, He captivated the hearts of millions throughout the centuries, so much so that many have considered it a supreme honor to die for Him.

PROOF 3—HE SPOKE WITH AUTHORITY AS "NO MAN SPOKE."

The first thing that impressed people about Christ when they heard Him was the authority with which He spoke. Although there was a remarkable tenderness in His voice, at the same time there was a directness about His words that pierced the hearts and consciences of men. When people heard His famous sermon, which he preached on the mountain, they were not only struck by the majestic simplicity of His words, but with the authority with which He spoke. "And so it was, when Jesus had ended these sayings, that the people were astonished at His teaching, for He taught them as one having authority, and not as the scribes" (Matthew 7:28, 29). Following this sermon on the mountain when Jesus came to Capernaum and spoke on the Sabbath day, the record says, "And they were astonished at His teaching, for His word was with authority" (Luke 4:32).

Soldiers, though hardened by their occupation, were affected as much as any by His Presence. When the religious leaders and chief priests heard about the stir His ministry was making, they sent officers to get Him. The officers returned without Him saying, "No man ever spoke like this Man" (John 7:46). When the soldiers came to arrest Jesus, after Judas had betrayed Him with a kiss, He said to the officers, "I am He." When He said this, "They drew back and fell to the ground" (John 18:6). When the army officer charged with oversight of the crucifixion witnessed the death of that noble figure hanging on the Cross, he could only exclaim, "Truly this was the Son of God" (Matthew 27:54).

PROOF 4—CHRIST KNEW THE INNERMOST
           THOUGHTS OF THE SINNER AND
           BESTOWED FORGIVENESS ON HIM.

"But Jesus did not commit Himself to them, because He knew all men, and had no need that anyone should testify of man, for He knew what was in man" (John 2:24, 25).

Sinners loved to be near Christ, not because they felt at ease in their sins, for indeed, His presence made them painfully aware of their sinfulness. But somehow, in Him, they saw a cure for their afflictions. They saw in Him their deliverance.

The Book of John speaks of a woman who met Christ while she was drawing water from a well. When she realized there was something unusual about Him, she began to ask Him questions. Christ had only to say a few words before the woman felt her soul had been exposed. Christ knew all about her, even though she had never seen Him before. He told her, "… for you have had five husbands, and the one whom you now have is not your husband; in that you spoke truly" (John 4:18).

Yet, the purity of Christ in contrast to her own sinfulness did not cause her to despair. So kind and compassionate was His voice that she saw hope and forgiveness in the very One Who had called attention to her sinful past. Her testimony to her neighbors carried such conviction that they also said, "Now we believe, not because of what you said, for we ourselves have heard Him and we know that this is indeed the Christ, the Savior of the world" (John 4:42).

Every evil deed and thought of man is open to the omnipotent God. As the Scripture says, "And there is no creature hidden from His sight, but all things are naked and open to the eyes of Him to whom we must give account" (Hebrews 4:13). Someday, men must stand before Him and give an account of their deeds, "And they were judged, each one according to his works" (Revelation 20: 13). But if our sins are confessed, they will be remembered against us no more. "If we confess our sins, He is faithful and just to forgive us our sins and to cleanse us from all unrighteousness" (1 John 1:9). "No more shall every man teach his neighbor, and every man his brother, saying, 'Know the Lord,' for they all shall know Me, from the least of them to the greatest of them, says the Lord. For I will forgive their iniquity, and their sin I will remember no more" (Jeremiah 31:34).

Christ paid the penalty for sin with His shed blood upon the cross. Today, He is our Savior; but if we do not accept Him, tomorrow He will be our Judge.

PROOF 5—CHRIST WAS THE ONLY SINLESS MAN.

Beyond the impact of His miracles, Christ impacted men because He was sinless. The only thing His enemies could charge Him with was His eating with sinners or doing good deeds on the Sabbath day. Because of their jealousy of his ability to perform miracles and to cause people to love and follow him, they wished to accuse Him of doing something wrong. When they accused Him of doing good deeds on their day of rest—the Sabbath—or eating with sinners, Jesus said to them, "Those who are well have no need of a physician, but those who are sick" (Matthew 9:12). Christ had come to help even the worst of men.

Christ being sinless is an amazing thing, for ours is a fallen race. The best of us, without Christ's redemptive power, find evil tendencies seeking place within us.

The Apostle Paul, whom God used to write much of the New Testament and who was one of the first to spread the Good News of Christ said,

> "For the good that I will to do, I do not do; but
> the evil I will not to do, that I practice. Now if
> I do what I will not to do, it is no longer I who

do it, but sin that dwells in me. I find then a law, that evil is present with me, the one who wills to do good" (Romans 7:19-21).

As a race we have all disobeyed, and therefore, sinned. So it is not possible to find a man who is perfect and without sin because everyone's root is in the human race.

PROOF 6—CHRIST PERFORMED MIRACLES NEVER BEFORE PERFORMED BY MAN.

"Since the world began it has been unheard of that anyone opened the eyes of one who was born blind. If this Man were not from God, He could do nothing" (John 9:32, 33).

The man who was healed had been born blind. The enemies of Christ tried to belittle the miracle by saying that He was a sinner. The man responded with unanswerable logic saying, "Whether He is a sinner or not I do not know. One thing I know: that though I was blind, now I see." (John 9:25). Christ proved He was unique by His power to perform miracles, even giving sight to the blind. By creating sight, He identified Himself as the Creator of the eye.

A miracle is the universal language understood by all people. When a genuine miracle takes place, it's a very convincing experience. As a result, most people believe. As Jesus said, "... but if I do, though you do not believe Me, believe the works, that you may know and believe that the Father is in Me, and I in Him" (John 10:38).

Some years ago, a minister was standing before a great audience. The people of this audience had been taught that Jesus was only a man, that He was dead in the tomb. The evangelist stood before the crowd and said, "You have been told that Jesus Christ is dead, that He was only a man. But if Christ were to come in Spirit and heal the sick, would you believe that He is alive?" The audience made it known that it was a fair test. The minister then began to pray for the sick. One person after another was healed. The blind saw, and the lame walked. When the people witnessed these things, they began to cry out, "Jesus is alive! Jesus is alive! He is healing our sick."

So it is; the great miracles which are taking place today through the power of Jesus' Name are proof that He is indeed alive today—He is the Son of God, seated at the right hand of God the Father in Heaven.

PROOF 7—JESUS PREDICTED THE FALL OF THREE CITIES: CAPERNAUM, CHORAZIN, AND BETHSAIDA.

> "Then He began to rebuke the cities in which most of His mighty works had been done, because they did not repent: 'Woe to you, Chorazin! Woe to you, Bethsaida! For if the mighty works which were done in you had been done in Tyre and Sidon, they would have repented long ago in sackcloth and ashes. But I say to you, it will be more tolerable for Tyre and Sidon in the Day of Judgment than for you. And you, Capernaum, who are exalted to heaven, will be brought down to Hades; for if the mighty works which were done in you had been done in Sodom, it would have

remained until this day. But I say to you that it shall be more tolerable for the land of Sodom in the Day of Judgment than for you" (Matthew 11:20-24).

At the beginning of the ministry of Jesus, He made the city of Capernaum, Israel, his home. Capernaum, along with Bethsaida and Chorazin, enjoyed privileges that few other cities ever had. The Son of God from Heaven dwelt in their midst. For a season, the people heard His words, saw His miracles, and rejoiced (Luke 8:40). But these cities situated in northern Galilee were at the crossroads of the great trade routes of the world. Many of the inhabitants were absorbed in sharing in the booming prosperity, and their attention was diverted to accumulating material wealth. So no deep work of repentance took place in their lives. This was the case, despite the fact that they had witnessed miracles that would have converted Sodom and Gomorrah—two cities which were destroyed because of their evil. In sorrow, Jesus warned them of their impending fate. Still, they gave no heed.

What happened to Capernaum, Bethsaida, and Chorazin? At the time of the Jewish rebellion in 65 A.D., the Fifth and Tenth Legions of the Roman army were brought in by the emperor Titus. The Romans began a systematic devastation of the country. One-by-one the cities of Galilee fell, including those cities that Jesus had denounced—Capernaum, Bethsaida, and Chorazin. Many of the inhabitants were killed in battle, and those who survived were sold into slavery.

No doubt some of the people who lived in the days when Christ preached on the shores of Galilee would still be alive and could remember His words. They could recall

His miracles. His invitation to repentance and His words of warning to those who would not repent could be remembered, too. Capernaum's prosperity and pride of life, which had been her downfall, were swept away forever. Ironically, an earthquake later shook the area and leveled all that was left standing.

Today, only one city, Tiberias, still stands on the Sea of Galilee, and it is not one of the three mentioned above. Capernaum, Bethsaida, and Chorazin have been gone for many centuries. Jesus said, "Heaven and earth shall pass away: but my words shall not pass away" (Luke 21:33). His words were fulfilled to the exact letter.

PROOF 8—JESUS PREDICTED THE FALL OF JERUSALEM TO TAKE PLACE WITHIN ONE GENERATION.

"Jesus stood on the Mt. of Olives overlooking the city of Jerusalem, Israel. The people had rejected Him as their Lord. He knew what it meant, and He wept over Jerusalem because they knew not the time of their visitation" (Luke 19:41-44).

"Now as He drew near, He saw the city and wept over it, saying, "If you had known, even you, especially in this your day, the things that make for your peace! But now they are hidden from your eyes. For days will come upon you when your enemies will build an embankment around you, surround you, and close you in on every side, and level you, and your children within you, to the ground; and they will not leave in you one stone upon another, because you did not know the time of your visitation" (Luke 19:41-44).

Jesus foresaw that this generation would pass away. "Assuredly, I say to you, this generation will by no means pass away till all things take place" (Luke 21:32). An enemy would come against the city and destroy it.

What happened? The Jews, unmindful of the warning, carried on a steady persecution of the followers of Christ, killing many and imprisoning others. Then, in the year 65 A.D., the fateful drama began to unfold. Becoming bolder, the more radical elements thought to throw off the yoke of their Roman masters. The spirit of rebellion flared throughout the country. The Jews had some preliminary successes and were encouraged to believe that they could win against those in power in Rome.

Then came the seasoned armies of Titus, who broke through the walls of Jerusalem and destroyed the city after a long siege. This event took place exactly forty years after Christ had made the prediction of its destruction, just one generation later.

PROOF 9—CHRIST FORETOLD OF THE DISPERSION OF THE JEWS.

After foretelling the siege of Jerusalem and the great catastrophe that was to overtake the city, Jesus then warned what would happen to the Jews because they had rejected Him. His followers were now to go to the whole world to acquaint all peoples with the Gospel. (Later, Christ would come back to the Jews after the other peoples, or Gentiles, had had an opportunity to accept Him.)

> "And they will fall by the edge of the sword, and be led away captive into all nations. And Jerusalem will be trampled by Gentiles until the times of the Gentiles are fulfilled" (Luke 21:24).

That is exactly what happened. The Jews, by their rejection of their Lord, had forfeited the Divine protection that God intended them to have. After the fall of Jerusalem, the survivors were herded together like animals and marched to the slave markets. The marts became so overflowing that their captors had to sell them at unbelievably low prices. Many died on the way because of the inhuman treatment they received.

From the slave markets, the Jews were dispersed throughout the nations of the world. And thus, it has been during what is called the Gentile Age. Jerusalem was demolished by the Gentiles, or non-Jewish people. Because the Jew, at long last, has returned to his homeland is startling proof that it is close to the time for Christ to return to Earth again. The Holy Scriptures said one of the signs of Christ's soon coming would be that the Jewish people would return to their country.

> "Thus says the Lord God: 'On the day that I cleanse you from all your iniquities, I will also enable you to dwell in the cities, and the ruins shall be rebuilt. The desolate land shall be tilled instead of lying desolate in the sight

of all who pass by. So they will say, 'This land that was desolate has become like the garden of Eden; and the wasted, desolate, and ruined cities are now fortified and inhabited'" (Ezekiel 36:33-35).

PROOF 10—CHRIST GAVE HIS OWN LIFE TO ESTABLISH HIS KINGDOM.

The pages of history are marked by illustrious men whose genius was dedicated to the building of great empires. Alexander the Great and his armies moved across the world in a conquering fury. In a series of battles, in which he demonstrated his remarkable generalship, he created an empire from Macedonia to the Indus River. Just before his death, Alexander is said to have wept because there were no more worlds to conquer.

Caesar conquered Gaul and became the father of the Roman Empire, and in a series of lightning maneuvers, subdued all of Europe to the Rhine River. Crossing the Rubicon against orders, he entered Rome and became its master.

All these sought to build their empires by shedding the blood of others. Christ, too, came to establish a Kingdom—one that is universal and eternal—not with the blood of others, but by giving His own life. Christ's Kingdom is not of this present age, except that it lives in the hearts of His people. Before He was crucified Christ told Pilate the Governor, "My kingdom is not of this world. If My kingdom were of this world, My servants would fight, so that I should not be delivered to the Jews; but now My kingdom is not from here" (John 18:36). And when His disciple Peter sought to prevent the officers from arresting him, Jesus said, "Put your sword in its place, for all who take the sword will perish by the sword (Matthew 26:52).

Christ is unique in that He inaugurated His own Kingdom, not by shedding the blood of others, but by giving His own blood.

PROOF 11—THE BIBLE PREDICTED ALL OF THE MAIN EVENTS THAT ACCOMPANIED CHRIST'S TRIAL, DEATH, AND RESURRECTION.

The Old Testament was written by God through prophets who lived 500 to 1500 years before Christ was born. They prophesied of His coming to Earth and of the many events in His life, even though Christ was not to be born for many more centuries.

The New Testament, inspired of God and written by devout followers of Christ, points out again and again how Christ's life fulfilled these prophesies.

Compare these Old Testament prophesies with the New Testament recordings of their fulfillment.

1. The Messiah was to be rejected (Isaiah 53:3; John 1:11).

2. He was to be betrayed by one of His dose followers and friends (Psalm 41:9; Mark 14:10).

3. He was to be sold for 30 pieces of silver (Zechariah11:12; Matthew 26:15).

4. He was to be silent before His accusers (Isaiah 53:7; Matthew 26:62, 63).

5. He was to be smitten and spat upon (Isaiah 50:6; Mark 14:65).

6. He was to bring healing to the people (Isaiah 53:4, 5; Matthew 8:14-17).

7. He was to be mocked and taunted (Psalm 22:6-8; Matthew 27:39-40).

8. He was to suffer with transgressors and pray for His enemies (Isaiah 53:12; Matthew 27:38; Luke 23:34).

9. His hands and feet were to be pierced (Psalm 22:16; John 20:27).

10. He was to be given gall and vinegar (Psalm 69:21; John 19:29).

11. His side was to be pierced (Zechariah 12:10; John 19:34).

12. They were to cast lots for His garments (Psalm 22:18; Mark 15:24).

13. He was to be buried with the rich (Isaiah 53:9; Matthew 27:57-60).

14. He was to be a sacrifice for sin (Isaiah 53:5, 8, 10, 12; John 1:29).

15. He was to be raised from the dead (Psalm 16:10; Matthew 28:9).

16. He was to ascend to the right hand of God (Psalm 68:18; Luke 24:50, 51).

17. He was to come again (Daniel 7:13, 14; Matthew 24:30).

Who can see all these detailed prophesies and their amazing fulfillments and not be compelled to say as the centurion of old did, "Truly this was the Son of God" (Matthew 27:54).

PROOF 12—HE PROVED HE WAS THE CHRIST BY HIS POWER OVER DEATH.

Many great men have lived and made their mark on the world; but they all died, and their bones still lie in their graves. Go to the Invalides in Paris, and you may gaze at the sealed tomb of Napoleon. His body is still there. In Westminster Abbey in London, one can see the Mausoleum that holds the bodies of many of Britain's greatest statesmen and kings. Their bones are all there moldering in the dust. Mount Vernon is the last resting place of George Washington, who was called the "Father of the United States." His body still lies sleeping in the tomb. One-by- one, the world's greatest men and women, as well as its small, have been laid away in their resting places.

Only in one place in the world is there an empty tomb. That is in Jerusalem, at the foot of Calvary where they once laid the Lord Jesus. It was there, three days later, that the angel appeared to some of His followers who had come to the tomb to weep. The angel said, "Why do you seek the living among the dead? He is not here, but is risen! Remember how He spoke to you when He was still in Galilee …" (Luke 24:5, 6).

Jesus said that one sign should be given to that generation: "'A wicked and adulterous generation seeks after a sign, and no sign shall be given to it except the sign of the prophet Jonah.' And He left them and departed" (Matthew 16:4). "For as Jonah was three days and three nights in the belly of the great fish, so will the Son of Man be three days and three nights in the heart of the earth" (Matthew 12:40).

It was this sign that gave faith and inspiration to the Early Church. Jesus had overcome, once and for all, the problem of death. It was upon this incontestable victory over death "And with great power the apostles gave witness to the resurrection of the Lord Jesus. And great grace was upon them all" (Acts 4:33).

PROOF 13—CHRIST HAD A NEW BODY

"And after eight days His disciples were again inside, and Thomas with them. Jesus came, the doors being shut, and stood in the midst, and said, 'Peace to you!' Then He said to Thomas, 'Reach your finger here, and look at My hands; and reach your hand here, and put it into My side. Do not be unbelieving, but believing'" (John 20:26, 27).

Christ was the first man who lived on Earth and received a resurrected body. The risen Christ was more than a spirit; He had a real body. In appearance, it looked like the same body He had previously had; although now, it also bore the marks of the nails in His hands and feet and the spear in His side. The voice was recognizable. When Jesus said, "Mary," to one of His followers, she knew the speaker was her Lord. Except when Jesus wished to conceal His identity, He was instantly recognizable as the "same Jesus." He could eat food as He did when He was in His physical body. He could walk at the same natural pace as others did. Yet, when He desired, He could travel instantaneously to distant places or go through locked doors.

At the resurrection, Christ's body underwent a fundamental change—a glorification. It was able to accommodate itself in two worlds. In other words, the Lord could adapt Himself to physical laws, but He was not bound by them.

The revelation we have of Christ's resurrection is relevant to the Christian. One day, when Christ returns to Earth, we shall receive a body like His, for it is written, "We shall be like him." It will be a distinctively different body from the one we have now. It will not be subject to disease, aging, or physical limitations. And like Christ, we shall never die.

PROOF 14—THE VERY CITY WHERE CHRIST WAS
         TO BE BORN WAS NAMED 500 YEARS
         EARLIER.

The only person in the world to have the city where He was to be born, identified centuries before the event took place, was Jesus Christ. Micah, the Jewish prophet, writing 500 years before Christ's birth tells of One "… whose goings forth have been from of old, from everlasting" (Micah 5:2). This is clearly a reference to Christ, Who as the Son of God had existence previous to His earthly birth. He was the God-man Who was to be born in the little town of Bethlehem, Israel.

> "But you, Bethlehem Ephrathah, Though you are little among the thousands of Judah, Yet out of you shall come forth to Me The One to be Ruler in Israel, Whose goings forth are from of old, From everlasting" (Micah 5:2).

Only a few weeks before His birth, Jesus' mother, Mary, was in the city of Nazareth. She had no plans to travel the many miles south to Bethlehem.

However, the Roman Emperor Augustus made a decree that the entire world should be taxed. Mary, to obey the law, even in the advanced stages of pregnancy, was forced to make the long trip south with her husband, Joseph, in order to register in the city of their lineage. Reaching Bethlehem after a tiring journey, Mary found she was about to give birth to her firstborn. Her husband, Joseph, looked about desperately for some kind of shelter. To his dismay, every room in the inn had been taken, and no other lodging was available. He finally found a manger among the animals to serve their purpose.

In these crude surroundings the greatest event of history occurred—the birth of the Christ-child. The inhabitants of Bethlehem, except some humble shepherds to whom angels appeared (Luke 2:8), were quite unaware of the stupendous event that had taken place in their little city. Yes, the child Jesus was born in the city of Bethlehem where the prophet Micah said He would be born some five centuries earlier.

PROOF 15—THE PROPHET ISAIAH PREDICTED 800 YEARS BEFORE CHRIST'S BIRTH THAT HE WAS TO BE BORN OF A VIRGIN.

Some eight centuries before Jesus was born, the prophet Isaiah predicted that a virgin should be with child, and they should call His name Immanuel.

"Therefore the Lord Himself will give you a sign: Behold, the virgin shall conceive and bear a Son, and shall call His name Immanuel" (Isaiah 7:14).

And that is exactly what took place. The angel Gabriel appeared to the Virgin Mary and told her that she would be with child by the Holy Ghost (Luke 1:26, 38). Her espoused husband, Joseph, became aware of her condition, and at first, not wanting to bring her to public shame, thought about secretly divorcing her. But the angel appeared in a dream to him saying, "Joseph, son of David, do not be afraid to take to you Mary your wife, for that which is conceived in her is of the Holy Spirit. And she will bring forth a Son, and you shall call His name JESUS, for He will save His people from their sins" (Matthew 1:20).

Christ was the only person in the world who was born of the Holy Spirit, rather than the will of man. Indeed, the fact is, that if Christ were the Son of God, He had to be born of the Holy Spirit. He could not have partaken of man's fallen state and still be our Savior. Christ was truly more than a man; He was the only begotten of the Father (God)

(John 3:16). We shall speak further on this important subject of the virgin birth in another chapter.

PROOF 16—THE TIME OF CHRIST'S BIRTH WAS PROPHESIED NEARLY 500 YEARS BEFORE HE WAS BORN.

The most amazing fact about Christ's birth was that prophecy predicted the very time He was to be born! From "the going forth of the commandment to restore and to build Jerusalem" there should be 69 weeks.

> "Know therefore and understand, That from the going forth of the command To restore and build Jerusalem Until Messiah the Prince, There shall be seven weeks and sixty-two weeks; The street shall be built again, and the wall, Even in troublesome times. And after the sixty-two weeks Messiah shall be cut off, but not for Himself; And the people of the prince who is to come Shall destroy the city and the sanctuary. The end of it shall be with a flood, And till the end of the war desolations are determined" (Daniel 9:25, 26).

Daniel, a prophet, living five centuries before Christ, prophesied under the inspiration of God what the future held. He said that Jerusalem, which lay in ruins, would be rebuilt. Another prophet, Isaiah, had even foretold who would give the command to rebuild Jerusalem—King Cyrus.

"Who says of Cyrus, 'He is My shepherd,

And he shall perform all My pleasure, Saying to Jerusalem, 'You shall be built,' And to the temple, 'Your foundation shall be laid'" (Isaiah 44:28).

History records that the time the command was given for the restoration of the city of Jerusalem was during the reign of Cyrus.

Therefore, the question is, when does history say that the command from Cyrus to restore and to rebuild Jerusalem was actually given? The commonly accepted chronologies, which differ slightly among themselves, show the event to be just before the 5th century B.C. Bible chronology sets the time in the 5th century. One thing is certain—the order to rebuild Jerusalem took place either shortly before or shortly after the beginning of the 5th century B.C. There is no question about this.

With this being the case, then according to the prophet, Daniel, "69 weeks" (of years later), after the order to restore Jerusalem was given, the Messiah was to come. The question we ask then is—Did the Messiah appear to Israel at this time?

Before we answer this question, we must define what is meant by "69 weeks." Plainly, they could not be weeks of 24 hour days, since 69 weeks of days is 483 days, or only a little over a year. In Bible times, a period of seven years, instead of seven days, is often spoken of as a "week" of years. This is shown in the Book of Genesis, where Laban bargains with Jacob to work another "week" or "seven other years" for his younger daughter, Rachel.

"Fulfill her week, and we will give you this

one also for the service which you will serve with me still another seven years" (Genesis 29:27).

If a "week" of years is truly seven years, then 69 weeks would be 483 years. So the prophet Daniel is saying, 483 years after the commandment went forth to rebuild Jerusalem, the Messiah would appear. Now, when did these 483 years run out? Did the Messiah, the Son of God, appear about 5 centuries later? The only Messiah the world knows anything about did appear at about that time—and that was Jesus Christ! Although the secular calendar may be a little uncertain, so that the date is not exactly determined, nevertheless, it definitely indicates the years as running out at the era of Christ!

Could we want a more irrefutable proof that Jesus is the Messiah? Could a fraud possibly have been perpetrated? And if so, how could it? Daniel's prophecy was given many centuries earlier. Either the Messiah had to appear at that time, or Daniel's prophecy was false.

The fact is that Jesus came at that time, and His life had such an impact upon the world that people from many nations have accepted Him as the Christ!

PROOF 17—CHRIST'S DEATH AS THE MESSIAH WAS PREDICTED 900 YEARS BEFORE HIS BIRTH.

There is another very remarkable thing about the prophecy of Daniel 9:24. The children of Israel supposed that when the Lord, whom the Jewish people called the Messiah, came, He would set up His Kingdom on Earth.

Even the apostles of Christ assumed that He would at once sit on His throne (Acts 1:6-7). But instead, the prophecy says that the Messiah was to be "cut off, or killed" (Daniel 9:26). Rather than setting up a visible Kingdom at His first coming, prophecy declared He was going to die! There is only one person in history that could possibly have fulfilled that prophecy at that time, and He was Jesus Christ.

Even the kind of death the Messiah was to die was foretold. His hands and feet were to be pierced—that is by crucifixion. The psalmist, David, 900 years before it happened, said:

> "For dogs have surrounded Me; The congregation of the wicked has enclosed Me. They pierced My hands and My feet ..." (Psalm 22:16).

So not only the manner of His birth was predicted, but also the kind of death—many centuries in advance. Only the One Who created this world could make these prophecies come to pass in this fashion.

PROOF 18—CHRIST GIVES A PERSONAL EXPERIENCE TODAY.

Beyond all else, the teachings of Christ satisfies, because the believer possesses Christ Himself. Jesus promised He would come into our life, change it so that we become a new creature, take away our burden of sin, and bring peace into our hearts. Some may argue against Christianity, but they cannot argue against the experience Christ gives. Christ is able to do what no other religion can—live and dwell within the human heart, and so it has been that way through the ages. Millions have accepted Christ and found Him to be their all-in-all.

Again and again, the Apostle Paul referred to his own experience of meeting Christ on the Damascus Road (Acts, chapter 9). It was the high point of his preaching. He told and retold the story wherever he went. The Christian's personal experience with Christ is the greatest proof of His reality. It is as the poet wrote:

"He lives, He Jives.
Christ Jesus lives today.
He walks with me, and talks with me,
Along life's narrow way.
He lives, He lives,
Salvation to impart.
You ask me how I know He lives.
He lives within my heart."

Chapter 2

THE MIRACLE
OF THE VIRGIN BIRTH

In the first chapter, we presented 18 different areas that prove that Jesus Christ is the Son of God. The central pillar of the whole matter of His peculiar origin and destiny is His virgin birth—a circumstance which is uniquely different from the birth of any other human being. While Christ received His human nature through His mother Mary, His God identity came by reason of His supernatural conception by the Holy Spirit. The whole structure of Christianity must rest upon this fact. For while the Scriptures teach that Christ took upon Himself human nature through His mother, Mary, nevertheless, if He Himself had been of the seed of the first man Adam, He would have been a fallen human being, just like every other human being. This would have made Him completely unable to redeem humanity. Thus, the first foretelling of Christ's birth was written 1500 years before by Moses referring to Christ as "the seed" of the woman, rather than the seed of Adam, or man (Genesis 3:15).

This fundamental truth is so important to the Gospel that we present, according to Scripture, seven great proofs of the virgin birth of Christ.

1. Christ's Name in prophecy was called

Immanuel, "God with us." The words of Isaiah clearly declared that this Immanuel should be born of a virgin:

"Therefore, the Lord himself shall give you a sign; Behold, a virgin shall conceive, and bear a son, and shall call his name Immanuel" (Isaiah 7:14).

2. Matthew 1:23, declares that the birth of Jesus of the Virgin Mary was a fulfillment of prophecy.

3. Joseph, the betrothed husband of Mary, discovered before they were married that she was with child. While pondering over what he should do about the matter, the angel of the Lord appeared to him and informed him that which had been conceived in Mary was not of man, but by the Holy Ghost (Matthew 1:18-20).

4. Luke 1: 26-38, tells of the angel's visit to Mary during which she was acquainted with the fact that she would be with child by the Holy Ghost, and this child would be called the Son of God.

"Then Mary said to the angel, 'How can this be, since I do not know a man?' And the angel answered and said to her, 'The Holy Spirit will come upon you, and the power of the Highest will overshadow you; therefore, also, that Holy One who is to be born will be called the Son of God'" (Luke 1:34-35).

5. It was prophesied that the Messiah would comefrom the line of David, the greatest king to have ever ruled the Hebrew nation (2 Samuel 7:12-19; Psalm 89:3, 4, 34-37; 132:11; Acts 2:30; 13:22, 23). These prophecies were fulfilled in Jesus as the son of Mary, who came from the line of David. Joseph, Mary's espoused husband, also of the royal line, was the legal father, but not the real father.

Jesus, the King of Israel, could not be the son of Joseph in the flesh because of a very significant circumstance. Joseph was a descendant of Jeconiah, a particularly wicked king. Because of the extreme flagrance of his evil reign, God said that none of the seed of Jeconiah (also called Coniah) would sit upon the throne of David, forever.

"O earth, earth, earth, Hear the word of the Lord! Thus says the Lord: 'Write this man down as childless, A man who shall not prosper in his days; For none of his descendants shall prosper, Sitting on the throne of David, And ruling anymore in Judah'" (Jeremiah 22:29-30).

If, therefore, Jesus had actually been the son of Joseph in the flesh, He would not have been eligible to the throne of David. Thus, Christ was the son of David through the maternal line of His mother, Mary.

Through His mother, Jesus became eligible to the throne of David. Thus, we see the amazing preciseness of the fulfillment of the Scriptures. Another supporting fact of His birth that is mentioned in the Scriptures shows its significance to anyone who would doubt the virgin birth of Christ.

6. Jesus was not the son of David on His paternal side is further proved by the words of Jesus Himself. He asked the Pharisees whose son they thought Christ was. They answered, "The son of David," thinking of him as a direct seed of David through a human father. Jesus then asked them a question as to why David, speaking in the inspiration of the Spirit, called Him Lord.

"He said to them, 'How then does David in the Spirit call Him 'Lord,' saying: 'The Lord said to my Lord, "Sit at My right hand, Till I make Your enemies Your footstool?"' If David then calls Him 'Lord,' how is He his Son?'" (Matthew 22:43-45).

The Pharisees could not answer this question. It certainly seemed inappropriate for David in the Spirit to call a descendant of his, after his own flesh, his Lord.

It is also evident from these words that Jesus knew of His own virgin birth, and that He was not the son of Joseph.

7. Finally, the Early Church fathers believed in the virgin birth. The belief is found in the Apostles' Creed, which was written in the early part of the second century.

Great historians, such as Ignatius, believed in the virgin birth and defended it against the heresies of his time. Origen, in his treatise against Celsus and Tertullian, believed it and defended the virgin birth.

We need not lengthen the list of names, since the Early Church fathers consistently put themselves on record as believing in the virgin birth. Moreover, they vigorously defended it against all heresies.

The virgin birth is the clue as to why Christ is uniquely different from all of mankind. He was a man through His mother Mary; but He was also God by being conceived by the Holy Spirit and not of the will of the flesh.

THE BOY JESUS BEGINS HIS MINISTRY

Joseph, Mary's husband, was a righteous man according to the Scriptures. He worked in his carpenter shop, supporting his large family to the best of his ability. As Jesus and His brothers grew older, they joined Joseph in the shop. Jesus, as a youth, made no real impression upon the community.

His early years, although he wasn't ministering yet, were not idle years. During the day, He was busy in the carpenter shop. In the evening, He would study the Holy Scriptures. And so the years went by as Jesus came to full manhood. Finally, there came a day when Jesus laid down His tools and left the carpenter shop forever.

He went to the river Jordan where an evangelist, who was strangely dressed in a girdle of camel's hair, was preaching a fiery message of repentance. It was John the Baptist. Against John's initial protest, Jesus was baptized by him in the waters of the Jordan. Then, being led by the Spirit, He disappeared into the wilderness for 40 days and 40 nights, fasting and meditating in solitude.

When His ministry made its first impact upon the nation, "He came back to Nazareth, where He had been brought up. And as His custom was, He went into the synagogue on the Sabbath day, and stood up to read. And He was handed the book of the prophet Isaiah. And when He had opened the book, He found the place where it was written:

'The Spirit of the LORD is upon Me,
Because He has anointed Me
To preach the gospel to the poor;
He has sent Me to heal the brokenhearted,

To proclaim liberty to the captives
And recovery of sight to the blind,
To set at liberty those who are oppressed;
To proclaim the acceptable year of the
LORD.'

"Then He closed the book, and gave it back to the attendant and sat down. And the eyes of all who were in the synagogue were fixed on Him. And He began to say to them, "Today this Scripture is fulfilled in your hearing." So all bore witness to Him, and marveled at the gracious words which proceeded out of His mouth. And they said, 'Is this not Joseph's son?'"

Indeed, it appears from John 7:3-5 that His own half-brothers in the flesh were not convinced of His Divine mission. Later on, however, they did come to believe He was Who He said He was and received the Baptism of the Holy Spirit on the Day of Pentecost. (Acts 1:14).

Even though Jesus may have announced to the people in Nazareth Who is really was, His ministry did not begin His hometown. "But Jesus said to them, "A prophet is not without honor except in his own country, among his own relatives, and in his own house" (Mark 6:4).

Then reappearing once more, He began a ministry in Capernaum, located on the Sea of Galilee. There among the growing population of the cities that lay along the Galilean shore, Christianity was cradled. And in three short years, not only did He rock that nation, but the entire world.

Along the sea, Jesus began the proclamation of the Good News of the Gospel. At times, He preached from a small ship, anchored a short distance from the shore. On other occasions, He ministered upon the neighboring hills that overlooked the sea. There in Galilee, the multitudes came to hear Him teach and to be healed of their diseases. The Good News of His work soon spread far and wide. It was a ministry, which in a few months' time, resulted in thousands of followers.

Chapter 3

THE MISSION OF CHRIST

After Christ appeared, it became possible to compare the actual events of His life with the passages in the ancient writings, which confirms our faith that the One Who came was indeed the Christ, the Son of the living God.

There was another purpose served in Christ's being born at the time that He was. The world by this time had been given an opportunity to establish its abilities and accomplishments. Many notable results were achieved in the development of the varied civilizations. It was proved that man could rise to higher levels in the arts and refinements of life, in literature, in painting, and in architecture; but in the religious realm, it became a matter of fact that man could not rise unaided to God. While man had made great progress in other fields of knowledge — improving his intellect, refining his tastes, and correcting his manners — he could not purify his heart. The sad story of the moral decline of mankind is drawn by the inspired writer in Romans 1:21-23:

> "... because, although they knew God, they did not glorify Him as God, nor were thankful, but became futile in their thoughts, and their foolish hearts were darkened. Professing to be wise, they became fools, and changed the glory of the incorruptible God into an image

made like corruptible man—and birds and four-footed animals and creeping things."

Man must have a Savior; he is not complete in himself. Contrary to the speculations of blind philosophers who contend that there is an upward force in nature, the sad fact is, that apart from Christ, the inherent tendency in the moral life of mankind is downward.

So although Christ performed many marvelous miracles, it was not His purpose to just heal the afflicted who might become sick again or to raise the dead that they might die again. Nor did He come to satisfy the physical appetite of men, only to have them hunger again. He came into the world to give men the bread of life—bread for the soul, so that they might never again hunger or thirst for those things of the spirit. He came to preach a Gospel of repentance to save men from their sins, so they should never perish.

When people told Him stories of the Governor Pilate, who had slain certain people, or of the tower of Siloam that had fallen on 18 others, causing their death, He said,

"And Jesus answered and said to them, 'Do you suppose that these Galileans were worse sinners than all other Galileans, because they suffered such things? I tell you, no; but unless you repent you will all likewise perish'" (Luke 13:2, 3).

Not all accepted Christ's call to repentance. There, in northern Galilee, where the great trade routes crossed, the temptation was strong for men to become deeply engaged in the pursuit of riches and the material things of life. Although the inhabitants seemed deeply impressed with Christ's miracles and His teachings, the drive or motivation to get their part of the prosperity outweighed, for most of them, Christ's call to "forsake all and follow me."

Some who were drawn by Christ's appeal followed Him for a time; but they had not fully counted the cost. A rich young ruler came to Him and asked, "Good Teacher, what good thing shall I do that I may have eternal life?" Looking with deep emotion at the earnest young man, Jesus told him to leave his riches and follow Him. (Matt. 19:16-22). Christ said this because He knew the young man loved his money more than God. Sadly, the youth turned away; the price was too great for him to pay. He wanted to give God second place in his life.

> "Then Jesus, looking at him, loved him, and said to him, "One thing you lack: Go your way, sell whatever you have and give to the poor, and you will have treasure in heaven; and come, take up the cross, and follow Me." But he was sad at this word, and went away sorrowful, for he had great possessions" (Mark 10:21, 22).

But whether men accept or reject Him, Christ is the stone by which the destinies of men are forever settled. He spoke to the religious leaders saying, "And whoever falls on this stone will be broken; but on whomever it falls, it will grind him to powder" (Matthew 21:44). In other words, whoever accepts Christ, will be broken, but only so their life might be reshaped and made new. However, anyone who rejects Christ will be ground to powder, and that can't be changed.

The teachings of Christ are beautifully illustrated in His conversations with people who came to Him with their questions. He always knew how to go straight to the heart of the person's need or problem.

Peter, under deep conviction, said to Him, "Depart from me, for I am a sinful man, O Lord!" (Luke 5:8). Jesus replied saying, "Do not be afraid. From now on you will catch men" (Luke 5:10). Why did Jesus give Peter this answer instead of reproaching him for his sinful past? Because Peter was already convicted of his sins; he knew that without Christ he was a lost man. Actually, the last thing he desired was for the Lord to depart from him. What Peter really wanted was to follow Jesus. The Lord told him that he would still be a fisherman, but from then on he would be fishing for men.

Nicodemus, a religious leader, came to Christ at night to talk about the miracles and Christ's standing as a prophet. But the Lord ignored this and turned the conversation around to the spiritual need of Nicodemus saying, "Most assuredly, I say to you, unless one is born again, he cannot see the kingdom of God" (John 3:3). At this statement Nicodemus expressed deep surprise, and his manner abruptly changed. "How can a man be born when he is old? Can he enter the second time into his mother's womb, and be born?" Nicodemus asked.

Christ went on to say that although Nicodemus was a ruler in a high religious court called the Sanhedrin, this would not give him entrance into the Kingdom of God. No one can enter the Kingdom of God unless he is born of the spirit. This rebirth takes place when a person accepts Christ into his soul and life as Savior and Lord. Jesus said, "Do not marvel that I said to you, 'You must be born again'" (John

3:7). All must have a radical change in their nature.

Nicodemus was overwhelmed by these words, which seemed to be so revolutionary. Three years later, however, Nicodemus dared to risk his position in the Sanhedrin court when He and Joseph of Arimathea went to Pilate and claimed the body of Christ for burial (John 19:38-40).

At another time, they brought to Jesus a woman who had been taken in adultery. As she cringed before her accusers, they craftily asked Jesus whether or not she should be stoned according to the Law of Moses. The Lord bent down and began to write something in the sand. Finally, He stood up. He turned to the self-righteous, religious leaders who were using the miserable woman as a means to trap Him, and said, "…'He who is without sin among you, let him throw a stone at her first.' And again He stooped down and wrote on the ground. (John 8:7, 8).

It has been speculated that Jesus was writing the sins of each of the Pharisees, religious leaders, in the sand. The Word tells us it was the older ones in the crowd who left first. Why would that be? Could it be that they had more sins than the younger ones simply because they had lived more years to commit them? The direction the Lord gave was, "He who is without sin, let Him be the first one to throw a stone." Obviously, these men were guilty. Convicted, her accusers had nothing further to say and shamefully made a hurried departure. Jesus asked the woman, "Where are your accusers?" As she raised her head to see that all of them had left, He said to the woman, "Neither do I condemn you; go and sin no more" (John 8:11).

To a man who came and asked Jesus to speak to his brother to divide the inheritance, He gave a sharp rebuke saying, "Take heed and beware of covetousness, for one's life does not consist in the abundance of the things he possesses" (Luke 12:15). He then described the fate of a rich fool who tore down his barns to build greater ones. He wanted more room to store his goods. The rich man said to his soul, "Soul, you have many goods laid up for many years; take your ease; eat, drink, and be merry." Jesus told how on that very night "But God said to him, 'Fool! This night your soul will be required of you; then whose will those things be which you have provided?'" (Luke 12:19, 20).

When Jesus heard that his close friend Lazarus was dead, and He saw the people mourning and weeping, He groaned in the spirit and was troubled. After they showed Him the tomb, He wept (John 11:35). But then, He raised Lazarus from the dead.

Again, on the way to the cross, Jesus saw the women weeping because of Him, and He said, "Daughters of Jerusalem, do not weep for Me, but weep for yourselves and for your children" (Luke 23:28). He was always thinking of others, rather than Himself.

On either side of Him on the Cross, were two soldiers (Matthew 27:44). As the crowds cried out to Jesus to save Himself, if He were the Son of God, these two men joined in. "Then Jesus said, 'Father, forgive them, for they do not know what they do.' And the soldiers who waited at the foot of the Cross divided His garments and cast lots" (Luke 23:34).

Then one of the criminals, who was hanging on His left side said, "If You are the Christ, save Yourself and us" (Luke 23:39). But the other, soon convinced that Jesus was the Son of God, rebuked his companion and sought the Lord for mercy. Jesus, forgetting His own suffering, spoke words of peace telling him, "Assuredly, I say to you, today you will be with Me in Paradise" (Luke 23:40-43).

The fateful afternoon passed; darkness descended upon the Earth. Death had finally overtaken the Prince of Life. Men took His body down from the cross and wrapped it in a linen garment to prepare it for the tomb. Again, word came to Pilate, the governor, reminding Him that Christ was supposed to rise from the grave in three days. The question was: What if the disciples just come and steal the body? Who would really know what had happened to Him? So Pilate agreed to station soldiers around the tomb to make certain there was no disturbance to His body.

For three days and nights, they guarded the tomb. But early in the morning of the third day, something happened that shook the Earth, as well as the spirit world. The powers of Satan were broken; death had to loosen its grip; and Christ rose from the grave with the keys to death, hell, and the grave! When two grief-stricken women came to the tomb to perform what they thought was the last service for the dead, two men in bright, shining clothes stood by them. Full of fear, the women bowed down to the ground. The men said to them: "Why do you seek the living among the dead? He is not here, but is risen! Remember how He spoke to you when He was still in Galilee, saying, 'The Son of Man must be delivered into the hands of sinful men, and be crucified, and the third day rise again'" (Luke 24:5-7).

Christ was indeed raised from the dead and is now a live forever. The risen Savior then appeared before the disciples and gave them the Great Commission by which they were to preach the Gospel to all the world.

> "And He said to them, 'Go into all the world and preach the gospel to every creature. He who believes and is baptized will be

saved; but he who does not believe will be condemned. And these signs will follow those who believe: In My name they will cast out demons; they will speak with new tongues; they will take up serpents; and if they drink anything deadly, it will by no means hurt them; they will lay hands on the sick, and they will recover.' So then, after the Lord had spoken to them, He was received up into heaven, and sat down at the right hand of God. And they went out and preached everywhere, the Lord working with them and confirming the word through the accompanying signs. Amen" (Mark 16:15-20).

Chapter 4

WHY WE MUST ACCEPT CHRIST

There is only one, true God. God, Creator of the universe, existed before the beginning of the world. God is a good God, a God of love. He created mankind to be a companion and friend to Him.

But since Satan deceived man and caused him to rebel and sin against God, sinful man is separated from God, which is a most terrible punishment.

Because God is holy and perfect, He cannot associate with anyone who has sin in his life. Thus, our sins will cause us to be eternally separated from God. In order to bring man back into communion with Himself, He allowed His only Son, Christ, to pay the penalty of death for our sins. If we accept His Son, God will forgive our sins, and we will be as though we have never sinned. As redeemed men, we can now commune with God while we live on this Earth, and when our life on Earth is finished, we will go to live with Him forever.

WHAT DOES CHRIST'S DEATH ON THE CROSS MEAN TO YOU PERSONALLY?

Let us think back upon the day when Christ was crucified. There, He hung between Earth and Heaven—a spectacle to mankind and angels, receiving torturous treatment that reached far beyond what anyone should have endured. Death by crucifixion includes the sum total of all the suffering a body can experience: thirst, fever, open shame, long and continual torment.

It was the noon hour, ordinarily the brightest hour of the day. But instead, a darkness began to descend upon the Earth. Nature itself, unable to bear the scene, withdrew its light, and the heavens became black. This darkness had an immediate effect upon the onlookers. There were no more jeers and taunts. People began to slip away silently to leave Jesus alone to experience the deepest depths of suffering and humiliation. Yet, a greater horror was yet to come. Instead of a joyful communion with God, there was a cry of distress. Jesus found himself utterly deserted by both man and God. His cry even today brings a shudder of terror. It was ...

"My God, my God. Why have You forsaken me?"

There was apparently one thing that God had held back from His Son Christ. The terrible truth came to Him only in the last hours of darkness. As the sun withdrew its rays, the Presence of God was also being withdrawn. Though sometimes forsaken of men, He could always turn in confidence to His Heavenly Father. But now, even God had forsaken Him. Although it was only for a moment, the reason is clear.

At that moment the sin of the world with all its hideousness rested upon Jesus. He became sin. "For He made Him who knew no sin to be sin for us, that we might become the righteousness of God in Him" (2 Corinthians 5:21).

There we have the answer to what happened. Christ

was made sin for us. He took upon Himself the sin of the world, which includes both yours and mine. Therefore, He had to receive the judgment which is the result of sin.

Finally, the end drew near. Losing that amount of blood produces an indescribable thirst. Jesus cried out, "I thirst." The One Who hung on the cross thirsted. He is the same One Who now satisfies our souls' thirst—"If anyone thirsts, let him come to Me and drink" (John 7:37).

The final moment came. Jesus bowed his head in death, saying as He died, "It is finished!" Salvation had been completed. It was a salvation—not of works to be earned by fasting, by penances, or by pilgrimages. Salvation is forever a finished work. We need not complete it by our own efforts. There is nothing more to do, but to accept it. There is no need to struggle and to labor, but to take quietly what God has prepared at an indescribable sacrifice.

Christ died for our salvation. He raised again three days and nights, later in glorious triumph to die no more. Therefore, He says, "Because I live, you will live also" (John 14:19, emphasis added).

God has done all that is possible to bring you eternal life. He paid the full price of punishment for your sins. It is now your turn to accept Him. God sees your mind and soul. He knows all of your thoughts. If you sincerely want to accept Jesus Christ, the Son of God, into your life, you will be reborn. You will become a child of God, and God the Father will become your Father.

Chapter 5

THE BIRTH OF JOHN THE BAPTIST

"There was in the days of Herod, the king of Judea, a certain priest named Zacharias, of the division of Abijah. His wife was of the daughters of Aaron, and her name was Elizabeth. And they were both righteous before God, walking in all the commandments and ordinances of the Lord blameless. But they had no child, because Elizabeth was barren, and they were both well advanced in years. So it was, that while he was serving as priest before God in the order of his division, according to the custom of the priesthood, his lot fell to burn incense when he went into the temple of the Lord. And the whole multitude of the people was praying outside at the hour of incense. Then an angel of the Lord appeared to him, standing on the right side of the altar of incense. And when Zacharias saw him, he was troubled, and fear fell upon him. But the angel said to him, "Do not be afraid, Zacharias, for your prayer is heard; and your wife Elizabeth will bear you a son, and you shall call his name John" (Luke 1:5-13).

The angel's announcement of John the Baptist's coming broke the 400 years of silence of the spirit of prophecy. In all ways, John was unique. Compared with the other prophets, Jesus said, "There were none greater born of women." His incorruptible sincerity, his humility, his fearlessness and courage, combined with the tragic story of his death, all give him a distinctive place in the Bible narrative. We are told that he came to Israel in the power and the spirit of Elijah. He stood alone between the Jewish dispensation and the Christian dispensation. But his greatest work and the ministry by which he will ever be remembered was that he was the forerunner of the Messiah.

The Book of Luke begins with relating events associated with the birth of John the Baptist. High up in the hill country near Jerusalem, there lived a certain priest by the name of Zacharias with his wife, Elizabeth. They were a godly couple, well advanced in age at the time of the events narrated. They had long desired a child, but this had been denied them. Nevertheless, they had prayed many times about the matter. At last, their best years had passed, and they ceased to have hope. They reconciled themselves to the fact that they would live and be childless (Luke 1:13).

Zacharias was a priest "of the division of Abijah," and twice a year it was his duty to journey to Jerusalem to fulfill his office of a week of six days and two Sabbaths. At this time in history, according to Josephus, there were about 20,000 priests in and around Judea. Many were no credit to the priesthood, but were, in fact, "blind leaders of the blind." On the other hand, there were those priests who were deeply sincere and led devout lives. Of this latter class was Zacharias, as well as his wife, Elizabeth. "And they were both righteous before God, walking in all the commandments and ordinances of the Lord blameless" (Luke 1:6).

As we have noted, the couple had long prayed for a son, but their prayer had not been answered. Although they did not know it, their petition had been heard, but the answer had been withheld because the hour set by Providence had not yet come. Elizabeth was to bear a son, who was to be the forerunner of the Messiah. The fullness of time when the Messiah was to appear, and therefore, also His forerunner was to appear, was settled in the Divine plan God prepared before the foundation of the world.

At last the time came. So it was that on this memorable occasion when Zacharias left his home in the hills to fulfill his duty in the Temple service, he knew little of the strange event which awaited him. Among the priestly duties was the offering of incense in the Holy Place at the time of prayer. The priest who offered the incense was determined by lot. And none in a lifetime offered it twice. But on this day, it so happened, the lot was cast, and it fell to Zacharias.

It was a great honor indeed. Zacharias was chosen from all of Israel to enter the Holy Place and minister at the altar and make intercession for the people. Since Zacharias had never before performed this solemn task, his mind was naturally in a state of awe and suppressed excitement. At the time of offering, Zacharias went into the Holy Place with his head covered and his shoes removed. Taking his censer full of incense in his hand, he poured it upon the perpetual fire of the altar. Then, he made intercession for the people, even as the whole multitude outside was also praying.

Suddenly, Zacharias looked up, and behold, an angel of the Lord was standing at the right side of the altar of incense. The priest, already in a state of emotional suspense, "... was troubled, and fear fell upon him." (Luke 1:12).

The angel was none other than Gabriel, who stands in the Presence of God. The angel reassured Zacharias and told him to fear not, for his prayer had been heard. His wife, Elizabeth was to bear him a son, and he was to call his name John.

> "But the angel said to him, 'Do not be afraid, Zacharias, for your prayer is heard; and your wife Elizabeth will bear you a son, and you shall call his name John. And you will have joy and gladness, and many will rejoice at his birth. For he will be great in the sight of the Lord, and shall drink neither wine nor strong drink. He will also be filled with the Holy Spirit, even from his mother's womb. And he will turn many of the children of Israel to the Lord their God. He will also go before Him in the spirit and power of Elijah, 'to turn the hearts of the fathers to the children, and the disobedient to the wisdom of the just, to make ready a people prepared for the Lord'" (Luke 1:13-17).

The event, the angel declared, would bring great joy to the household of Zacharias. He went on to give further instructions. The child was to be brought up a Nazarite and was not to drink wine nor strong drink of any kind. He would be filled with the Holy Ghost from the time of his conception. When the child grew up, he would become a great prophet who would turn many souls to the Lord. But most importantly, he was to be a forerunner of the Messiah, preparing a people for His coming. In the accomplishment of this great task, he would go forth in the power and the spirit of Elijah.

As the angel continued speaking, the priest composed himself. Beginning to realize the astonishing significance of the angel's message, his human reasoning began to assert itself. True, he had prayed for a son, but had not the angel come too late, much too late? The time when Elizabeth could bear a son was passed. How could these things possibly be?

And so, Zacharias, as many others have done, tried to reason out how a miracle could take place. "How shall I know this? For I am an old man, and my wife is well advanced in years" (Luke 1:18). Zacharias wanted a sign, and he got it. The angel in rebuke told him he would be mute until the birth of the child took place.

> "And the angel answered and said to him, 'I am Gabriel, who stands in the presence of God, and was sent to speak to you and bring you these glad tidings. But behold, you will be mute and not able to speak until the day these things take place, because you did not believe my words which will be fulfilled in their own time.' And the people waited for Zacharias, and marveled that he lingered so long in the temple. But when he came out, he could not speak to them; and they perceived that he had seen a vision in the temple, for he beckoned to them and remained speechless. So it was, as soon as the days of his service were completed, that he departed to his own house" (Luke 1:19-23).

The people marveled that the priest stayed so long

in the Temple. When Zacharias finally came out, they saw he could not speak. He made signs to them, and finally they understood that he had seen a vision. Zacharias stayed in the Temple until he had fulfilled the days of his ministration, then returned to his own house.

Since he could not speak, when Elizabeth, his wife, saw him, she must have been quite dismayed. But after he had written down on paper the story of what happened and Elizabeth read it, her alarm gave way to joyful anticipation. The couple decided, however, that all circumstances considered, it was best for them to say nothing to anyone. It would be an awkward thing to explain, and despite their happy anticipation of the coming event, they felt that any explanation at the moment would be misunderstood. For the next five or six months, they kept it to themselves, and said nothing of these things.

However, at the end of six months, they had an unexpected visitor. She was certainly a welcomed one. It was none other than Mary, the mother-to-be of the Christ Child! Whether the cousins had met before, we do not know for certain. Probably so, for Mary though she made the trip by herself, apparently knew the place where the elderly couple lived. As Mary stood at the door, two remarkable things happened. At the moment Mary spoke, the babe leaped in Elizabeth's womb. Then suddenly, the Spirit of God came upon the elderly woman, and a beautiful prophecy came forth acknowledging Mary as the mother of the Messiah.

It was a happy meeting, indeed, as the women exchanged all the little details and secrets of the wonderful events that had taken place. These two women, along with Zacharias, were for the time being, in almost exclusive possession of the secret of the destiny of the world! No doubt, Elizabeth and Mary talked about nothing else, other than the meaning of these strange things that had happened to them. Poor Zacharias sat mute, saying nothing, although he probably conveyed his thoughts to them from time-to-time in writing.

Zacharias was probably busy studying from a scroll, the Psalms, and the Prophets. Everything that he could find that related to the coming of the Messiah and his forerunner was searched out, and then, of course, shared with the women. The prophecy that Zacharias gave, after John was born, makes it appear that his spirit had been enriched with the great Messianic truths of the Old Testament.

Mary remained with Elizabeth for about three months, for traveling as the days of her pregnancy increased were to become increasingly difficult.

On the eighth day after Elizabeth gave birth to a son, the neighbors and cousins came to rejoice with the parents and to circumcise the child. They wanted to call him Zacharias after the father. The mother said that he should be called John. The relatives were not pleased with this, for they had a name already selected. But when they made signs to Zacharias, he wrote the words, "His name is John." In his answer all former hesitation was gone. He told them what his name was—not what it would be! And no sooner had he done this than his tongue was loosed and he gave forth a beautiful Messianic prophecy:

> "Now his father Zacharias was filled with the
> Holy Spirit, and prophesied, saying:
> 'Blessed is the Lord God of Israel,
> For He has visited and redeemed His people,
> And has raised up a horn of salvation for us

In the house of His servant David,
As He spoke by the mouth of His holy prophets,
Who have been since the world began,
That we should be saved from our enemies
And from the hand of all who hate us,
To perform the mercy promised to our fathers
And to remember His holy covenant,
The oath which He swore to our father Abraham:
To grant us that we,
Being delivered from the hand of our enemies,
Might serve Him without fear,
In holiness and righteousness before Him all the days of our life.
'And you, child, will be called the prophet of the Highest;
For you will go before the face of the Lord to prepare His ways,
To give knowledge of salvation to His people
By the remission of their sins,
Through the tender mercy of our God,
With which the Dayspring from on high has visited us;
To give light to those who sit in darkness and the shadow of death,
To guide our feet into the way of peace'"
(Luke 1:67-79).

These events had a solemn effect upon the people who lived in that region. It was something they would not quickly forget. Thirty years later, when John the Baptist began his preaching, many of those who had heard the prophecy would be dead, including his mother and father. However, there may have been some who were still alive, and they would have remembered.

We can believe that the boy growing up would find a home noted for its piety and devotion. His recollection in after-years would be of the constant perusal of the sacred books by his father and of his teaching them to him, even as God had instructed by the hand of Moses:

> "And these words which I command you today shall be in your heart. You shall teach them diligently to your children, and shall talk of them when you sit in your house, when you walk by the way, when you lie down, and when you rise up" (Deuteronomy 6:6, 7).

Each day, the aged priest would pray with fervent spirit that God would indeed use their son in the ministry the angel had spoken about. And that the Messiah would come and bring salvation to Israel.

Zacharias probably knew he would never live to see it himself, but he was sure that it would come to pass. As for the lad, we are told that "… the child grew and became strong in spirit, and was in the deserts till the day of his manifestation to Israel" (Luke 1:80).

Chapter 6

THE VOICE CRYING IN THE WILDERNESS

"In those days John the Baptist came preaching in the wilderness of Judea, and saying, 'Repent, for the kingdom of heaven is at hand!' For this is he who was spoken of by the prophet Isaiah, saying: 'The voice of one crying in the wilderness: 'Prepare the way of the Lord; Make His paths straight.' Now John himself was clothed in camel's hair, with a leather belt around his waist; and his food was locusts and wild honey. Then Jerusalem, all Judea, and all the region around the Jordan went out to him and were baptized by him in the Jordan, confessing their sins" (Matthew 3:1-6).

As son of a priest and a direct descendant of Aaron through Elizabeth, John the Baptist would have been in line to become a priest of the Temple. The Temple life would have brought him honor and security, rich robes, and jewels. But he turned his back on all of this and renounced his right to the priesthood.

Apparently, John was a silent, lonely boy. An old

man's only child, he was without brothers or sisters, without playmates, or companions. Learning from his parents the work that was before him, he wandered in solitude, thinking. Assuming that John the Baptist's parents died when he was a youth, it is probable that he made it his habit to retire to the desert for long seasons of meditation and prayer. This does not necessarily mean that he entirely avoided village life. It is probable that he came out on occasions.

While in the wilderness, he learned to survive on meager food, wild honey and flying locusts, which are cooked as food by the Bedouins of the desert. His appearance was uncouth, his dress was of camel's hair, and a leather girdle was about his loins.

John was not alone in the great wilderness of Judea. There was the Essene, Palestinian sect, who had left civilization and lived a life of poverty and self-denial. Josephus the historian in his early life had come under the influence of the Essenes, and he gives us an accurate account concerning their beliefs and practices.

The Essenes were recruited from among people who were tired of the world and its vanities. They evolved an idea of communal life, which later, was followed for a while by the Early Church. Some of the Essenes were married, but others practiced celibacy. One of the features of their belief was their strong faith in the coming Messiah.

The discovery of the Dead Sea Scrolls gave us much additional light on the habits of the Essenes. For it was the members of this sect who prepared these documents and hid them in the caves beside the Dead Sea, where they would be rediscovered by a wandering Bedouin in the year 1947. The total number of the Essenes, according to Josephus, was about 4,000. While they had disciples in many cities in Palestine, their main community was Eneglaim, located south of Jericho. The Essenes set a common table, had a commissary, and when someone needed clothes, they were permitted to take as much as they desired from the common storehouse.

Although the Essenes participated in Temple worship, they also conducted their own sacrificial rites. Each day at sunrise, they had special prayers. Grace was said before and after each meal. Above all, the Essenes gave great importance to the studying and copying of the Scriptures.

While we do not have proof that John the Baptist was an Essene, his strict, self-disciplined life corresponds to that of this sect. It is likely that he was influenced by them, and probably, when he began preaching, he drew many of his disciples from among their followers.

So now, John the Baptist reaches manhood, a hermit, of the wilderness, living far from civilization—except for the Essenes—who themselves lived an isolated existence. He may have come into the community to study the Scriptures because they kept copies available. Then, he'd go back again into solitude, giving his time to fasting, repenting, and praying.

We can only imagine that during this time he would meditate on the words of the prophets and how God had spoken to them. There was a central thought in the prophecies—the coming of the Kingdom of God. How soon would its King, the Messiah, appear?

His father and mother, while they were alive, must have told him about his mysterious birth and the angel's appearance, proclaiming that "he (John) should go before Him in the spirit and power of Elijah." Isaiah referred to John as the "voice crying in the wilderness." (When they found the Dead Sea Scrolls there was also a manuscript of the Book of Isaiah. It is identical with what we have today.)

John must have accepted that his ministry was to be a forerunner to that of the Messiah. Even while John was in the wilderness, there was an unusual spiritual awakening going on in Israel. Many people were becoming concerned about the coming Messiah. Their first thought when John the Baptist began preaching was to ask whether he was Elijah, or the Christ. "Who are you? …What then? Are you Elijah? … Are you the Prophet?" (John 1:19-22)

Then, the time came when John began to preach the message of the Kingdom of God. Perhaps, on occasion, he spoke in the surrounding cities, but mostly, he preached on the banks of the Jordan River. His voice rang out against sin, as he called the nation to repent and to prepare themselves for the Coming One. When people asked him who he was, he would say, "… as it is written in the book of the words of Isaiah the prophet, saying: 'The voice of one crying in the wilderness: 'Prepare the way of the Lord; Make His paths straight" (Luke 3:4).

What kind of person did the people see when John spoke? They saw a fiery young man tanned by wind and sun. They saw a man consumed with a vision, preaching his heart out, calling men to repentance and righteousness, telling them to make their crooked ways straight and to get ready for Christ. "Repent," he repeated, again and again, "for the kingdom of heaven is at hand."

It is significant that John began his message of repentance near the city of Jericho. During the reign of the wicked Herod, Jericho had gained a position of economic and political importance. Under his son Archelaus, the city overflowed with a life filled with sensual gratification. Its rich lands were farmed out by the Romans, while revenues from them were collected by the publicans. Josephus and others describe the beauty of its gardens and the splendor of its palaces and places of entertainment. It was a city of wealth and luxury of a decadent society. A hippodrome and an amphitheater offered exciting pleasures. Jericho became a resort of the rich, a place where they gave themselves to amusement, revelry, and abandonment to sensual delights.

Only John the Baptist was capable of raising an effective protest against this way of living. The Essenes, sick at heart with the luxury and irresponsibility of the times, could do nothing but withdraw themselves from it. But John, sparing none, struck at the heart of the evil. When his preaching created such excitement that the people came out of the cities in large numbers to hear him, he spoke words that made them shake with terror and conviction:

> "Then he said to the multitudes that came out to be baptized by him, 'Brood of vipers! Who warned you to flee from the wrath to come? Therefore bear fruits worthy of repentance, and do not begin to say to yourselves, 'We have Abraham as our father.' For I say to you that God is able to raise up children to Abraham from these stones. And even now the ax is laid to the root of the trees. Therefore every tree which does not bear good fruit is cut down and thrown into the fire'" (Luke 3:7-9).

What powerful words, coming from a man who preached from the sand dunes of a river that flowed into the Dead Sea! However, this was an appropriate place for this kind of preaching. No other land compared, except those guilty cities of Sodom and Gomorrah.

There stood John, a weird figure with flowing locks—clothed in a rough garment, presenting a vivid picture of wrath to come. But instead of frightening off the hearers, the multitudes, even from Jerusalem and the cities of Judea, continued to flock to him. There was greatness in John, grandeur in his mission, an authority in his message, which compelled the people to listen.

The alarm caused by his strong words as he presented the issues of life and death, stripped of all pretense, was penetrating. Because of his powerful preaching, the consciences of people were laid bare. What were they to do? John told them to repent. Not only were they to repent, but they were to bring forth fruits as evidence of repentance. After they had confessed their sins, they were to be baptized as a symbolic act, showing that their past sins had been washed away and a new life begun.

John cut through hypocrisy and pretense without compromise. The Pharisees and Sadducees also came to his baptizing. He was thoroughly familiar with their hypocrisies, how they devoured "… widows' houses, and for a pretense made long prayers" (Matthew 23:14). To them he said, "O generation of vipers, who has warned you to flee from the wrath to come?"

He warned the self-righteous not to say that "we have Abraham to our father," for God was able to raise up children to Abraham from the very stones that lay by the river bank. "What must we do?" said the people in the throng who stood listening. "He answered and said to them, 'He who has two tunics, let him give to him who has none; and he who has food, let him do likewise'" (Luke 3:11).

The tax collectors also said, "What shall we do?" "And he said to them, 'Collect no more than what is appointed for you'" (Luke 3:13).

"Likewise the soldiers asked him, saying, "And what shall we do?" So he said to them, "Do not intimidate anyone or accuse falsely, and be content with your wages" (Luke 3:14).

At no time did he advise the people to change their livelihood, but to go on in their present work and to be just, honest, and to show mercy.

When a man repented and said that he wanted to live a new life, John took him by the hand and plunged him into the waters of the Jordan. This was a symbol of the washing away of sin, and a preparation for the new kingdom.

John brought his sermons to a close with words about the coming Messiah. He explained that he was only the forerunner, that while he baptized in the water, the One who would come after him would baptize in the Holy Ghost and with fire.

> "John answered, saying to all, 'I indeed baptize you with water; but One mightier than I is coming, whose sandal strap I am not worthy to loose. He will baptize you with the Holy Spirit and fire. His winnowing fan is in His hand, and He will thoroughly clean out His threshing floor, and gather the wheat into His barn; but the chaff He will burn with unquenchable fire'" (Luke 3:16, 17).

Not since the days of Amos, Isaiah, and Jeremiah had there been such a prophet! The fire of his message swept through the land! Young men from every side flocked to him. Disciples multiplied with such speed that 30 years later, they were found in faraway places such as Asia Minor and Egypt (Acts 18:24-25; 19:3). Caiaphas and his father, Annas, became alarmed. It caused King Herod to send messengers to find out what the excitement was all about.

But an event was about to take place. Even though it involved John's ministry, it completely overshadowed John's ministry. News of the Baptist's teaching had gone abroad to a hundred villages and cities in Israel. One of these towns was Nazareth. There in that village, a workman in a carpenter shop heard the rumors. He knew what it was all about. He knew by heart the words that John quoted from Isaiah:

> "The voice of one crying in the wilderness:
> "Prepare the way of the Lord; Make straight
> in the desert A highway for our God. Every
> valley shall be exalted And every mountain
> and hill brought low; The crooked places
> shall be made straight And the rough places
> smooth ..." (Isaiah 40:3, 4).

Jesus, the carpenter, realized that at last His time had come. He was now to leave the shop in Nazareth forever.

For the last time, Jesus gathered up His tools and put them in their place. He bid His family farewell, and began His journey down the hill that led toward the Plain of Esdraelon. After a while, He turned east, and going through the gap of Jezreel, He went down toward the Jordan River.

Chapter 7

JOHN AND JESUS

Did Jesus and John ever meet in their boyhood days? If Zacharias and Elizabeth were still alive and in good health when Joseph and Mary went on their annual visits, it is almost certain that they did. Mary who had been so close to Elizabeth would certainly desire to see her and exchange experiences. Both Mary and Elizabeth would have an intense interest in the welfare of each other's sons, who they knew were destined to fulfill established roles in human destiny.

Since Zacharias and Elizabeth lived not far from Jerusalem, it is highly probable that nothing except the infirmities of old age would keep them away from the Passover. Still, it might be that in the providence of God, Jesus and John were to be kept apart in their youth. At all events, the two did grow up apart, each moving toward his own peculiar mission. Both would accomplish a great work, but one was to soar higher than the other. One would increase, and then decrease. But of the other, "Of the increase of His government and peace, there will be no end ..." (Isaiah 9:7).

Having traveled for several days since He left Nazareth, Jesus came to the banks of the Jordan. He then moved south along the path to where the crowds had gathered to hear John. Immediately, he went up to John and asked to be baptized. Although both men were related in the flesh, there was no visual appearance that they recognized each other. However, John, possibly by the Spirit, knew who He was. John immediately said, "I need to be baptized by You, and are You coming to me?" (Matthew 3:14)

This candidate for water baptism needed no repentance or a better way of life. John knew that He was no ordinary candidate. This was none other than the Messiah, Himself! As John surveyed the solemn majesty of the Sinless One Who stood before him, he obviously felt the need for this Man to baptize him. And, since there were no sins to wash away, baptism for the visitor seemed inappropriate.

But Jesus had subjected himself to all forms of human jurisdiction. He was circumcised according to the Law. He was obedient to the Law. According to the Mosaic Law, those who came in contact with anyone ceremonially unclean were required to submit to the appointed cleansing. Jesus had been in touch with men. He was willing to be baptized to fulfill all righteousness. He recognized John's baptism as a symbol of purification. But more than purification, baptism was a testimony. It was a symbol of the soul's consecration to God's will forever. It was a dedication on Jesus' part to become the Lamb of God—slain from the foundation of the world.

So when Jesus said, "Permit it to be so now, for thus it is fitting for us to fulfill all righteousness" (Matthew 3:15). John obeyed His command, and baptized Him.

BAPTISM OF THE SPIRIT

As Jesus rose up out of the water, a wonderful thing happened to Him. It was the glorious coming of the Holy Spirit in all His fullness.

"When He had been baptized, Jesus came up immediately from the water; and behold, the heavens were opened to Him, and He saw the Spirit of God descending like a dove and alighting upon Him. And suddenly a voice came from heaven, saying, 'This is My beloved Son, in whom I am well pleased'" (Matthew 3:16, 17).

Jesus was not the only person who saw the Spirit descending as a dove upon Him. John saw the same thing, which confirmed to him that Jesus was the One Who was to come, the Son of God (John 1:32-34).

In this event at the Jordan, the trinity of the Godhead was revealed. God the Son being baptized; God the Holy Spirit coming upon Him in the form of a dove; God the Father saying, "This is my beloved Son, in whom I am well pleased."

One other thing should be noted concerning a remark of John's. He said that God had sent him to baptize. Some have assumed that John on his own initiative had adopted baptism as an appropriate rite to symbolize his ministry. This is untrue. John baptized because God had specifically called him to do it. It is true that the ancients in some of their rituals used water as a symbolic act of purification. But it never included repentance. John's baptism was a baptism of repentance. It was something altogether new.

Jesus Himself certified that the baptism of John was of Heaven when he reasoned with the Pharisees. They demanded to know by what authority did He do the things He did. Jesus answered them by asking a question, "The baptism of John—where was it from? From heaven or from men?" (Matthew 21:25).

This put the chief priest and the elders in a tough spot. The inference was that John's baptism was of Heaven. But if they agreed to that, then Jesus would want to know, "Why did you then not believe him?" On the other hand, if they said "of men," they would have trouble with the people, "for all held John as a prophet." Therefore, they did not answer.

THE APOSTLE JOHN'S RECORD OF JOHN THE BAPTIST

The Book of John was written a number of years after the other gospels and was intended to fill in some of the details not covered by the evangelists. The apostle also provides some additional information concerning the ministry of John the Baptist.

He begins with a statement that John was a man sent from God, that he was not the Light, but was sent to bear witness of that Light. The Baptist's knowledge evidently included the fact of the pre-existence of Christ when he said, "He who comes after me is preferred before me, for He was before me" (John 1:15).

In the midst of John's ministry at the Jordan, the Jews sent a committee of priests and Levites from Jerusalem to make an investigation of what was happening. They asked John if he was Elijah. Or was he the prophet that Moses spoke of? To each of these questions, John answered in the negative. Then they questioned him further, asking that if he were neither Christ nor Elijah, why then did he baptize?

John's answer was to tell them that he was "a voice crying in the wilderness," warning the people to make straight the way of the Lord, that the Christ, Israel's Messiah, was already standing in their midst.

These events took place at Bethabara on the other side of Jordan. The very next day, after John's interview with the Levites and priests, who should appear before him but Jesus Himself. Immediately, John cried out and said, "Behold! The Lamb of God who takes away the sin of the world!" (John 1:29).

The next day, Jesus appeared again, and John said, "Behold the Lamb of God!" (John 1:36). This time, two of John's disciples heard him say this, and they turned and followed Jesus. One was the Apostle John and the other was Andrew, Simon's brother. The latter went and found his brother Peter and said to him, "We have found the Messiah!" From that day they were no longer the disciples of John, but disciples of Jesus.

THE RISE OF CHRIST'S MINISTRY AND THE DECLINE OF JOHN'S

John continued carrying on his ministry the same as he had been doing. He chose a place "… in Aenon near Salim, because there was much water there. And they came and were baptized" (John 3:23).

More and more of his disciples left him to join Jesus. But some remained with him, even if the One John had pointed out to them was the Messiah.

News reached them that Jesus and His disciples were baptizing more disciples than John (John 4:1-2). The followers of John, called this to his attention: "And they came to John and said to him, 'Rabbi, He who was with you beyond the Jordan, to whom you have testified—behold, He is baptizing, and all are coming to Him!'" (John 3:26).

But noble John the Baptist rose fully to the occasion, and in a mild manner, he not only fully justified what Christ was doing, but made the most definitive statement of the Lord's divinity and position as the Messiah:

"John answered and said, 'A man can receive nothing unless it has been given to him from heaven. You yourselves bear me witness, that I said, 'I am not the Christ,' but, 'I have been sent before Him.' He who has the bride is the bridegroom; but the friend of the bridegroom, who stands and hears him, rejoices greatly because of the bridegroom's voice. Therefore this joy of mine is fulfilled. He must increase, but I must decrease. He who comes from above is above all; he who is of the earth is earthly and speaks of the earth. He who comes from heaven is above all. And what He has seen and heard, that He testifies; and no one receives His testimony. He who has received His testimony has certified that God is true. For He whom God has sent speaks the words of God, for God does not give the Spirit by measure. The Father loves the Son, and has given all things into His hand. He who believes in the Son has everlasting life; and he who does not believe the Son shall not see life, but the wrath of God abides on him'" (John 3:27-36).

A careful look at John's words shows that he had a comprehensive understanding of the nature and ministry of Christ.

1. John understood that he was but the forerunner; therefore, he said "He must increase, but I must decrease" (verse 30).

2. John resisted all efforts to make him take the pre-eminence, and he called his disciples' attention to the fact that all along he had said that, "'I am not the Christ,' but, 'I have been sent before Him'" (verse 28).

3. His office was that of a "friend of the bridegroom" and in that position he could say, "Therefore this joy of mine is fulfilled" (verse 29), and that in fulfilling that office his purpose in life had been attained.

4. John followed with a statement of Christ's divinity, saying that He was from above, that is, from heaven (verse 31).

5. He stated that "God does not give the Spirit by measure" (verse 31).

6. Christ was beloved of the Father and He "… has given all things into His hand" (verse 35).

7. To have faith in Jesus was to have everlasting life; to reject Him was to have the wrath of God abiding on him:

> "He who believes in the Son has everlasting life; and he who does not believe the Son shall not see life, but the wrath of God abides on him" (John 3:36).

In this remarkable declaration of faith in the Messiah, John the Baptist rose above any petty, human jealousies and rivalries that could have been present. He completely renounced personal ambition and reaffirmed his absolute faith in the One Who he had praised and identified as the Messiah of Israel.

Just what the future course of his ministry held for him, John did not know. He saw it as his duty, however, to continue to carry on as before, until he had received instructions otherwise.

Chapter 8

JOHN THE BAPTIST AND HEROD

"... for Herod feared John, knowing that he was a just and holy man, and he protected him. And when he heard him, he did many things, and heard him gladly" (Mark 6:20).

King Herod, the tetrarch, had for some time been watching with great interest the ministry of John the Baptist. There were two contrasting sides to this man Herod, a better nature that responded to John's earnest preaching, and also an evil side which more often than not, controlled the man. When Herod first heard John, he was very impressed, which may have surprised his own court by his favorable attitude toward John. They no doubt had misgivings as to how Herod would react to the straight preaching of the Baptist. It seemed that Herod was not offended, but rather took to the Baptist's preaching. We are told that "when he heard him, he did many things, and heard him gladly."

But Herod's religious impressions didn't last long. In the first place, his wife Herodias, whom he had taken from his brother Philip, had no interest in John. If she thought of him at all, it was to consider him as an uncouth fanatic. But when she learned that John had the nerve to denounce her marriage publicly, she was furious. Herodias demanded that Herod have the Baptist taken into custody at once and executed. He refused her demand. But when he perceived that she was determined to accomplish her evil purpose one way or another, he had John put in prison.

Failing to achieve her objective immediately, she apparently played on Herod's fears by insinuating that the Baptist was a revolutionary, who was bent on inciting a rebellion. Josephus seems to bear this out, saying that Herod "feared lest the great influence John had over the people might put it in his power and inclination to raise a rebellion; for they seemed ready to do anything he should advise."

John's faithfulness in preaching the truth to King Herod shows him at his very highest moment. It is common for preachers to preach straight to ordinary people. But it is also true that some, who have been vocal in denouncing the sins of the lower classes, often change their tone when they come face-to-face with sinners in high places. Herod probably presumed that John the Baptist would follow this policy and would refrain from saying anything about him of a personal nature. But John was not made that way. All men were alike to him. He bluntly told Herod that it is not lawful to have your brother's wife."

The interviews Herod had with John left him in an unhappy frame of mind. The uncompromising Baptist completely dominated the conversation. There was something about the prophet that stirred Herod's slumbering conscience so that "he did many things." But the evil genius of Herodias held him back. With all the spitefulness of a thoroughly bad woman, who was angry because John had dared to denounce her adulterous marriage, she yearned for his death.

Herod was torn between these forces, the one good and the other bad. Finally, he made the imprisonment as easy as possible on John by permitting his disciples free access to their master. In this way, the Baptist was kept in close touch with all that was taking place on the outside.

The black fortress of Machairus where John was imprisoned was not a scene to inspire a man who was used to freedom as the prophet was. It was located in an area surrounded by fields of black lava, which overlooked the desolate waters of the Dead Sea.

Above the valley, there rose at this point the sheer precipices of black volcanic rock. One of these was surrounded on three sides by deep chasms, and on the summit, Herod the Great had reared Machairus Castle. Its vast cellars were stocked with grain and food capable of withstanding a long siege. Its armory was crammed with swords, javelins, and shields for a great army. Surely with such an impenetrable fortress, Herod could beat anyone who dared to challenge his authority.

Nevertheless, Herod was bothered by many fears. Every day, rumors came to him about the Arabs who were gathering against him. In marrying Herodias, Herod had sent his former Arab bride back to her father Aretas. The proud Arab was furious at this insult to his daughter, and began working to draw the Arab tribes together for a fight to the death against Herod.

Tiberius Caesar was also interested in what was happening. He had his spies out to keep an eye on his vassal-king to find out the reason for all the restlessness on the Arab frontier. Would Tiberius give Herod assistance, or would he, being displeased with his actions, decide to remove him from his throne?

These were the reasons for Herod's fear. He dared not risk any disturbances in his kingdom, which might arise from John's preaching. And so Herod, stilling the voice of conscience, did nothing. Therefore, John remained in prison. Still he had hope. Wouldn't Jesus, the Messiah, come soon to get involved in the matter? His prison days could not last much longer.

From time-to-time, John's disciples would come to him to give him the latest word on what was happening on the outside. On each occasion, John would listen eagerly, but each time the report was the same; nothing exciting was happening. It seemed Jesus was spending most of his time teaching. There was no indication that he was taking any steps to restore the kingdom to Israel, or to help John out of his present predicament.

Then, for the first time, a question arose in John's mind. The days were swiftly passing, and his hopes apparently were not being fulfilled. He had called the people to repentance assuring them that the Kingdom of God was at hand. But now it seemed as if he were going to remain in prison indefinitely.

It was a dark hour for the great prophet. Shut up in prison, deprived of his liberty, it was hard for him to believe the sun was shining anywhere. At last he felt that he must have a definite word from Jesus on how matters stood. Was Jesus the Messiah after all? He sent two of his disciples to say to him, "Are You the Coming One, or do we look for another?" (Luke 7:19-23).

Christ's answer to John's messengers just confirmed the truth about Who He was and His wisdom. He 'might have sent John a list of proofs of His divinity. He might have reminded the prophet of the supernatural signs that took place at the Jordan River to confirm that He was the Messiah. He might have called John's attention to the revelations that

God had given to John himself, concerning Him. But He did no such thing. Instead, he asked the messengers to observe His ministry that day, and then to go back and report to John what they had seen. The prophet could judge whether or not it had the marks and qualifications of being the Messiah. Let them tell John that the blind receive their sight, the lepers are cleansed, the dead are raised, and the poor have the Gospel preached to them. In other words, the needs of humanity were being met, the wounds of the suffering were being bound up, the sorrows of the broken-hearted were being comforted, and the sick and diseased were being made whole.

Here is a lesson for the Church today. It is a curious thing to see sects and denominations in labored attempts trying to prove that they and they only represent the true Church. One group claims that they have inherited the mantle of Christ through apostolic succession and they alone are God's elect, and all others are imposters.

Christ showed that the proper way to prove that His ministry was of God was by His works. His credentials were: "Believe Me that I am in the Father and the Father in Me, or else believe Me for the sake of the works themselves" (John 14:11). Men need to cease arguing over which Church is the true Church, and instead, begin to let the world see the signs following their ministry.

The disciples of John went back and told him all things that they had seen and heard. We are certain that John was reassured by His answer and was strengthened for the final tragic scene in his life.

The martyrdom of John was now at hand. The weak Herod was about to climax his evil career with a crime that must forever blacken his name and relegate him to the lowest hall of infamy. Like his father, Herod the Great, he could be cruel and crafty, but unlike his father, he was weak. He was a man in whom many of the worst features of fallen human nature were compounded. Although Herod was not all bad, and there were times when he thought to do better, whatever good there was in him was destroyed by his marriage to the horrible Herodias. It has been well said that what Jezebel was to Elijah in the Old Testament, Herodias was to the John the Baptist in the New Testament. But whereas Elijah escaped the deadly hatred of Jezebel, John the Baptist was to be the victim of the murderous Herodias.

Herodias had sound reasons for hating John. If Herod followed John's instructions for putting her away, where would she go? She would be a disgraced and ruined woman. Her hatred was merciless and she waited for the right time with one consuming purpose: to vent her fury upon the head of the faithful prophet.

Chapter 9

DEATH OF THE PROPHET

"Then an opportune day came when Herod
on his birthday gave a feast for his nobles, the
high officers, and the chief men of Galilee.
And when Herodias' daughter herself came in
and danced, and pleased Herod and those who
sat with him, the king said to the girl, 'Ask me
whatever you want, and I will give it to you.'
He also swore to her, 'Whatever you ask me, I
will give you, up to half my kingdom.' So she
went out and said to her mother, 'What shall
I ask?' And she said, 'The head of John the
Baptist!' Immediately she came in with haste
to the king and asked, saying, 'I want you to
give me at once the head of John the Baptist
on a platter.' And the king was exceedingly
sorry; yet, because of the oaths and because
of those who sat with him, he did not want
to refuse her. Immediately the king sent an
executioner and commanded his head to be
brought. And he went and beheaded him in
prison, brought his head on a platter, and
gave it to the girl; and the girl gave it to her
mother. When his disciples heard of it, they
came and took away his corpse and laid it in

a tomb" (Mark 6:21-29).

The birthday of Herod had come and to celebrate the occasion, he invited as guests a number of the lords and captains of his kingdom to his princely castle at Machairus, where John was imprisoned.

Herodias was there with him at the castle, and still mad about the stinging rebuke John gave, regarding her marriage, she had plans which she hoped would bring a quick end to the prophet and his career.

While Herod and his nobles and officers were in the midst of their banqueting, Herodias introduced an unexpected diversion. She had a daughter by the name of Salome by her former husband whom she had so shamelessly abandoned. The young princess was sent by her mother to the banquet hall to perform before the wine-inflamed eyes of the revelers a lustful dance. This lewd performance evoked an enthusiastic applause from the audience. The gratified Herod summoned the girl before him, and oblivious of the fact that he was only a vassal-king and had no right to transfer anything of the kingdom without the Emperor Tiberius' sanction, vowed that he would grant her anything she might ask, even up to half of his kingdom.

Salome then went to her mother and sought her advice as to what she should request, and the wicked woman, exulting in the success of her strategy asked for the head of John the Baptist. It might be wondered why a young girl would not shrink from so gruesome a request as this. However, the mother persuaded her daughter that John the Baptist endangered their own security, that if his advice were followed by Herod, they would be left out in the cold, banished and exiled.

Herod the king was deeply distressed by this unexpected request, and would gladly have withdrawn his promise, were it not for those that were present. With the greatest of reluctance, he made good his ill-considered promise. Soon a soldier appeared at the cell of John the Baptist. Made aware that the vengeance of Herodias had at last succeeded, the great prophet committed himself into the hands of God and prepared for his fate. Moments later, the deed was done; and the head of the prophet was presented to Salome who carried the ghastly trophy to Herodias where she might gloat over it in triumph.

John the Baptist was as Moses, who led the children of Israel into the Promised Land, which he himself could only see afar off; or like King David who prepared the materials for the Temple, which he himself could not build. He had begun a great work, but it was not for him to finish. As a forerunner of Christ, John accurately described his place in the unfolding order of events when he said, "He must increase, but I must decrease."

The mean and cowardly crime had been committed. The disciples of John, at the risk of their own lives, came to the prison, and after securing the body of the prophet, they sorrowfully buried it. But Herod was far from happy with himself. His conscience now rose up to taunt and punish him. Before long, news came to him of the works of Jesus. When Herod's servants talked to him about it, he said, "This is John the Baptist; he is risen from the dead, and therefore these powers are at work in him" (Matthew 14:2). The unhappy king didn't have many more years to enjoy the position of power he held and had proved himself so unworthy to receive.

In the end, Herod received what he deserved.

Ironically, it came from Herodias' brother, Agrippa. Herod had treated the young man as a pauper relative, and he had departed, vowing that Herod would pay dearly for his insults. When, by a stroke of fortune, the adventurer was made king of Palestine by the erratic Emperor Caligula, Herodias filled with envy, gave her husband no rest until they went to Rome to also ask the emperor for a larger kingdom. It was their undoing. Due to Agrippa's treachery, Caligula was made to believe that Herod planned a rebellion. Immediately, Herod and Herodias were banished into exile, to reap the harvest of evil they had sown. How unhappy the miserable Herodias must have been, knowing that their misfortune had been caused by her own brother and her insatiable desire for ambition.

Herodias had followed a pattern of evil throughout her life. It was payment-in-full that she and her husband spent their last days in poverty and misery.

Chapter 10

JOSEPHUS' RECORD OF JOHN THE BAPTIST AND HEROD

"… for Herod feared John, knowing that he was a just and holy man, and he protected him. And when he heard him, he did many things, and heard him gladly" (Mark 6:20).

There is only one other source of knowledge of John the Baptist apart from the Gospels, and that is Josephus. For the most part, his records are considered accurate. Therefore, we shall include his story of Herod and John the Baptist.

WHY THE SAMARITANS WERE EXCLUDED FROM THE TEMPLE

"As the Jews were celebrating the Feast of Unleavened Bread, which we call the Passover, it was customary for the priests to open the Temple gates just after midnight. When, therefore, those gates were first opened, some of the Samaritans came privately into Jerusalem, and threw about dead men's bodies in the cloisters; on which account the Jews afterwards excluded them out of the Temple, which they had not used to do at such festivals; and on other accounts also they watched the Temple more carefully than they had formerly done."

HEROD BUILDS TIBERIAS

"And now, Herod the tetrarch, who was in great favour with Tiberius, built a city of the same name with him, and called it Tiberias. He built it in the best part of Galilee, at the lake of Gennesaret. There are warm baths at a little distance from it, in a village named Emmaus. Strangers came and inhabited this city; a great number of the inhabitants were Galileans also; and many were necessitated by Herod to come thither out of the country belonging to him, and were by force compelled to be its inhabitants; some of them were persons of condition. He also admitted poor people, such as those that were collected from all parts, to dwell in it. Nay, some of them were not quite freemen, and these he was a benefactor to, and made them free in great numbers; but obliged them not to forsake the city, by building them very good houses, at his own expense, and by giving them land also; for he was sensible, that to make this place a habitation was to transgress the ancient Jewish laws, because many sepulchers were to be here taken away in order to make room for the city Tiberias:

whereas our law pronounces that 'such inhabitants are unclean for seven days.'" (Numbers 19:11)

JOSEPHUS' RECORD OF CHRIST

"Now, there was about this time, Jesus, a wise man, if it be lawful to call him a man, for he was a doer of wonderful works—a teacher of such men as receive the truth with pleasure. He drew over to him both many of the Jews, and many of the Gentiles. He was (the) Christ; and when Pilate at the suggestion of the principal men amongst us, had condemned him to the cross, those that loved him at the first did not forsake him, for he appeared to them alive the third day as the Divine prophets had foretold these and ten thousand other wonderful things concerning him; and the tribe of Christians so named from him, are not extinct at this day."

HOW HEROD MARRIED THE ADULTEROUS HERODIAS

"About this time Aretas (the king of Arabia Petrea) and Herod had a quarrel, on the account following; Herod the tetrarch had married the daughter of Aretas, and had lived with her a great while; but when he was once at Rome, he lodged with Herod, who was his brother indeed, but not by the same mother;

for this Herod was the son of the High Priest Simon's daughter.

"However, he fell in love with Herodias, this last Herod's wife who was the daughter of Aristobulus, their brother and the sister of Agrippa the Great. This man ventured to talk to her about a marriage between them; which address when she admitted, an agreement was made for her to change her habitation, and come to him as soon as he should return from Rome: one article of this marriage also was this, that he should divorce Areta's daughter.

"So Antipas, when he made this agreement, sailed to Rome; but when he had done there the business he went about, and was returned again, his wife having discovered the agreement he had made with Herodias, and having learned it before he had notice of her knowledge of the whole design, she desired him to send her to Macherus, which is a place on the borders of the dominions of Aretas and Herod, without informing him of any of her intentions. Accordingly, Herod sent her thither, as thinking his wife had not perceived anything.

"Now she had sent a good while before to Macherus, which was subject to her father, and so all things necessary for her journey were made ready for her by the general of

Areta's army, and by that means she soon came to Arabia, under the conduct of the several generals who carried her from one to another successively; and she soon came to her father, and told him of Herod's intentions.

"So Aretas made this the first occasion of his enmity between him and Herod, who had also some quarrel with him about their limits at the country of Gamalitis. So they raised armies on both sides, and prepared for war, and sent their generals to fight instead of themselves, and when they had joined battle, all Herod's army was destroyed by the treachery of some fugitives, though they were of the tetrarchy of Philip, joined with Areta's army."

THE MINISTRY OF JOHN THE BAPTIST

"Now, some of the Jews thought that the destruction of Herod's army carne from God, and that very justly, as a punishment of what he did against John, that was called the Baptist; for Herod slew him, who was a good man and commanded the Jews to exercise virtue, both as to righteousness toward one another, and piety towards God, and so to come to baptism; for that the washing (with water) would be acceptable to Him, if they made use of it, not in order to the putting away (or the remission) of some sins (only), but for the purification of the body: supposing still that the soul was thoroughly purified beforehand by righteousness.

"Now, when (many) others came to crowd about him, for they were greatly moved (or pleased) by hearing his words, Herod, who feared lest the great influence John had over the people might put it into his power and inclination to raise a rebellion (for they seemed ready to do anything he should advise), thought it best by putting him to death, to prevent any mischief he might cause, and not bring himself into difficulties, by sparing a man who might make him repent of it when it should be too late.

"Accordingly, he was sent a prisoner, out of Herod's suspicious temper, to Macherus, the castle I before mentioned, and was there put to death. Now the Jews had an opinion that the destruction of this army was sent as a punishment upon Herod, and a mark of God's displeasure against him."

HEROD'S TREATMENT OF HEROD AGRIPPA

"For these reasons he went away from Rome, and sailed to Judea, but in evil circumstances, being dejected with the loss of that money which he once had, and because he had not wherewithal to pay his creditors, who were many in number, and such as gave no room for escaping them. Whereupon, he knew not what to do; so for shame of his present condition, he retired to a certain tower at Malatha, in Idumea, and had thoughts of killing himself: but his wife Cypros perceived his intentions, and tried all sorts of methods to divert him from his taking such a course: so she sent a letter to his sister Herodias, who was now the wife of Herod the tetrarch, and let her know Agrippa's present design, and what necessity it was which drove him thereto, and desired her as a kinswoman of his, to give him her help, and to engage her husband to do the same, since she saw how she alleviated these her husband's troubles all she could, although she had not the like wealth to do it withal.

"So they sent for him and allotted him Tiberias for his habitation, and appointed him some income of money for his maintenance, and made him a magistrate of that city, by way of honor to him. Yet did not Herod long continue in that resolution of supporting him, though even that support was not sufficient for him; for, as once they were at a feast at Tyre, and in their cups, and reproaches were cast upon one another, Agrippa thought that was not to be borne, while Herod hit him in his teeth with his poverty, and with his owing his necessary food to him. So he went to Flaccus, one that had been consul, and had been a very great friend to him at Rome formerly, and was now president of Syria."

HEROD AGRIPPA MADE KING OF TIBERIUS

"However, there did not many days pass, ere he sent for him to his house, and had him shaved, and made him change his raiment; after which he put a diadem upon his head, and appointed him to be king of the tetrarchy of Phillip. He also gave him the tetrarchy of Lysanias, and changed his iron chain for a golden one of equal weight. He also sent Marullus to be procurator of Judea.

"Now in the second year of the reign of Caius Caesar, Agrippa desired leave to be given him to sail home, and settle the affairs of his government; and he promised to return again when he had put the rest in order, as it ought to be put. So, upon the emperor's permission, he came into his own country and appeared to them all unexpectedly as a king, and thereby demonstrated to the men that saw him, the power of fortune, when they compared his former poverty with his present happy affluence; so some called him a happy man; and others could not well believe that things were so much changed with him for the better."

HOW HERODIAS' ENVY LED TO HEROD'S RUIN

"But Herodias, Agrippa's sister, who now lived as wife to that Herod who was tetrarch of Galilee and Perea, took this authority of her brother in an envious manner, particularly when she saw that he had a greater dignity bestowed on him than her husband had; since, when he ran away, he was not able to pay his debts; and now he was come back, it was because he was in a way of dignity and of great fortune. She was therefore grieved and much displeased at so great a mutation of his affairs; and chiefly when she saw him marching among the multitude with the usual ensigns of royal authority, she was not able to conceal how miserable she was, by reason of the envy she had towards him; but she excited her husband, and desired him that he would sail to Rome, to court honors equal to his; for she said that she could not bear to live any longer, while Agrippa, the son of that Aristobulus, who was condemned to die by his father, one that came to her husband in such extreme poverty, that the necessaries of life were forced to be entirely supplied him day by day; and when he fled away from his creditors by sea, he now returned a king.

"But let us go to Rome, and let us spare no pains nor expenses, either of silver or gold, since they cannot be kept for any better use than for the obtaining of a kingdom.

"But for Herod, he opposed her request at this time, out of the love of ease, and having a suspicion of the trouble he should have at Rome; so he tried to instruct her better. But the more she saw him drawback, the more she pressed him to it, and desired him to leave no stone unturned in order to be king: and at last she left not off till she engaged him, whether he would or not, to be of her sentiments, because he could not otherwise avoid her importunity.

"So he got all things ready, after as sumptuous a manner as he was able, and spared for nothing, and went up to Rome, and took Herodias along with him. But- Agrippa, when he was made sensible of their intentions and preparations, he also prepared to go thither; and as soon as he heard they set sail, he sent Fortunatus, one of his freedmen, to Rome, to carry presents to the emperor, and letters against Herod, and to give Caius a particular account of those matters, if he should have any opportunity. This man followed Herod so quick, and had so prosperous a voyage and came so little after Herod, that while Herod was with Caius, he came himself, and delivered his letters; ... wherein he accused him, that he had been in confederacy with Sejanus, against Tiberius's government, and that he was now confederate with Artabanus, the king of Parthia, in opposition to the government of Caius; as a demonstration of which he alleged that he had armor sufficient for seventy thousand men ready in his armory.

"Caius was moved at this information and asked Herod whether what was said about the armor was true; and when he confessed there was such armor there, for he could not deny the same, the truth of it being too notorious, Caius took that to be a sufficient proof of the accusation, that he intended to revolt. So he took away from him his tetrarchy, and gave it by way of addition to Agrippa's kingdom; he also gave Herod's money to Agrippa, and, by way of punishment, awarded him a perpetual banishment, and appointed Lyons, a city of Gaul, to be his place of habitation.

"But when he was informed that Herodias was Agrippa's sister, he made her a present of what money was her own and told her that it was her brother who prevented her being put under the same calamity with her husband, but she made this reply—'Thou indeed, O emperor! actest after a magnificent manner, and as becomest thyself, in what thou offerest me; but the kindness which I have for my husband, hinders me from partaking of the favor of thy gift; for it is not just that I, who have been made a partner in his prosperity, should forsake him in his misfortunes.'

"Hereupon, Caius was angry at her, and sent her with Herod into banishment, and gave her estate to Agrippa. And thus did God punish Herodias for her envy at her brother, and Herod also for giving ear to the vain discourses of a woman."

Thus, the curtain was rung down on the lives of two of the most abhorrent characters found in the entire Bible.

Chapter 11

THE WORLD WHEN JESUS WAS BORN

There was a remarkable woman in the city of Jerusalem by the name of Anna who lived in the days just before the coming of Christ (Luke 2:36-38). She stayed in the Temple, and there she prayed night and day for her people. She had married in the year 91 B.C., but her husband had died seven years later. She, with a few others like her, had interceded to God continually with fasting for the Messiah to come. During her lifetime, she had witnessed the world passing through great political convulsions. Rome was shaken again and again by bloody civil wars. Kingdoms rose and fell in their march to world power.

In 63 B.C., Pompey invaded Palestine and besieged Jerusalem. The Roman army broke down the wall with battering rams. The battle had been fought on the Sabbath when many of the Jews refused to fight. The slaughter that followed was terrible. After breaking into the Temple, Pompey went into the holy place where only the priest was supposed to go. Eleven years later, another general by the name of Crassus entered the Temple and plundered it again. Then came Julius Caesar. Caesar crossed the Rubicon and made himself the master of Italy. Pompey, who had profaned the Temple, fought desperately, but his army was crushed in the battle of Tapsus. Three years later, it was Caesar's turn to meet his fate. He was assassinated in Rome on the Ides of March. More civil war followed, and Mark Antony came to power, but he and his paramour, the ambitious and unscrupulous Cleopatra, lost the battle at Actium. Augustus Caesar was the victor. All these things took place in Anna's life time, but she prayed on. In time, her prayers, and those of others like her, changed the world more than all the armies of the Caesars.

During Augustus Caesar's reign, a man by the name of Herod had watched these events, and he was always careful to throw his support to the winning side. As a reward for his services, Augustus made him king of Palestine. Ambitious and ruthless, he beautified Jerusalem and authorized the building of a new and magnificent Temple.

From the time it was built, Anna worshipped in it, both day and night. She was in the Temple fasting and praying for the Messiah to come. Then, one day, she went to that part of the Temple where the priests were getting the offerings ready for the people. The Spirit had witnessed to her that a certain child, who was being presented in the Temple, was none other than the One Who would bring redemption to Jerusalem. She went in and gave thanks to God and told the people that it was He Who would save Israel. At about the same time a man called Simeon had also received a similar revelation. After seeing the Baby and taking Him in his arms, he blessed God and said, "Lord, now You are letting Your servant depart in peace, According to Your word; For my eyes have seen Your salvation" (Luke 2:29, 30).

THE STATE OF THE NATION ISRAEL

With the appearance of the Messiah, an altogether new force came into the world. If we are to understand the impact of this significant event, we must know something of the state of Israel at that time. Let us, therefore, take a brief view of those conditions existing in the nation within whose borders the life of the Messiah was to be passed. As one reads through the Bible and passes from the Old Testament to the New Testament, he may think that the people of Israel in Jesus' day were much the same as they were in the earlier period. However, during the four centuries that elapsed after the days of Malachi, the greatest change took place in Israel that has ever occurred in the history of any nation. Even the language of the people had changed, as well as many of its customs and institutions.

Politically, Israel had passed through evil times. In the days of Ezra and Nehemiah, the nation had been organized as a sort of theocratic state. One conqueror after another had passed through the land, gradually changing everything. The brave Maccabees had raised the battle cry of freedom, and for a certain period, they had thrown off the yoke of the oppressor. However, within a century after the Maccabees, the Jewish state had fallen completely under the power of Rome.

The Herod dynasty, which came to power a few years before Christ's birth, held the nation under subjection. But shortly after Jesus was born, the country was divided into three parts. Galilee and Paraea were ruled by vassal kings. Judea, after suffering the misrule of Archelaus, was ruled by a governor. The iron heel of Rome was now felt everywhere. Roman soldiers were stationed throughout the country.

Roman standards waved over the nation's fortresses. Roman tax gatherers were in every town of any size.

The Sanhedrin, which was the supreme religious body of the nation, retained only a shadow of power because they were just puppets of Rome and subject to the imperial rulers and their ever-changing minds. Religious and national patriotism burned with a fierce passion at that time in Israel's history.

Religiously, the people were more orthodox than in any previous period. Prior to the Babylonian captivity, the nation had been cursed with idolatry. But the captivity had cured them of that. The priestly orders had since been reorganized, and the Temple services and the annual feasts were regularly observed.

Although Herod the Great had built a new Temple in Jerusalem that rivaled that of Solomon's, a new institution sprung up. There were synagogues wherever the Jews worshipped in Israel, as well as throughout the civilized world. People filled the synagogues on Sabbath days, where they prayed, heard the Scriptures read, and listened to an exhortation from a rabbi. Schools of theology had sprung up where rabbis were trained and the sacred books interpreted. Even with all this religious activity, true spirituality in Israel declined. While there had been periods of total religious desertion in ancient Israel, there had also arisen great prophets who spoke to the conscience of the nation and maintained a contact with Heaven. But for 400 years, there hadn't been a prophet in Israel.

During this period, there had arisen several new religious sects; one was the Pharisees, who elevated themselves to be almost superior Jews. Characterized by an extreme narrowness, they were committed to legalism—

strictly obeying the laws of Moses—and their outward appearance or perception. They despised and hated other races and came to look upon themselves as the special favorites of Heaven, simply because they were descendants of Abraham.

There were the scribes, who were associated with the Pharisees, and who devoted their lives to copying the Scriptures. They professed great reverence for the Scriptures, counting every word and letter in them. However, their interpretation of the Old Testament was entirely legalistic, and much of what was spiritual and noble in it, they passed by.

The rabbis added their mass of opinions to the Scriptures, and in the course of time, the scribes came to regard these traditions as being as authoritative as the Holy writings themselves. The multiplication of interpretations finally reached such proportions that it regulated every detail of human life—personal, domestic, and social. The learning of a scribe consisted of memorizing a vast number of these opinions. It was these traditions that the scribes taught the people in the synagogues, which became such a burden that the people were unable to bear it. The spiritual and moral issues were forgotten as rituals and ceremonies multiplied and grew excessively.

The Sadducees were the "modernists" of their day. They rejected the authority of tradition, but their protest was mainly negative. They had nothing to offer in the place of the traditions. They were a worldly group of men, many of whom were wealthy. They ridiculed the exclusiveness of the Pharisees, but at the same time, they had lost all faith in that which had once been the hope of the nation. They did not believe in miracles or angels. The

Sadducees were entirely materialistic in their thinking and even denied the Resurrection. They are best described as a worldly, sophisticated group with a superficial appearance of religion, who reflected Greek culture and enjoyed foreign amusements. They worshipped wealth and worldly position. One special section of the Sadducees flattered Herod; they sought his favor, and for that reason were called Herodians.

Outside of these religious parties were the masses of the lower social scale—the publicans, harlots, and sinners—the odds and ends of humanity that no one cared about, including the condition of their souls. These were the people that God had once called the children of Abraham. These were the people God had promised the Messiah would come to save. There were still some among them who cherished the hope of Israel. There were those such as Anna and Simeon who prayed night and day with fasting and tears that the Lord might come and redeem His people from their sins.

Chapter 12

MARY, THE MOTHER OF JESUS

As the mother of Jesus, Mary stands apart from all other women. No other in history has ever been so honored. Both the angel Gabriel and Mary's cousin Elizabeth said to her, "... blessed are you among women!" (Luke 1:28, 42) To get the true picture of Mary, we must escape the legend and fancy of centuries and confine our attention to what the Scriptures actually say about her.

Mary had a humble beginning. She was an obscure, peasant girl, living in the village of Nazareth, from a poor family, although of the royal, Davidic line. She seemed to be reserved, shrinking from public view.

When we first see Mary, she is a young girl having scarcely crossed the threshold of womanhood. Marriage came early in the East; and a Jewish maiden just betrothed could hardly have been out of her teens. To this young woman, born in a peasant's home, accustomed to doing the domestic duties, and completely ignorant of the world and its ways, came a startling and overwhelming revelation.

"Now in the sixth month the angel Gabriel was sent by God to a city of Galilee named Nazareth, to a virgin betrothed to a man whose name was Joseph, of the house of David. The virgin's name was Mary. And having come in, the angel said to her, 'Rejoice, highly favored one, the Lord is with you; blessed are you among women!' But when she saw him, she was troubled at his saying, and considered what manner of greeting this was" (Luke 1:26-29).

The first thoughts Mary had could only have been those of bewilderment and dismay. First the appearance of the archangel—which in itself would have startled anyone, and then his message of pregnancy—virgin motherhood—must have astonished her beyond measure. But she managed to recover her composure, and bowing in submission to the angel, she listened to what he had to say:

> "Then the angel said to her, 'Do not be afraid, Mary, for you have found favor with God. And behold, you will conceive in your womb and bring forth a Son, and shall call His name Jesus. He will be great, and will be called the Son of the Highest; and the Lord God will give Him the throne of His father David. And He will reign over the house of Jacob forever, and of His kingdom there will be no end.' Then Mary said to the angel, 'How can this be, since I do not know a man?' And the angel answered and said to her, 'The Holy Spirit will come upon you, and the power of the Highest will overshadow you; therefore, also, that Holy One who is to be born will be called the Son of God. Now indeed, Elizabeth your relative has also conceived a son in her

old age; and this is now the sixth month for her who was called barren. For with God nothing will be impossible.' Then Mary said, 'Behold the maidservant of the Lord! Let it be to me according to your word.' And the angel departed from her" (Luke 1:30-38).

It is the artists, rather than the theologians, who have tried to convey to us the feeling of the Nazarene maiden at the time of the announcement. The painter, Rosselli, shows Mary shrinking from the angel, almost cowering at his feet. However, it's not because she is dazzled by coming into the presence of such a great being, for she keeps her eyes upon him in a steadfast gaze. The terror that is portrayed in her dark eyes is not from Gabriel, but the overwhelming message he brings to her.

Mary recovered her thinking capacity, and humbly answered the angel with simple dignity. She did not say as Zacharias did, "Whereby shall I know this?" Instead, she asked, "How shall this be?" The first statement was one of unbelief, but Mary took the words of the angel for granted. She only inquired how the event would come about.

The angel informed Mary that the conception would occur by the power of the Holy Ghost Who would overshadow her, and that the child that was to be born would be called the Son of God. In humble submission the young maiden said, "Behold the maidservant of the Lord! Let it be to me according to your word" (Luke 1:38).

We are then told that, "Now Mary arose in those days and went into the hill country with haste, to a city of Judah ..." (Luke 1:39). What was the reason for this haste in departure? Was her mother a person that she could not confide in? Or was Mary already an orphan? Since the Scriptures are silent on this point, we cannot be sure. But the fact that Mary left "in haste" is significant. It was important to her that she should have time to ponder the meaning of her strange experience and adjust herself to it. It would seem that there was no one in Nazareth that she could fully confide in. Plus, women have a way of quickly discovering when another woman is pregnant. Although she was betrothed to Joseph, she did not feel the subject was one that she could tell him about at that particular time.

The Angel Gabriel had mentioned that her cousin Elisabeth had "conceived a son in her old age." Mary apparently felt that a visit to Elisabeth's home at that time would provide her with wisdom and counsel for the events that were to come. She made the trip southward to the home, which was located in the hill country not far from Jerusalem. The warm welcome she received at the household of Elisabeth and Zacharias was reassuring. Even as Mary entered the house and gave her salutation, her cousin was filled with the Holy Ghost. Elisabeth began to prophesy, speaking of Mary as the "mother of my Lord."

> "Then she spoke out with a loud voice and said, 'Blessed are you among women, and blessed is the fruit of your womb! But why is this granted to me, that the mother of my Lord should come to me? For indeed, as soon as the voice of your greeting sounded in my ears, the babe leaped in my womb for joy. Blessed is she who believed, for there will be a fulfillment of those things which were told her from the Lord'" (Luke 1:42-45).

The words of Elisabeth, spoken under the anointing of Holy Spirit, were just the encouragement Mary needed at the time. Following Elisabeth's prophecy, Mary spoke in the Spirit:

And Mary said: 'My soul magnifies the Lord, And my spirit has rejoiced in God my Savior. For He has regarded the lowly state of His maidservant; For behold, henceforth all generations will call me blessed. For He who is mighty has done great things for me, And holy is His name. And His mercy is on those who fear Him From generation to generation. He has shown strength with His arm; He has scattered the proud in the imagination of their hearts. He has put down the mighty from their thrones, And exalted the lowly. He has filled the hungry with good things, And the rich He has sent away empty. He has helped His servant Israel, In remembrance of His mercy, As He spoke to our fathers, To Abraham and to his seed forever'" (Luke 1:46-55).

These Scriptures are referred to as the Magnificat, Mary's hymn of praise to God, and they showed that apart from being the mother of the Lord, Mary was a prophetess in her own right. This jubilant song pouring from her lips revealed Mary's wonderful breadth of spiritual experience. Her words remind us of the song of Hannah, but as the mother of the Lord, her song reaches even more supreme heights.

Mary found in Elisabeth a true mother in Israel. They spent many a holy hour together, discussing the tremendous significance of the events that had come into their lives.

Zacharias sat near them with sealed lips, mute evidence of the goodness and severity of God. (Luke 1:18-23). Then, the three happy months Mary spent in Elisabeth's home came to an end.

Mary, although a pure virgin, was soon to face the problem that a young, unmarried girl does when she becomes pregnant. She could not keep the news from others for long. With natural delicacy and reserve, she hesitated to say anything. Indeed, how could Mary reveal to a suspicious world, or even to Joseph, an experience that must have seemed utterly impossible?

And then came that awful day when Joseph became aware of her condition, and though he may have said nothing, she knew he doubted her. Or she may have told him her story, but how could he believe it? Despite her great faith, that night must have been dark indeed with only the light of her knowledge that she was pure and innocent of any wrong doing.

It must have been a black night also for Joseph. There is evidence that he was much older than Mary, and she was his first real love. His discovery could only have left him crushed and bewildered. Yet, despite his grief, his thoughts were on how he could help the poor girl in the hour of shame that seemed to be upon her.

> "Then Joseph her husband, being a just man, and not wanting to make her a public example, was minded to put her away secretly" (Matthew 1:19).

To Joseph there seemed only one thing left to do— to make some arrangement where Mary could be sent away from the village to have her baby, and to be spared the humiliation and embarrassment of bearing the child in Nazareth. But God had not forgotten Mary, the holy virgin, for the child she was to bear was the very Son of God. At that fateful moment, the angel of the Lord appeared to Joseph in a dream and said,

> "Joseph, son of David, do not be afraid to
> take to you Mary your wife, for that which
> is conceived in her is of the Holy Spirit. And
> she will bring forth a Son, and you shall call
> His name Jesus, for He will save His people
> from their sins." (Matthew 1:20, 21).

When dawn came, what a morning it must have been for both Joseph and Mary! Joseph was at her door, his face beaming with joy and reassurance to tell her he knew the truth, and that all was well.

However, there are some religions that have exalted Mary above her position, while others have considered her to be only common and ordinary. Neither view is correct. Mary was a person of strong character. She possessed the gifts and graces that make for womanly greatness. Because some have exalted her beyond her place, we must not allow this to keep us from granting her the full honor that belongs to her. The record of her in the Scriptures, even though relatively brief, shows her to be a woman of unusual spiritual depth and piety. The fact that she conducted herself well in the presence of the angel showed her to be a person of courage.

Faith was a great element in Mary's character. If it is hard for some to believe in the Incarnation, it would have been far more difficult for her. Yet she believed it with all that was within her. Jesus Himself said that no mighty work could be done where there was unbelief (Mark 6:5,

6). Therefore, her faith must have had a part in the great miracle of the Incarnation. It was the greatest of all miracles performed in the history of the human race. So it was for her as Elisabeth had said, "Blessed is she that believed, for there will be a fulfillment of those things which were told her from the Lord" (Luke 1:45).

Mary's humility is another of her striking virtues which manifested itself, not so much in devaluing herself, as it was in abandoning herself. She did not seem to think of herself as either worthy or unworthy. Her soul was lifted away from herself, and she thought of God only.

Standing at the forefront of Mary's greatness was her purity, as it is revealed in the Magnificat. There is no confession, but a wonderful joy. Only the pure heart rejoices when God is near.

Mary's life was filled with mysteries that were beyond her. Yet, she never ceased to ponder them as she waited their unfolding. When possible, she was nearby to watch the developments in her son's ministry. She witnessed the soul-piercing scenes of the crucifixion. She shared in the first revelations on the resurrection morn. She waited with the 120 in the Upper Room. She, along with the others, received the blessed Baptism in the Spirit.

There was patience in Mary in her long years of waiting. After the birth of her child, there were no more angel choirs, strange stars, or miraculous escapes. No pilgrims came to Nazareth to search Him out; no kings came to bow before Him. Silence fell on the scene as 30 years came and went. What were Mary's thoughts in those days? Through all those years, did she ponder in her heart the things the angel had spoken to her? It appears she never doubted because even before His ministry began, she turned to those who were serving at the wedding and said, "Whatever He says to you, do it" (John 2:5).

Chapter 13

THE BIRTH OF JESUS

Mary, according to the genealogy given in Luke, was the daughter of a man by the name of Heli. The family was poor, but we may assume that their standard of living was not much different from that of their neighbors. They came from a devout stock. Mary and Elisabeth were cousins, although it doesn't seem possible that they were first cousins because of the differences in their ages, which would mean that their fathers had been brothers.

On each Sabbath day, Mary went with her parents to the synagogue to listen to the Scriptures. She didn't realized at the time that certain Scriptures referred to her personally (Isaiah 7:14). We do not have a record of what kind of education Mary received, though probably it wasn't much. However, her song in Luke 1:46-55 indicates that she was not unlearned.

What kind of man was Joseph? As far as the record shows, he was only a humble carpenter, probably much older than Mary, but the Scriptures describe him as a "just man." Like his ancestor Joseph, after whom he was named, he too seemed to have a special gift of dreams. Several times the revelations he received in dreams gave him information of the utmost importance.

Where did Mary first meet Joseph? Was it at the spring in Nazareth where she went to draw water? Or did she first meet him at the carpenter's shop? We don't know for sure, but quite possibly he brought her a gift he had made for her in the carpenter's shop. From that time, Mary began making simple preparations for her wedding. Then, the strange events began that changed her life completely.

In the city of Rome, on the great throne sat Augustus Caesar, the ruler of an empire that was greater than any the world had ever known. It might appear that this powerful figure was complacent in his victory in the great power struggle for control of the world. But actually, he was puzzled with the problem of how to finance his unmanageable kingdom. The cost of maintaining the army and his widely dispersed administration required great sums of money. Many provinces were paying tribute, but Palestine was among those that were not. The emperor decided that each country must share its part of the burden.

So Augustus set the wheels in motion for carrying out his plan with a universal tax. This decree went down from one official to another until eventually the news reached the ears of Joseph and Mary. They realized that they immediately would have to go to the city of their ancestors, despite the fact that Mary was in the latter stages of her pregnancy.

It was a familiar road, for Mary had returned on the route just six months before from her visit to Elisabeth. She was seated on the back of a donkey; and with Joseph leading, they began their trip down the road that led to the plain of Esdraelon. Not all the people on the route were friendly. While passing through Samaria, no hospitality was offered them. At Shechem they saw Ebal and Gerizim, the mountains of curse and blessing where the Samaritans worshipped. Perhaps they stopped and refreshed themselves at the well of Sychar, the one that Jacob dug. Then, they went on, passing Shiloh, Gibeon, and Bethel. At last as they drew near Jerusalem, the magnificent Temple burst into view. Though it was still in the process of being built, the outer courts shone with a dazzling whiteness.

It was an unforgettable experience to visit Jerusalem, but they were not yet at their destination. Bethlehem was still five miles away. Within an hour after leaving the outskirts of Jerusalem, they were in view of the city. In another half hour, they were passing the tomb of Rachel, and then, finally, they entered the city. They stopped to find a room at the inn, but many visitors were there ahead of them for the same purpose. Every spare room was taken. Joseph, almost in despair, at last found a manger which the innkeeper permitted them to use. The best that Mary could have was a rug and a little covering thrown over the straw. Thus, the humble couple, who would someday be the world's most famous family, laid down to rest.

Who would have believed that in that humble surrounding the greatest event in history had just taken place!

WAS CHRIST BORN IN THE WINTER?

The traditional date of the birth of Christ is celebrated on December 25. Of course, this is not what the Bible says, and the evidence supports that this is not the truth. Jerusalem and Bethlehem are at an altitude of 2,500 feet. Snow often falls in this area. The winters were severe enough for Christ to have warned the Jews who were to flee the Romans when they surrounded Jerusalem to pray "… that your flight may not be in winter …" (Matthew 24:15-22). The weather at that time of the year would have been very severe for a prospective mother to travel the long distance from Nazareth to Bethlehem. The child Jesus was born in an open manger, and it must be noted that the shepherds, on their own volition, were out in an open field. It was not customary for shepherds to be out with flocks at night in the winter. Historical evidence indicates that Christ was born in September.

THE VISIT OF THE ANGELS

> "Now there were in the same country shepherds living out in the fields, keeping watch over their flock by night. And behold, an angel of the Lord stood before them, and the glory of the Lord shone around them, and they were greatly afraid. Then the angel said to them, 'Do not be afraid, for behold, I bring you good tidings of great joy which will be to all people. For there is born to you this day in the city of David a Savior, who is Christ the Lord. And this will be the sign to you: You will find a Babe wrapped in swaddling cloths, lying in a manger.' And suddenly there was with the angel a multitude of the heavenly host praising God and saying: 'Glory to God in the highest, And on earth peace, goodwill toward men!'" (Luke 2:8-14).

The visit of the angels to the humble shepherds was an interesting event, but it may also be asked: Why didn't the angels appear to the priests at Jerusalem who sat in Moses' seat instead of the shepherds? The priests were informed of the event, but they were not interested enough to make the five-mile-journey to Bethlehem to find out for themselves (Matthew 2:4-5). Why did the angels appear to the shepherds? Undoubtedly, the shepherds, like Simeon, were among those who were watching for the consolation of Israel. In the quietness of their occupation, they had time to meditate and prepare their hearts for the great event. However, the effect of the sudden, heavenly visitation certainly made them "afraid."

> "So it was, when the angels had gone away from them into heaven, that the shepherds said to one another, 'Let us now go to Bethlehem and see this thing that has come to pass, which the Lord has made known to us.' And they came with haste and found Mary and Joseph, and the Babe lying in a manger" (Luke 2:15-16).

They told the remarkable story of their angelic visitation to Mary and Joseph. It is most certain that Mary and Joseph weren't the only ones who heard of the visitation. They repeated the story to anyone who wanted to listen.

THE POVERTY OF CHRIST

The Scriptures tell us that He Who was rich became poor that we might through His poverty become rich. By our standards today, the family of Jesus was poor indeed, although probably not much poorer than the average family of Nazareth.

One incident which occurred in the Temple gives us a glimpse of Joseph's financial condition. When it came time for the circumcision of the child, the Law required that the parents bring a lamb and offer it for atonement. But the Scriptures, taking notice of the poor added, "And if she is not able to bring a lamb, then she may bring two turtledoves or two young pigeons ..." (Leviticus 12:6-8). The poverty of the family of Jesus is thus evident. The devoted couple would have certainly brought a lamb had their means permitted. The most they could afford was two turtledoves.

Considering their limited finances, they could have not made their way to Egypt to escape from Herod. Because of the providence of God the wise men had brought gifts—gold, frankincense, and myrrh, were they able to make the trip.

THE VISIT OF THE WISE MEN

"When they heard the king, they departed; and behold, the star which they had seen in the East went before them, till it came and stood over where the young Child was. When they saw the star, they rejoiced with exceedingly great joy" (Matthew 2:9-10).

The wise men and the Star of the East are inseparably associated with the birth of Christ. What was this Star of Bethlehem? The verses above indicate that the wise men saw the star at different times—first, in their homeland in the East, and then later, after they left Jerusalem, on the way to Bethlehem. Since Christ was born in 4 B.C., the wise men saw the star at least two years earlier according to verse 16. This would mean the date that they first saw it was 6 B.C., or perhaps late 7 B.C.

Was this star a comet with its bright tail sweeping across the sky? Comets have always made a deep impression upon men's minds. They were believed to portend special events. It would not be surprising that men of that day would consider an especially brilliant comet as a prediction of some extraordinary event. Comets, however, do not linger long in the sky. Drawn by the powerful attraction of the sun, a comet revolves around that massive body, and then, after gathering great momentum, it swings out into space. It would not have reappeared two years later.

History records a brilliant comet in 44 B.C., just before the Ides of March when Caesar was assassinated. Another appeared in 66 A.D., just before the Christians fled to Pella to escape the siege of the city of Jerusalem by the Romans. Halley's Comet appeared in 12 B.C., and is described in great detail by Chinese astronomers. This, however, is too early to be associated with the birth of Christ in 4 B.C.

Astronomers inform us, however, that there was a conjunction of planets at about this time. Jupiter, Saturn, and Venus came so close together in the year 7 B.C. that "they appeared as one." But such a planetary configuration lasts only a few days. Matthew 2:9 declares that "the star, which they saw in the cast, went before them, till it came and stood over where the young child was." This wording would indicate that the star actually appeared to change its position as they traveled from Jerusalem to Bethlehem, much as the Pillar of Cloud and the Pillar of Fire arose from the tabernacle and went before the children of Israel.

And who were the wise men, or magi, as they are sometimes called? They were a priestly class from a region of Persia, who specialized in interpreting dreams and supernatural visitations. It is hardly possible that they were Jews, since they did not seem to be familiar with the Old Testament Scriptures. When they reached Jerusalem, they went to the Temple priests to inquire where Christ the King was to be born. The Wise Men were typical of the great multitude of Gentiles who were to believe on Him.

It is strange that the wise men of the East should travel all the way to Bethlehem to see the newborn Babe, while the scribes and chief priests in Jerusalem only five miles away, who knew where He was to be born, did not bother to investigate the report of His birth.

There was one person, however, who took their quest seriously. This was none other than Herod the king. Slowly dying in his bed, he hoped to perpetuate his dynasty and would stop at no cruelty to accomplish his purpose. To maintain his grip over the country, Herod had spies stationed everywhere to bring him the news of anything that might jeopardize his interests. When word of the Magi's arrival came to him, he sent for the scribes and the priests to learn where Christ was to be born.

> "So they said to him, 'In Bethlehem of Judea, for thus it is written by the prophet: 'But you, Bethlehem, in the land of Judah, Are not the least among the rulers of Judah; For out of you shall come a Ruler Who will shepherd My people Israel'" (Matthew 2:5-6).

Having obtained this information, he called for the wise men. He told them he knew where the King of the Jews was to be born. They were to go to Bethlehem and search out diligently where the child was. Then craftily he asked them to return and give him the information as to where the Child was so that he might also worship Him.

> "Then Herod, when he had secretly called the wise men, determined from them what time the star appeared. And he sent them to Bethlehem and said, 'Go and search carefully for the young Child, and when you have found Him, bring back word to me, that I may come and worship Him also'" (Matthew 2:7, 8).

The Magi turned and left the palace of Herod. They took their gifts they had brought from Persia and mounted their animals for the short trip from Jerusalem to Bethlehem. The star they had seen in the East went before them and led them directly to the place where the child was born.

By this time, Joseph had found a house, Mary was no longer occupying a stable. And when the wise men came in, they fell down on the floor and worshipped the Babe. Then they took their gifts of gold, frankincense, and myrrh and laid them at His feet.

But as they were ready to return to Jerusalem, one of them was visited by a dream which warned them not to return to Herod, and they departed down the valley east of Bethlehem and returned to their country another way.

Joseph also had a dream. In the vision, he received a warning to take the Child and His mother and flee at once from Herod to go down to Egypt. There was no time to be lost. Herod had a fortress palace close to Bethlehem, and at any hour the word might go out to slay the Child.

In the dead of night, Joseph sat Mary and the Child upon the back of the animal, and they began the journey south to Egypt. By morning light, they would not be far from the valley of Elah where Mary's ancestor David once fought the giant Goliath. It could not have been easy for Mary to hold the Child in her arms, hour-after-hour, all through the night, but it had to be done. Every mile brought them closer to safety. By the time they reached Beersheba, they had put danger well behind them.

Meanwhile in Jerusalem, Herod waited impatiently for the return of the wise men. At last a messenger brought him the disconcerting news that the wise men had defied his command and had returned to their country by another way. Filled with rage, Herod determined on a fiendish act which was in keeping with his cruel spirit. His officers were to go to Bethlehem and slay all the children in that part of the country from two years old and under. Then was fulfilled the prophecy of Jeremiah:

> "A voice was heard in Ramah, Lamentation,
> weeping, and great mourning, Rachel weeping
> for her children, Refusing to be comforted,
> Because they are no more" (Matthew 2:18).

This is a remarkable prophecy, and it refers to Rachel, Jacob's wife. In her earlier years of marriage, she had been barren and had once cried out to Jacob, "Give me children, or else I die!" (Genesis 30:1). Finally, her prayer to God was heard, and she gave birth to Joseph, and later, to Benjamin. Rachel's passionate love for children seemed to project itself down the ages to her descendants, and so it is said that the cry of mourning over the slaughter of the innocents is spoken of as "Rachel weeping for her children, and could not be comforted because they were not."

It was one of the last acts of the wicked Herod. To the very end of his life, his wicked and cruel nature could not be satisfied. He ordered fires to be kindled in Jerusalem, and 42 students were consigned to the flames. About the same time, he wrote a letter to his son Antipas, asking him to come home. When the boy arrived, Herod made terrible accusations against him. After putting him in prison, he sent word for him to be put to death. As Herod's death drew near, spies came and told him that the people were rejoicing. Furious over this, he gave a command that when he died, soldiers were to kill all who rejoiced at his death—a command that was never carried out. The agonies of the dying king were beyond description. Finally, when he died, the people breathed a sigh of relief.

ARCHELAUS REIGNS, AND JOSEPH AND MARY RETURN TO ISRAEL

"Now when Herod was dead, behold, an angel of the Lord appeared in a dream to Joseph in Egypt, saying, 'Arise, take the young Child and His mother, and go to the land of Israel, for those who sought the young Child's life are dead.' Then he arose, took the young Child and His mother, and came into the land of Israel. But when he heard that Archelaus was reigning over Judea instead of his father Herod, he was afraid to go there. And being warned by God in a dream, he turned aside into the region of Galilee" (Matthew 2:19-22).

Herod had made a total of four wills. At his death, Archelaus was chosen as king of Judea, while the other sons, Herod Antipas and the half-brother Philip, inherited other provinces of the kingdom. All this, of course, had to be ratified by Emperor Augustus. But even before Archelaus could get away to Rome, violent demonstrations broke out in Jerusalem with the rioters demanding special concessions from Archelaus. The ringleaders of the mob were captured and burned alive.

Joseph and Mary of course did not intend to remain in Egypt. As soon as the angel of the Lord appeared to him in a dream, assuring him that Herod was dead, he made the decision to return.

When the family had crossed the desert and began to climb the hills of Judea, Joseph received word of further events occurring in Judea. He heard the terrible news that thousands of pilgrims who had gone to the city had been massacred by the soldiers.

It did not appear safe to pass through the land. When he learned that Archelaus was king over Judea, he decided to follow the road that went up the lowlands and around Mt. Carmel. From there he crossed the Plain of Esdraelon to Nazareth where their former home had been.

Chapter 14

THE BOY JESUS

The city of Nazareth was to be the home of Jesus, until He was thirty years of age. Writers of the life of Christ generally regret the fact that so little is recorded about His youthful days. There was, however, a reason for this. The early life of Jesus was Divinely intended to not be any different from that of any other boy in Israel. Although it is probable that people recognized Jesus as an unusual child, it was certainly furthest from their thoughts that the youth who dwelt in their midst was the very Son of God, whose impact on the world would be greater than any other person who ever lived.

The inhabitants of Nazareth may have noticed that, although all children at times are given to misbehaving, yet they could never recall Jesus acting improperly. Those who were especially close to the family probably observed His devotion to Mary and Joseph. Others, perhaps, noticed His interest in the Scriptures. It seems probable that Jesus grew up in Nazareth without attracting any extraordinary attention.

THE APOCRYPHAL GOSPELS

Although the Gospels have little to say about the boyhood of Jesus, some of the apocryphal New Testament gospels profess to show this period of His life. In the days of Paul, there were evidently those who tried to find out about the early life of Jesus. The apostle cautioned against too much zeal in this saying, "Therefore, from now on, we regard no one according to the flesh. Even though we have known Christ according to the flesh, yet now we know Him thus no longer" (2 Corinthians 5:16). It was His ministry and message that were significant, not His boyhood days.

The apocryphal gospel of Thomas records a number of miracles that were supposed to have transpired during Jesus' childhood. These are nothing but fabrications, and poor ones at that. Not a single historian considers them anything but fiction. These fables only show how unequal the imagination of man is to such a task. The stories are crude caricatures in comparison to the majestic narratives of the four Gospels. They make Jesus a worker of frivolous and useless marvels. According to these apocryphal stories, Jesus made birds of clay and caused them to fly. He was supposed to have raised a boy from the dead to prove he was innocent of a crime. He changed playmates into animals. In short, the apocryphal gospels are compilations of mere chaff; and some of the tales are not only incredible, but are almost blasphemous.

Such miserable concoctions of fantasy warn us to stay clear of trying to peer too far into the hallowed enclosure of His early life. It was the purpose of God that Jesus should grow up quietly in an obscure village and drew no special attention to Himself. We are told that He grew in wisdom and stature and in favor with God and man, thus passing through all the stages of normal development.

As for the miracles which were supposed to have been performed during His boyhood, the Gospel of John specifically tells us that the first miracle of Christ was that of turning the water into wine (John 2:11).

THE HOME OF JESUS

The home of Jesus was a godly one. According to Scripture, "Joseph was a righteous and just man." It is probable that as Jesus and each of His brothers grew older, they joined Joseph in the carpenter shop to help in the task of providing for the family.

Mary was certainly a woman of faith, as she demonstrated by her beautiful response to the angel Gabriel in Luke 1:38. She showed knowledge of the Scriptures, possessed poetic genius, and yet, was a humble woman. She was highly conscious of the great and totally unexpected honor that had been bestowed upon her as the mother of the Messiah.

Despite her large family, it's probable that she took time to teach the children all she knew about spiritual things. The great secret she kept in her heart spurred her to do everything possible for her Firstborn. In return, we see Him thinking of her, even during the last hours of His life. While He suffered on the cross, He told John, His disciple, that he was to be a son to her.

THE SYNAGOGUE SCHOOL

About the age of eight, Jesus was sent to the teacher of the synagogue who taught the children from the sacred rolls of the Scriptures. The teacher would write Aramaic letters in the sand with a pointed stick, and the students sitting down cross-legged repeated together the letters that were spelled out. The teacher also read the boys stories of the Bible characters, such as Abraham, Isaac, Jacob, and Joseph. Jesus listened to these stories with rapt attention. He let nothing that was read from the Scriptures fall to the ground.

On the day before the Sabbath, Joseph put away his saw, his chisel, and his hammer, and as night came on, the men of the village went to the synagogue. On the following morning, the boys and girls attended special services. The ruler of the synagogue usually appointed someone to read the Scriptures. Anyone who could read was qualified to take his turn at this task. The cylinder that contained the sacred scroll was brought out and unrolled. Then the one appointed chose a certain portion of the Scriptures to read to the congregation.

When the Scriptures were read, Jesus took the greatest interest. It was during these hidden years at Nazareth that His mind became richly endowed with the knowledge of the Old Testament.

It appears from Luke 4:16 that on numerous occasions He was the One to read. "And as his custom was, he went into the synagogue on the Sabbath day and stood up for to read."

THE FEASTS OF ISRAEL

There was another activity in which Jesus participated that must have had an unusual interest for Him —the annual feasts of Israel.

The Jews of this period were very faithful in the observance of these feasts. One of these was the Feast of the Dedication of the Temple, or the Feast of Lights. This occurred during the winter time. People lit their lamps, and the young men marched down the streets with blazing torches. On the following day, they went to the synagogue and sang joyful songs. The people recounted the stirring stories of the great hero, Judas Maccabeus, who vanquished Israel's enemies and purified the Temple. The Temple had once been defiled by the wicked, Syrian tyrant Antiochus Epiphanes, and the Jews celebrated its purification by this eight-day Feast of Dedication.

There were other festivals, including the Feast of Purim, in which they remembered how Queen Esther overthrew the wicked Haman who plotted to destroy the Jews from the face of the Earth. During this feast, the story of Esther was read from a scroll in the synagogue.

Then of course, there was the greatest of all feasts, the Passover. This feast was held each year at about the same time as our Easter. Many pilgrims went to Jerusalem to celebrate this notable event. Those who remained home ate the Passover feast in their houses with unleavened bread.

Following the Passover was the feast of Pentecost, a little over a month later. Finally, in the fall was the Feast of Booths or Tabernacles. People left their houses and camped out in the open under the tree branches. This was something a small boy would relish. And so these various feasts in which the people celebrated the goodness of God were important events in the lives of the people of Israel. It was a time when parents would teach their children about God and about His peculiar dealings with their nation. We may be sure that the Boy Jesus gave all these occasions His most thoughtful attention. Each of these feasts had a meaning to Him, and He let nothing get past Him.

THE REBELLION OF JUDAS

When Jesus was about 10-years-old, news reached Nazareth that Augustus had removed Archelaus as the King of Judea. Archelaus had apparently inherited the worst traits of his father Herod, and at the same time, he lacked his political finesse. Having little interest in trying to help the impoverished subjects of his kingdom, Archelaus embarked on an extravagant building program. He divorced his wife and married his brother's spouse. At last, the news of his misgovernment reached the ears of the Emperor Augustus. The emperor had Archelaus recalled to Rome and then exiled to Vienne where he died a few years later. Augustus decided he no longer would have a king over Judea, but a governor. Thus, it was at the trial of Jesus that Pilate the governor ruled, instead of a king.

The year following the removal of Archelaus there was a rebellion in Galilee. News had come to Nazareth and other Galilean cities that the Roman government had ordered a census to be taken. Great anger was aroused among the Galileans. In every town and village, young nationalist patriots arose and gathered in groups to curse Rome and swear revolt.

In the neighboring town, Sepphoris, only three miles from Nazareth, a man by the name of Judas raised the standard of revolt (Acts 5:37). Young men throughout Galilee poured into the city to gather around Judas. They shouted the cry of war and vowed to give their lives to free the Jews from the Roman yoke. 10,000 of them marched across the land to Tiberias, the new city where Herod's palace was soon to be built, and after overpowering the guards broke into the armory and took the spears, swords, and shields. Then they went out to face the Romans.

The news of the revolt quickly reached the ears of Varus, who commanded the Roman legions in the hills above Gadara. His veterans marched against the undisciplined mob that Judas had gathered. There could only be one result. The Galilean recruits split up and fled. Then Varus went to Sepphoris and set the town on fire. That night, every person in Nazareth went to the top of the hill to see the whole city of Sepphoris going up in flames. By morning, nothing was left but a smoldering ruin. The people of the city were driven like cattle to the sea coast. There they were forced to board ships to be taken to the slave markets. Two thousand of the young prisoners were crucified on crosses.

But the saddened Jews who survived continued to hope that someday the Messiah would come, and He would drive out the hated Romans and set up the Kingdom of God on Earth. But the Boy Jesus, who even then was learning what the prophets had taught, knew that freeing the land of the Romans was not the Messiah's first task. Soon, He would have His first opportunity to go to Jerusalem and learn from the teachers of the Temple more about the hopes and aspirations of His countrymen.

Chapter 15

THE VISIT TO JERUSALEM

In the days of Jesus, the 13th birthday of a Jewish boy marked a great milestone in his life. He then became "a son of the Law." At that age, the responsibility for keeping the Law shifted from his father to him. He stepped over the threshold into a new world. It was the greatest day in his life. When a boy reached 13 years of age, it was customary for pious parents to take him with them to Jerusalem to celebrate the Passover. In the case of Jesus, his 12th birthday had occurred about six months before the Passover. Even though He was not yet 13, He was allowed to go with Joseph and Mary.

Ever since the crescent of the new moon had appeared in the western sky, there was great activity in Nazareth. Pilgrims were making preparations for the journey to Jerusalem before the full moon of the Passover came. Joseph and Mary, like many others, were getting ready for the journey. The donkey, besides carrying Mary, also bore sleeping mats and the food that was needed.

The journey to Jerusalem was a long trip for a boy of 12. Despite the artists who tend to make the Jesus appear weak and frail, He must have been of a strong constitution. During His ministry, He constantly made long trips from one part of the country to the other. The record says, "… the Child grew and became strong in spirit …" (Luke 2:40).

The road from Nazareth was a steady downhill path to the Plain of Esdraelon. As the procession passed the bluffs, the pilgrims could see other caravans moving southward far down the valley. By the time they were well into the plain, the noon hour had come, and the whole company paused for lunch. Then they moved on. As night came, the caravan leader called a halt. By this time, they were into the foothills of Samaria. The evening meal was eaten; prayers were said, and the people laid their mats on the ground to sleep.

The Samaritan people were generally hostile and had no dealings with the Jews, but if a caravan was large, there was little danger that any of the Samaritan raiders would attempt to attack the party. As the first rays of dawn were seen in the east, the caravan was up and around.

Late in the afternoon of the second day, they came to the city of Sychar which stood between Mount Gerizim, the mount of blessing, and Mount Ebal, the mount of cursing. Nearby was Jacob's well where Jesus later was to meet and talk with the Samaritan woman.

As they continued on the third day to journey southward, they passed many historic spots. There was the Valley of Ajalon, where Joshua commanded the Sun and the Moon to not move for 24 hours. Further south were the ruins of Bethel, where Jacob in a dream saw a ladder reaching to Heaven. Other places marked historic events in the lives of Saul and Samuel. At last, Jerusalem came into view. As many of the pilgrims as possible camped on the Mount of Olives, where a magnificent view of the Temple and its court could be seen.

The Passover must have been a time of intense interest to Jesus. There was the visit to the Temple—that dazzling edifice built by Herod which stood almost as one of the wonders of the world. Joseph and Jesus walked into the outer court and looked around, admiring the magnificent architecture. They continued until they came to the inner court. There was a sign carved in Greek letters, "Let no foreigners enter within the screen and enclosure around the holy place. Whosoever is taken in so doing will himself be the cause of the death that overtakes him."

This meant, of course, that God was only for the Jews. Since He was only a young lad, Jesus could go no further than the Court of the Women. Joseph, however, was allowed to go into the inner court where the heads of families offered their lambs for sacrifice. He received the sacred parts of the Passover lamb and came out again through the Gate Beautiful. Then, they went to a place where the family and the other Nazareth travelers celebrated the Passover supper.

Only two days were required for the essential observances of the Passover feast to be completed. Many might have wished to stay longer. Others were eager to get back home, since it was nearing the time of the wheat planting. Joseph's carpenter shop was without its master. At an agreed time, many of the Nazareth pilgrims started on their homeward journey, and Joseph and Mary joined the group. They took for granted that Jesus was with the other boys. All day long, the company moved northward.

As they neared a village, which is known as Ramaliah today, the caravan prepared to stop and camp for the night. It was then, to their great alarm, that Joseph and Mary discovered that Jesus was not with them. They ran quickly throughout the whole group, inquiring anxiously of everyone as to His whereabouts. No one had seen Him. What if something had happened to Him? Would not the wrath of Heaven be visited upon them if through their carelessness something had happened to Him?

However, there was nothing they could do, but wait for morning to come. At dawn, they started to retrace their steps, reaching Jerusalem before the day was over. But neither that day nor the next could they find the lost boy. They went from one place to another, walking and looking. Finally, on the third day, they went to the Temple, and there to their relief, they saw Him talking with the doctors and elders.

What happened? The Passover supper had absorbed the whole soul and spirit of the boy Jesus. He wanted to ask the religious leaders what they believed was God's will and plan for the nation. It was His golden opportunity to ask them questions that were pounding in His soul. As He went into the Temple, He found one of the groups of rabbis who were teaching. For a while He said nothing, but listened quietly. Then the questions began.

The rabbis were astounded by His insight and comprehension, and in turn, began asking Him questions. We do not know all the things they discussed.

One day passed, then two. On the third day, suddenly, Jesus heard a familiar voice. It was His mother reproaching Him for not being in the company (Luke 2:48). The answer the young lad gave marks the beginning of a new era in the life of Jesus. They are Jesus' only recorded words before He began public ministry. "Why did you seek Me? Did you not know that I must be about My Father's business?" (Luke 2:49).

Christ's humanity clearly shows here. He had not meant to displease His mother. He had tried to make the most of His trip to Jerusalem. When Mary and Joseph found Him, He dutifully returned with them to Nazareth. But from that time on there was a change in His life. He began to think about His mission in the world.

The next 18 years in Nazareth are called the silent years, but they were by no means idle years. Jesus worked with His hands at the carpenter's trade, and at the same time, He was making preparation for His life's work. When that was completed He would go forth in His ministry, which in three short years would profoundly change the destinies of the human race.

Chapter 16

RETURN TO NAZARETH

Joseph and Mary returned to Nazareth from Jerusalem with Jesus, their son. At this point, the 18 silent years began. From the time of this visit to Jerusalem, they perceived that a notable change was taking place in Him. There was that ever-present feeling that He must be about His Father's business.

Luke says:

"Then He went down with them and came to Nazareth, and was subject to them, but His mother kept all these things in her heart" (Luke 2:51).

No doubt Jesus longed to remain in Jerusalem where He might sit at the feet of the great masters. However, it was not God's plan. Naturally, as His parents, Joseph and Mary expected Him to return to Nazareth with them, and that is what He did. The writer of the Hebrews said, "… though He was a Son, yet He learned obedience by the things which He suffered" (Heb. 5:8). It would seem that in Christ's return to Nazareth, God was teaching men that simple obedience and faithfulness in performing the normal duties of a son while growing into manhood was considered high and holy in His sight. Here is a pointed lesson to those who become irritated at what seems to be the dull routine of life.

Then one day, Joseph was home ill. He did not get better. Mary wept, for Joseph was dead. Jesus wept with the others, even as He would do someday at Lazarus' grave. Though He was to be the Resurrection and the Life, just as He reminded Martha later on in His life, at this time, His time had not yet come. It was His Heavenly Father's will for Jesus to share in all the sorrows of the human race — including death, the great enemy of man. Someday, He would come to grips with this enemy and destroy its power forever.

How do we know that Joseph died during the years that Jesus spent at Nazareth? For one thing, he no longer appears in the Gospel narrative. Mary, His brothers and sisters do, but Joseph does not. When they attended the wedding at Cana of Galilee, Mary went, but Joseph was not seen. Mary is mentioned several times in the Gospel narrative, after the visit to Jerusalem, but Joseph isn't. When Christ went to the Cross, He said to John the Beloved, "Behold your mother! "And then turning to her, He said, "Woman, behold your son!" (John 19:26, 27).

We can only suppose the responsibility of taking care of the family fell on Jesus. He was the oldest son. Perhaps He had the assistance of some of the younger brothers. He was known in the community as the "carpenter" and the "carpenter's son" (Mark 6:3; Matthew 13:55).

> "'Is this not the carpenter, the Son of Mary,
> and brother of James, Joses, Judas, and
> Simon? And are not His sisters here with us?'
> So they were offended at Him."

Perhaps, from His own family, He experienced

anxieties of the poor, or He heard the word which He later repeated in the Sermon on the Mount, "What shall we eat?" or "What shall we drink?" or "Wherewithall shall we be clothed?" He, too, had to learn to put His whole trust in the Heavenly Father, Who knew what those needs were. He, too, learned by experience that if He sought "... first the kingdom of God and His righteousness, and all these things shall be added to you" (Matthew 6:33).

Later after His ministry began, His peculiar ways brought disapproval from the family who was sensitive to what the neighbors thought:

> "But when His own people heard about this, they went out to lay hold of Him, for they said, 'He is out of His mind'" (Mark 3:21).

> "Then His brothers and His mother came, and standing outside they sent to Him, calling Him. And a multitude was sitting around Him; and they said to Him, 'Look, Your mother and Your brothers are outside seeking You'" (Mark 3:31, 32).

> "For even His brothers did not believe in Him" (John 7:5).

Having taken into consideration all these events and circumstances that went into the formation of the character of Jesus, there is still something unaccounted for. There was an original dimension of personality that was not given Him by any part of His environment. It was His spirit-awareness that because His body was entirely human, His Spirit was something more than human. He was conscious that God was His Father in a way that was different from anyone else. He was the only begotten Son of the Father. But the full significance of that truth, the great purpose of His mission, the exact manner by which that mission would be accomplished, all had to be worked out. This is why the Scriptures read, "But when the fullness of the time had come, God sent forth His Son ..." (Galatians 4:4, 5). Everything with God has a perfect time and season.

We must not overlook the fact that Joseph and Mary went up every year, not just the one time recorded, to celebrate the Passover at Jerusalem (Luke 2:41). It was customary for pilgrims arriving in Jerusalem to camp on the Mount of Olives. Over toward the east and south only a short distance was the village of Bethany. It was on a road on the other side of the hill that led down to the Jordan River.

During the years Jesus lived in Nazareth, He was in continual communion with His Heavenly Father. We are told that "Jesus increased in wisdom and stature, and in favor with God and man" (Luke 2:52). Later, in the days of His ministry, we find Him oftentimes retreating to the mountains or the desert where He could commune with His Father. During those 18 silent years, we may be certain that there were many such seasons in which He was alone with God.

From time to time, Jesus went out on the hilltop above Nazareth. Mary saw Him go and watched Him return, but what took place in His visits to the summit she did not know. She probably noticed that there was a widening gulf—a realm that her Son was entering into that she herself could not invade. Yet, His attitude toward her was always the same—one of great love, gentleness, and deference.

Chapter 17

JESUS AND THE SCRIPTURES

As we have noted, there can be no doubt that Jesus, from His early childhood, was aware of His divinity. He must have realized early in His years that His great source of knowledge of the Divine plan of God was to be found in the Scriptures, which He had access to when He was at the synagogue in Nazareth. It is more than likely, He carefully studied the Scriptures. His constant reference to what Moses and the prophets had written, His absolute belief in their inspiration, and that "not one jot or tittle should pass away until all of it was fulfilled," proves this.

To what extent were the Old Testament Scriptures able to enlighten Him on the character and manner of His future ministry? Would this enlightenment make it possible for Him, upon whose shoulders rested the fate of the world, to orient His life to His great calling?

Before we answer these questions, we should first take note of what Jesus had learned by the time He had reached manhood, concerning Israel's expectation of the advent of the Messiah. Regular attendance at the annual festivals at Jerusalem made Jesus intimately familiar with the nature of the Jews' religious worship.

There was also a hardening of the moral life of the nation into a system of formality and rituals. There was the outward offering of sacrifice, but no inward piety. The people as a whole were ignorant and superstitious, yet faithful to such ideals that they had.

When Jesus, on His occasional trips to Galilee, visited the hot baths on its shores, He witnessed the heart-breaking scenes of human misery and physical suffering. What he saw revealed the little world of men, women, and children, worn and wasted with sickness and disease. It produced a great compassion in His heart for those who were suffering.

A vision of the world was formed in His mind—a world lost and perishing, yet with possibilities. He felt the weight of its wretchedness, its suffering, and its unavailing sorrow. He saw the failure and despair of the race. He witnessed its violence, its lust for riches, the desire for luxury, and the selfish pursuit of pleasure. He saw also the patient toil, the servitude, the poverty of the downtrodden, and the desire for better things. He saw the longing in the human heart for immortality on one hand, and the cynicism and materialism that existed on the other. And in the background were the everyday sorrows of a race that had fallen, the sobbing of women and little children, the grief of the bereaved who stood beside the cold form of their loved one.

W. P. Livingston, in his volume The Master Life, sums up what Jesus saw and His interpretation of the need of the human race whose burdens He was to share and whose souls He had come to rescue:

> "That world needed no political potentate, or military colossus, who would strut through a petty hour of blood and triumph and then vanish into the abyss. Nor did it need a master of learning who would expound the philosophy of the universe or the constitution of matter or the solution of economic

and industrial problems, or the principles underlying art. These things did not touch its essential life. They left unaffected its spiritual palate. They were appropriate to the intellectual sphere and it was the privilege of man to enlighten himself. ... but to inform him out of season, regarding the origin and physical history of the earth, the processes that shaped it into being ... would be inviting the natural evolution of mind and interfering with the divine scheme."

What then was to be the nature of the mission of Christ? What was needed was someone who could speak with authority and tell mankind what was truth, the purpose for which people were born, how they might live in accord with the law of their being, and how they might have immortality. Jesus was to be God's evangelist, proclaiming to the world the principles of the Kingdom of God and of eternal life. In Him was the desire of all nations. He was the One Who had come to redeem men from their sin and set them free.

Jesus would then reveal God to mankind, show them His real nature—God was a Father to whom every child could go. He would show men that before they could enjoy Heaven, Heaven had to first be born within their hearts. He would teach them to know that before the visible Kingdom of God would appear on the Earth, that Kingdom must first be set up in the human heart. He would declare to them that the soul was worth more than the body, which would soon perish, and that men could not live by bread alone, but by every Word that proceeds from the mouth of God, that loss of the body meant little, but the loss of the soul was catastrophic.

However, Jesus was becoming aware that this was not the message Israel was looking to hear. Men were impatient for the throne of Israel to be set up. So the task of Jesus would be very difficult due to their twisted thinking. The Messiah they were looking for was not one who would teach, but one who would lead them to victory on the battlefield. There was little desire for a purely spiritual kingdom.

What wisdom Jesus needed to present His message to the people! How He would have to make allowance for their ignorance and shallowness! He would have to agree and even partake in their religious customs. He would have to use simple illustrations, such as those from nature, so they could understand. And above all, He would have to lead them back to the Scriptures to lay a foundation for His teachings.

Jesus knew He was born to be a King. Later, when Pilate asked Him the question, "Are you a king then?" He would answer, "For this cause I was born ..." But, at the same time, He would also say that His Kingdom was not of this world.

> "Jesus answered, 'My kingdom is not of this
> world. If My kingdom were of this world, My
> servants would fight, so that I should not be
> delivered to the Jews; but now My kingdom
> is not from here'" (John 18:36).

Jesus recognized in Jacob's prophecy a reference to the scepter of Israel descending to Him.

> "The scepter shall not depart from Judah, Nor
> a lawgiver from between his feet, Until Shiloh
> comes; And to Him shall be the obedience of

the people" (Genesis 49:10).

In Balaam's prophecy He saw Himself as a Star rising out of Jacob, who would someday overthrow the enemies of Israel.

> "I see Him, but not now; I behold Him, but not near; A Star shall come out of Jacob; A Scepter shall rise out of Israel, And batter the brow of Moab, And destroy all the sons of tumult" (Numbers 24:17).

But it was also clear to Jesus that He had to come first as a prophet, a Savior to save the nation from their sins. He first had to reign over the people's hearts before He could rule over them in a Kingdom. This great truth must have come to Him very early. He certainly knew all the facts of the terrible power struggle that had taken place in the establishment of the Roman Empire. Judas' insurrection and the ghastly consequences were an illustration close to home that the Kingdom of God could not be established by using those same methods. Jesus, undoubtedly, foresaw that there would be attempts to make Him King, as indeed there were, and He would have to be on His guard against them (John 6:14, 15).

Jesus, therefore, saw that His ministry was to have its beginning as a prophet. And indeed, He referred to Himself as a prophet when He spoke to Nazareth saying, "No prophet is accepted in his own country." He must have carefully studied the life of Moses, for He saw Himself typed in the Scriptures by this prophet:

"The Lord your God will raise up for you a Prophet like me from your midst, from your brethren. Him you shall hear, according to all you desired of the Lord your God in Horeb in the day of the assembly, saying, 'Let me not hear again the voice of the Lord my God, nor let me see this great fire anymore, lest I die.' 'And the Lord said to me: 'What they have spoken is good. I will raise up for them a Prophet like you from among their brethren, and will put My words in His mouth, and He shall speak to them all that I command Him. And it shall be that whoever will not hear My words, which He speaks in My name, I will require it of him" (Deuteronomy 18:15-19).

At Sinai, God had spoken directly to the children of Israel. But this approach had frightened them, and they begged Moses to let God speak to him, rather than directly to the people. However, Moses was only the prototype who portrayed the prophet that was to come. So as Moses spoke to the people, so did Jesus. He spoke the Words of God to the people of Israel.

Jesus saw His own life in Moses; He was imperiled at birth, rejected by His brethren, and chosen of God to deliver Israel. He saw Moses as an intercessor, as the giver of the Law of God, as leading the children of Israel up to the very doors of the Promised Land, yet, not as being permitted to go over himself. So He, the deliverer of Israel would lead His people into a land of rest and of plenty, but at the price of His own life.

THE MINISTRY OF THE MESSIAH

It must have come early to Jesus the type of ministry that He was to have. He saw that it was ministries of deliverance, not to rid the nation of the Romans, but to set free the spirits and bodies of men from sin and sickness. The Book of Isaiah, which refers so often to the Messiah, must have held His attention. The passage in Isaiah 61:1, 2 was one that He must have pondered often and indeed it was the text He chose for His first recorded sermon:

> "The Spirit of the Lord God is upon Me, Because the Lord has anointed Me To preach good tidings to the poor; He has sent Me to heal the brokenhearted, To proclaim liberty to the captives, And the opening of the prison to those who are bound; To proclaim the acceptable year of the Lord, And the day of vengeance of our God; To comfort all who mourn …"

This prophecy told Him many things. First, He was to receive a special anointing of the Spirit, by which He would be given power to perform the work that lay before Him. It reminds us of the Words He spoke to His own disciples after His resurrection, when He gave them the Great Commission: "But you shall receive power when the Holy Spirit has come upon you; and you shall be witnesses to Me …" (Acts 1:8). Jesus' task wasn't to just speak words, as all the other religious teachers and reformers had done before Him. He was to demonstrate His authority with a ministry of power. How His heart must have gone out to the sick, lying about the warm-water springs near Tiberias. As the Messiah, He would restore sight to the blind, heal the brokenhearted, give liberty to those who were bruised, and to those bound by Satan's power, He would bring deliverance.

HIS REJECTION

But just as certainly as the poor and the down-trodden were to receive this ministry with joy, it was surely made plain to Him from the prophecies that the religious authorities would reject Him. In chapter 53 of Isaiah, He saw His fate foretold clearly and unmistakably. Many of the Psalms also revealed the sufferings and peculiar destiny of the Messiah.

Looking backward in time, we are able to see how perfectly all these prophecies were fulfilled in the suffering, death, and resurrection of Jesus Christ. To us they proclaim salvation and redemption. To the youth, who had reached manhood in Nazareth, they spelled out the many sorrows and griefs He was to bear in fulfilling His appointed mission.

So that we might see through the eyes of Jesus, as He studied the prophecies and communed with His heavenly Father during the days He was in Nazareth, we list these prophecies of His betrayal, trial, death, resurrection, and their fulfillment. When Jesus read them, they were not yet fulfilled. He knew that if for any reason these failed to be fulfilled, the very heavens would fall.

Let us notice some of these prophecies that related to Christ's ministry and their later fulfillments:

1. THE MESSIAH WAS TO BE REJECTED.

The Prophecy:
"He is despised and rejected by men, A Man of sorrows and acquainted with grief. And we hid, as it were, our faces from Him; He was despised, and we did not esteem Him" (Isaiah 53:3).

The Fulfillment:
"He came to His own, and His own did not receive Him" (John 1:11).

2. THE MESSIAH WAS TO BE BETRAYED BY ONE OF HIS CLOSE FOLLOWERS AND FRIENDS.

The Prophecy:
"Even my own familiar friend in whom I trusted, Who ate my bread, Has lifted up his heel against me" (Psalm 41:9).

The Fulfillment:
"Then Judas Iscariot, one of the twelve, went to the chief priests to betray Him to them" (Mark 14:10).

3. THE MESSIAH WAS TO BE SOLD FOR 30 PIECES OF SILVER.

The Prophecy:
"Then I said to them, 'If it is agreeable to you, give me my wages; and if not, refrain.' So they weighed out for my wages thirty pieces

of silver" (Zechariah 11:12).

The Fulfillment:
"... and said, 'What are you willing to give me if I deliver Him to you?' And they counted out to him thirty pieces of silver" (Matthew 26:15).

4. THE MESSIAH WAS TO BE SILENT BEFORE HIS ACCUSERS.

The Prophecy:
"He was oppressed and He was afflicted, Yet He opened not His mouth; He was led as a lamb to the slaughter, And as a sheep before its shearers is silent, So He opened not His mouth" (Isaiah 53:7).

The Fulfillment:
"And the high priest arose and said to Him, 'Do You answer nothing? What is it these men testify against You?' But Jesus kept silent. And the high priest answered and said to Him, 'I put You under oath by the living God: Tell us if You are the Christ, the Son of God!'" (Matthew 26:62, 63)

5. THE MESSIAH WAS TO BE SMITTEN AND SPAT UPON BY HIS ENEMIES.

The Prophecy:
"I gave My back to those who struck Me,

And My cheeks to those who plucked out the beard; I did not hide My face from shame and spitting" (Isaiah 50:6).

The Fulfillment:
"Then some began to spit on Him, and to blindfold Him, and to beat Him, and to say to Him, 'Prophesy!' And the officers struck Him with the palms of their hands" (Mark 14:65).

6. THE MESSIAH WAS TO BRING HEALING TO THE PEOPLE.

The Prophecy:
"Surely He has borne our griefs And carried our sorrows; Yet we esteemed Him stricken, Smitten by God, and afflicted. But He was wounded for our transgressions, He was bruised for our iniquities; The chastisement for our peace was upon Him, And by His stripes we are healed" (Isaiah 53:4, 5).

The Fulfillment:
"Now when Jesus had come into Peter's house, He saw his wife's mother lying sick with a fever. So He touched her hand, and the fever left her. And she arose and served them. When evening had come, they brought to Him many who were demon-possessed. And He cast out the spirits with a word, and healed all who were sick, that it might be fulfilled

which was spoken by Isaiah the prophet, saying: 'He Himself took our infirmities and bore our sicknesses'" (Matthew 8:14-17).

7. THE MESSIAH WAS TO BE MOCKED AND TAUNTED.

The Prophecy:
"But I am a worm, and no man; A reproach of men, and despised by the people. All those who see Me ridicule Me; They shoot out the lip, they shake the head, saying, 'He trusted in the Lord, let Him rescue Him; Let Him deliver Him, since He delights in Him!'" (Psalm 22:6-8)

The Fulfillment:
"And those who passed by blasphemed Him, wagging their heads and saying, 'You who destroy the temple and build it in three days, save Yourself! If You are the Son of God, come down from the cross' (Matthew 27:39, 40).

8. THE MESSIAH WAS TO SUFFER WITH TRANSGRESSORS AND PRAY FOR HIS ENEMIES.

The Prophecy:
"Therefore I will divide Him a portion with the great, And He shall divide the spoil with the strong, Because He poured out His soul unto death, And He was numbered with the transgressors, And He bore the sin of many,

And made intercession for the transgressors"
(Isaiah 53:12).

The Fulfillment:
"Then two robbers were crucified with Him,
one on the right and another on the left"
(Matthew 27:38).

9. THE MESSIAH'S HANDS AND FEET WERE TO BE PIERCED.

The Prophecy:
"For dogs have surrounded Me; The
congregation of the wicked has enclosed
Me. They pierced My hands and My feet ..."
(Psalm 22:16).

The Fulfillment:
"Then He said to Thomas, 'Reach your finger
here, and look at My hands; and reach your
hand here, and put it into My side. Do not be
unbelieving, but believing'" (John 20:27).

10. THE MESSIAH WAS TO BE GIVEN GALL AND VINEGAR.

The Prophecy:
"They also gave me gall for my food, And
for my thirst they gave me vinegar to drink"
(Psalm 69:21).

The Fulfillment:
"Now a vessel full of sour wine was sitting there; and they filled a sponge with sour wine, put it on hyssop, and put it to His mouth" (John 19:29).

11. THE MESSIAH'S SIDE WAS TO BE PIERCED.

The Prophecy:
"And I will pour on the house of David and on the inhabitants of Jerusalem the Spirit of grace and supplication; then they will look on Me whom they pierced. Yes, they will mourn for Him as one mourns for his only son, and grieve for Him as one grieves for a firstborn" (Zechariah 12:10).

The Fulfillment:
"But one of the soldiers pierced His side with a spear, and immediately blood and water came out" (John 19:34).

12. THEY WERE TO CAST LOTS FOR THE MESSIAH'S GARMENTS.

The Prophecy:
"They divide My garments among them, And for My clothing they cast lots" (Psalm 22:18).

The Fulfillment:
"And when they crucified Him, they

divided His garments, casting lots for them to determine what every man should take" (Mark 15:24).

13. THE MESSIAH WAS TO BE BURIED WITH THE RICH.

The Prophecy:
"And they made His grave with the wicked—But with the rich at His death, Because He had done no violence, Nor was any deceit in His mouth" (Isaiah 53:9).

The Fulfillment:
"Now when evening had come, there came a rich man from Arimathea, named Joseph, who himself had also become a disciple of Jesus. This man went to Pilate and asked for the body of Jesus. Then Pilate commanded the body to be given to him. When Joseph had taken the body, he wrapped it in a clean linen cloth, and laid it in his new tomb which he had hewn out of the rock; and he rolled a large stone against the door of the tomb, and departed" (Matthew 27:57-60).

14. THE MESSIAH WAS TO BE A SACRIFICE FOR SIN.

The Prophecy:
"But He was wounded for our transgressions,

He was bruised for our iniquities; The chastisement for our peace was upon Him, And by His stripes we are healed" (Isaiah 53:5).

"He was taken from prison and from judgment, And who will declare His generation? For He was cut off from the land of the living; For the transgressions of My people He was stricken" (Isaiah 53:8).

Yet it pleased the Lord to bruise Him; He has put Him to grief. When You make His soul an offering for sin, He shall see His seed, He shall prolong His days, And the pleasure of the Lord shall prosper in His hand" (Isaiah 53:10).

"Therefore I will divide Him a portion with the great, And He shall divide the spoil with the strong, Because He poured out His soul unto death, And He was numbered with the transgressors, And He bore the sin of many, And made intercession for the transgressors" (Isaiah 53:12).

The Fulfillment:
"The next day John saw Jesus coming toward him, and said, 'Behold! The Lamb of God who takes away the sin of the world!'" (John 1:29)

15. THE MESSIAH WAS TO BE RAISED FROM THE DEAD.

The Prophecy:
"For You will not leave my soul in Sheol, Nor will You allow Your Holy One to see corruption" (Psalm 16:10).

The Fulfillment:
"And as they went to tell His disciples, behold, Jesus met them, saying, 'Rejoice!' So they came and held Him by the feet and worshiped Him" (Matthew 28:9).

16. THE MESSIAH WAS TO ASCEND TO THE RIGHT HAND OF GOD.

The Prophecy:
"You have ascended on high, You have led captivity captive; You have received gifts among men, Even from the rebellious, That the Lord God might dwell there" (Psalm 68:18).

The Fulfillment:
"And he led them out as far as to Bethany, and he lifted up his hands, and blessed them. And it came to pass, while he blessed them, he was parted from them, and carried up into heaven" (Luke 24:50, 51).

WHEN WAS THE MESSIAH TO COME?

There was one more prophecy in the book of Daniel that must have held a tremendous interest to Jesus. It concerned the time appointed for the Messiah to come. What must have been the thoughts of the young Man when He first read the prophecy in Daniel 9?

> "Know therefore and understand, That from the going forth of the command To restore and build Jerusalem Until Messiah the Prince, There shall be seven weeks and sixty-two weeks; The street shall be built again, and the wall, Even in troublesome times. "And after the sixty-two weeks Messiah shall be cut off, but not for Himself; And the people of the prince who is to come Shall destroy the city and the sanctuary. The end of it shall be with a flood, And till the end of the war desolations are determined" (Daniel 9:25, 26).

Here the prophet Daniel received word by the archangel Gabriel the very date that the Messiah was to be cut off—or put to death. Was Jesus born at the right time that the prophecy mentioned? It said that the Messiah was to be cut off just 69 weeks after "the going forth of the commandment to restore and to build Jerusalem" (Daniel 9:25). The event for the restoration of Jerusalem was clearly predicted by Isaiah in the Edict of Cyrus:

> "Who says of Cyrus, 'He is My shepherd,
> And he shall perform all My pleasure, Saying
> to Jerusalem, 'You shall be built,' And to

the temple, 'Your foundation shall be laid'"
(Isaiah 44:28).

Its fulfillment was recorded in Ezra 1:1-4. How long a period is the 69 weeks that were to begin with this event? If it were days, the period would only be a little over a year—far too short a time. In Genesis 29:27, we see that a "week" of years is seven years. 69 weeks of years is, therefore, 483 years. Jesus, using such chronologies as were available in His time, saw that indeed He had come on the scene at the exact time! Of course, He knew He was the Messiah. But it is notable that Jesus always supported His faith by the confirmation of the Scriptures. The knowledge that these 483 years were almost up must have spurred Him to renewed prayer and preparation. Apart from this, the prophecy declared the Messiah was to be cut off! He was to consummate His ministry with death!

THE PRIESTHOOD OF JESUS

The Scriptures also showed Jesus that He was to function as a priest, not as one of the tribe of Levi, for He was not of that tribe, but after the order of Melchizedek:

> The Lord has sworn and will not relent, 'You are a priest forever According to the order of Melchizedek'" (Psalm 110:4).

Jesus saw that the Levitical priesthood and the Law made nothing perfect (Hebrews 7:11; 18, 19). The Levitical priesthood died and did not continue. Therefore, the Messiah became a priest after the order of Melchizedek (Hebrews

7:17).

> "But He, because He continues forever, has an unchangeable priesthood. Therefore He is also able to save to the uttermost those who come to God through Him, since He always lives to make intercession for them" (Hebrews 7:24, 25).

As priest, Christ would mediate the better covenant (Hebrews 8:6), which would take the place of the old covenant (Hebrews 8:13). But before Christ could become priest, it was necessary that He reach the age of 30, the time when a priest was accepted for service (Numbers 4:3). If He entered His ministry at 30, how many years would that give Him before the prophecy said the Messiah would "be cut off" or die? Only about three years! Jesus would have to fulfill His tremendous task in the amazingly short period of three years! It would have been enough to stagger Him, or to overwhelm His humanity, if it weren't for His great faith in God. As it was, a few times He bent under the weight of His gigantic task. Little by little, as Jesus pondered the Scriptures, the form and nature of His ministry was taking shape. Yet, He was not limited to the Scriptures only, for indeed the Spirit of God was upon Him from the beginning to teach Him, and to bring all things to His remembrance.

> "For He whom God has sent speaks the words of God, for God does not give the Spirit by measure" (John 3:34).

The Scriptures were the basis of the ministry of

Christ, although the Spirit dwelling with Him made the Word alive and powerful and guided Him into all truth.

It is interesting to follow the Gospel narrative of the four evangelists and observe the manner in which the events in Christ's life were again and again related to a fulfillment of Old Testament prophecy.

- To the people He said, "You search the Scriptures, for in them you think you have eternal life; and these are they which testify of Me" (John 5:39).
- And to the unbelieving Jews He said, "For if you believed Moses, you would believe Me; for he wrote about Me. (John 5:46).
- To the Sadducees He said, "You are mistaken, not knowing the Scriptures nor the power of God" (Matthew 22:29).
- And after the Resurrection, when He opened the understanding of His three disciples, "Then He said to them, 'O foolish ones, and slow of heart to believe in all that the prophets have spoken! Ought not the Christ to have suffered these things and to enter into His glory?" And beginning at Moses and all the Prophets, He expounded to them in all the Scriptures the things concerning Himself" (Luke 24:25-27).

Chapter 18

THE DIVINITY OF CHRIST

One day, during the ministry of Christ, Jesus asked the Pharisees the question, "What do you think about the Christ?" (Matthew 22:42). They answered that they believed He was the son of David, which according to Christ's humanity was true. But Jesus' question regarded His divinity, and He called attention to the fact that David had called Him Lord. How could He then be His son?

The question of Who Christ is has been answered in many ways. Some have considered Jesus as only one of those especially gifted individuals who come into the world from time-to-time. They say He was a man with a unique personality and possessed with unusual talents—but still only a man. This view has been tenaciously held by a specific school of thought from the days of Christ on down to the present.

Unitarians believe that the physical laws of nature are invariable and constant; and all true knowledge is a product of the observation of these physical laws. This view, of course, excludes all miracles and denies the Divine inspiration of the Scriptures. If followed to its logical consequences, it destroys all grounds for belief in angels, spirits, and the immortality of the soul. Indeed, it denies the very possibility of the government of God. To them, God is the unknown and unknowable. Such a position inevitably leads to atheism.

There is a second class of people who look upon Christ as more than human, but less than Divine. They admit the grandeur of Christ's nature and the excellence of His teachings. They exalt Him above the angels, but not to the level of deity. This belief is a theory of compromise.

Then there is the medieval view which is still held by some that Jesus had a double soul—a human soul and a Divine soul in one body. This view represented a grasping for the truth, and is a closer approach to the truth than the first two. It is, however, a troublesome theory. The real truth, as we shall see, is actually very simple. Let us now turn to the Scriptures and see what they have to say on this all-important matter.

1. THE WORD WAS MADE FLESH

John the Apostle tells us that "the Word was made flesh, and dwelt among us." This is the explanation given by John who was the closest to Christ. The simple meaning of the above words is that the Divine Spirit clothed Himself with a human body, and in that condition, took on the limitations of mankind.

2. HE WAS MADE IN THE LIKENESS OF MEN

"Let this mind be in you which was also in Christ Jesus, who, being in the form of God, did not consider it robbery to be equal with God, but made Himself of no reputation, taking the form of a bondservant, and coming in the likeness of men. And being found in appearance as a man, He humbled Himself and became obedient to the point of death, even the death of the cross" (Philippians 2:5-8).

From this passage, we see the pre-existence of Christ in the form of God, and that He took upon Himself the form of man. In other words, Jesus, being a Divine person, took on a human body and became subject to all its laws and conditions.

3. HE TOOK ON SINFUL FLESH

"For what the law could not do in that it was weak through the flesh, God did by sending His own Son in the likeness of sinful flesh, on account of sin: He condemned sin in the flesh …" (Romans 8:3).

Here we are told that Christ took on sinful flesh. He took on human nature through Mary, so that in all respects His body was the body of a man, struggling with the same temptations mankind faces, but He remained without sin. The fact is these Scriptures simply teach that the Son of God came into the world in the person of Jesus. In so doing, He veiled His royalty and emptied Himself of the powers that belonged to Him in His pre-incarnate state. He did not bring with Him in the incarnation the attributes of deity; although after He was baptized in the Holy Ghost, He manifested more of the power of God.

Jesus, after He had received the Baptism of the Spirit at the Jordan River, "being found in fashion as a man," became subject to the gradual unfolding of those powers He once had. He came back to His original self little by little. As Henry Ward Beecher said in his Life of Jesus, the Christ:

> "Who shall say that God cannot put Himself
> into finite conditions? Though as a free spirit,
> God cannot grow, yet as fettered in the flesh,
> He may. Breaking out at times with amazing
> power in single directions, yet at other times
> feeling the mist of humanity resting upon His
> eyes, He declares, 'Of that day and that hour
> knoweth no man, no, not the angels which are
> in heaven, neither the Son, but the Father.'
> This is just an experience we should expect
> in a being whose problem of life was, not
> the disclosure of the full power and glory of
> God's attributes, but the manifestation of the
> love of God and of the extremities of self-
> renunciation ..."

Some early theologians believed suffering to be inconsistent with divinity. With such ideas of the Divine nature, how could they believe that Jesus, a Man of suffering, was then Divine? When God created man, He said, "Let us make man in our image, after our likeness" (Genesis 1:26).

Yes, Christ was very much God. When clothed with flesh and made subject to physical Laws, He was a Man of the same moral faculties, of the same mental powers, subject to the same physical weaknesses, trials and temptations—only without sin. What Christ was like on Earth in His sympathies, tastes, friendships, we shall find in Him in Heaven. But now the question is: When did Christ know He was Divine? Isaiah 7:15, 16, shows that Christ's knowledge came the same as any other child. "For before the child (Immanuel) shall know to refuse the evil, and choose the good ..." (verse 16). This verse makes it plain that His own human awareness, where memory would play a part, would not occur much before the age of three. Yet, once this had happened, simultaneously, there must have been an awareness of His pre-existence, as well.

Christ was very emphatic of His pre-existence in His personal testimony. Here are a few typical statements He made on the matter:

> "Jesus said to them, 'If God were your Father, you would love Me, for I proceeded forth and came from God; nor have I come of Myself, but He sent Me' ... Jesus said to them, 'Most assuredly, I say to you, before Abraham was, I AM ...' I came forth from the Father and have come into the world. Again, I leave the world and go to the Father ... And now, O Father, glorify Me together with Yourself, with the glory which I had with You before the world was ... 'Father, I desire that they also whom You gave Me may be with Me where I am, that they may behold My glory which You have given Me; for You loved Me before the foundation of the world'" (John 8:42; 58; 16:28; 17:5,24).

Not only did He testify of His pre-existence; but He declares His actual deity:

> "I and My Father are one ... Do you not believe that I am in the Father, and the Father in Me? The words that I speak to you I do not speak on My own authority; but the Father

who dwells in Me does the works ... Jesus said to her, 'I who speak to you am He' ... Jesus heard that they had cast him out; and when He had found him, He said to him, 'Do you believe in the Son of God?' ... All things have been delivered to Me by My Father, and no one knows the Son except the Father. Nor does anyone know the Father except the Son, and the one to whom the Son wills to reveal Him"(John 10:30; 14:10; 4:26; 9:35; Matthew 11:27).

"... saying, 'What do you think about the Christ? Whose Son is He?' They said to Him, 'The Son of David.' He said to them, 'How then does David in the Spirit call Him 'Lord,' saying: 'The Lord said to my Lord, 'Sit at My right hand, Till I make Your enemies Your footstool'? If David then calls Him 'Lord,' how is He his Son?'" (Matthew 22:42-45)

It is apparent that Christ knew of His divinity in His childhood because of what He said to His mother after she and Joseph had been looking for Him. He was sitting with the elders in the Temple, "So when they saw Him, they were amazed; and His mother said to Him, "Son, why have You done this to us? Look, Your father and I have sought You anxiously" (Luke 2:48). Here, Mary refers to Joseph as Jesus' father. Jesus replied:

"And He said to them, 'Why did you seek Me? Did you not know that I must be about

My Father's business?'" (Luke 2:49)

He was not only emphasizing that they should know by now that He should be about His Father's business, but that indeed God was His true Father.

The 18 years expired; it was time for Christ's public ministry to begin.

Chapter 19

TEMPTATIONS IN THE WILDERNESS

"Then Jesus, being filled with the Holy Spirit, returned from the Jordan and was led by the Spirit into the wilderness, being tempted for forty days by the devil. And in those days He ate nothing, and afterward, when they had ended, He was hungry" (Luke 4:1, 2).

The Scriptures maintain almost complete silence about what happened during those 40 days in the wilderness, except that Satan came to visit Him personally. It is evident that Satan's appearance was timed to be at the right psychological moment. It took place when Christ, after the long days of fasting, was at His weakest. This strategy of the devil is not a matter to be overlooked, for most of us have moments of exhaustion and depression. It is well that we know the time when Satan usually chooses to attack.

The devil's first words are significant. "If You are the Son of God …" he said. The very first battle the devil ever began was over Christ's identity—His position as God's Son. Isn't this still questioned today? The devil tried to inject doubt about His divinity. The enemy thought if there was a good time to try to get Christ to doubt Who He was, it was right then. Even though Christ's physical man was weak, His Spirit was strong. This was something the devil never counted on.

When we hear Satan saying to Jesus, "If You are the Son of God ..." we are witnessing a bold attempt on his part to confuse Christ of His divinity by appealing to the human side of His nature. Only one other time would this temptation strike Him with the same force; that was on the Cross when He cried, "My God, my God, why have you forsaken me?" (Mark 15:34).

There is a remarkable parallel between Satan's words to Christ, "If You are the Son of God ..." and those spoken by the serpent to Eve in the Garden of Eden, "You will be like gods ..." The temptation in each instance was a suggestion to make one's own importance to be of greater significance. Adam and Eve yielded to the temptation to become as gods by giving in to their appetite, but Christ refused to act upon the devil's idea of the way He could reach His deity.

Christ's position as God's Son is still the great battle ground in God's plan to bring His salvation to mankind. God gives that truth to men by revelation of the Spirit and not through spectacular demonstrations like the devil suggested. The devil's strategy was to provoke Christ to attempt to prove His position as God's Son in a way that was contrary to the will of God. And the devil didn't quit with this test in the wilderness, for in the last hour, on the Cross, we hear voices flinging the very same words at Him. "If you are the Son of God, come down ..." (Matthew 27:40).

The importance of this temptation is seen in its persistent recurrence. If the devil, at any time, could have persuaded Him to act in an inappropriate manner, he would have accomplished his purpose.

It was essential that the Lord not assert His divinity in a carnal or fleshly way, but it should be accomplished in the Heavenly Father's way. At the Jordan River, Jesus had received the fullness of the Godhead bodily (Matthew 3:16, 17, Colossians 2:9). What He was doing in the wilderness was emptying His human will in order that the will of God might be fully operative instead. It was in emptying Himself that room was made for the fullness of God. The First Temptation:

THE SNARE OF BODILY HUNGER

The devil is exceedingly subtle in his temptations. This fact is seen in the first words He used to address Christ. He suggested the Lord prove His divinity by turning stones into bread. During a long fast, the desire for food is almost absent, but for some, towards the end, the appetite can return. The devil wanted to prompt Christ into making an unwarranted display of His power. It was a challenge on his part to provoke Christ into an attempt to prove His deity.

It is a fact that with the sense of physical weakness following a fast, there is also a feeling of spiritual power. There was the temptation of cutting the devil down by a demonstration of that power. In one, God-like act, He could have silenced the taunts of Satan. Moreover, the temptation was rational. Since Christ was so weak from exhaustion, he could have preserved Himself and His life for God's work. Such was the temptation that beset Esau and caused him to fail. He said, "Look, I am about to die; so what is this birthright to me?" (Genesis 25:32).

There is also a deeper side to the temptation. Christ came not to do His own will, but the will of the Father. He came into the world to be a man, to act like a man, to be limited as a man, and not to perform miracles for His own personal benefit. When Christ answered Satan, He answered him not as the Son of God whose rights had already been established on Earth, but as the Son of man. He quoted the Scripture, "… that man shall not live by bread alone; but man lives by every word that proceeds from the mouth of the LORD" (Deuteronomy 8:3). This showed His trustful reliance on God to meet His necessity.

It was certainly not a matter whether the stones could be turned into bread, for as John the Baptist said, "'We have Abraham as our father.' For I say to you that God is able to raise up children to Abraham from these stones" (Matthew 3:9). It was simply the method that Satan suggested was false. In Eden, we see Adam and Eve turning from the Tree of Life. Christ, on the other hand, turned from appetite to the will of God, so that He might lead men back to the Tree of Life. So, the choice in Eden was reversed by the second Adam—Christ.

Christ said, "If a son asks for bread from any father among you, will he give him a stone? Or if he asks for a fish, will he give him a serpent instead of a fish? Or if he asks for an egg, will he offer him a scorpion?"(Luke 11:11, 12). In this verse, Christ speaks about His experience. He once had been in the desert hungry, in a stony place where scorpions and serpents lurked. The devil pointed to a stone and said Jesus could find the answer to His need. If He took the stone, it might be bread in His hand. But Jesus rejected that His heavenly Father would answer His need in that manner.

Christ had to meet this temptation more than once in His life. He might have been ensnared by a natural desire to satisfy the physical hunger of his fellow men. Having fed the 5,000, they wanted to make Him king by force, but Jesus knew their real motive had been inspired because of the loaves and fishes they had eaten:

> "Jesus answered them and said, 'Most assuredly, I say to you, you seek Me, not because you saw the signs, but because you ate of the loaves and were filled. Do not labor for the food which perishes, but for the food which endures to everlasting life, which the Son of Man will give you, because God the Father has set His seal on Him'" (John 6:26, 27).

To want to end poverty is a noble thought, but how insignificant is the idea of just feeding the body when compared to giving men the "meat which endures to everlasting life." Christ never really touched the problem of the world's hunger and its need for physical bread. Not that this does not have its place, but He was concerned with something vastly more important:

> "Therefore I say to you, do not worry about your life, what you will eat or what you will drink; nor about your body, what you will put on. Is not life more than food and the body more than clothing?" (Matthew 6:25)

It was in these teachings that Christ offered His listeners the Bread of Life (John 6:41, 66). If He had only chosen a bread policy, He would have saved Himself from the death of the cross.

That is the fate the devil designed for Christ. But in failing to bring the world its bread, Christ brought the Bread from Heaven, which if any man eat, he shall have everlasting life. Man needs bread, but not bread alone. His higher life and his moral and spiritual capacities must be provided for. They have a far greater importance than simple physical wants.

THE TEMPTATION OF THE FOURTH DIMENSION

The second time Jesus was tempted was different from the first, and it involved an occurrence which some describe as a temptation of the fourth dimension. By some strange means, the person of the Lord was moved from the wilderness to the pinnacle of the Temple in Jerusalem. To some people, this incident is hard to perceive, and they are inclined to regard the physical transportation of Jesus as an imaginary one—that is, it was supposedly a scene presented to His imagination.

While the event was contrary to the laws of the natural world, this should not hinder us. There are laws of nature which have remained hidden through the ages which have only recently been discovered. As to the laws in the spirit world, our knowledge is extremely limited. But we do know in this atomic age that energy transcends matter, and life transcends both and controls both. The method by which Christ was transported to Jerusalem is outside the bounds of our present knowledge, but this does not remove it from the sphere of possibility. The fact is that such an experience belongs in the realm of the fourth dimension. Scientists laboring with the theory of relativity now agree there is a realm in which the fourth dimension operates, although admittedly they have a difficult time explaining it.

In a sense, matter is bondage. Our material

embodiment is a great limiting factor as to what we can do. Man is engaged in the tremendous undertaking of going to the moon. To break away from the earth's gravitation requires a rocket's thrust to overcome its powerful attraction.

The physical body is a cumbersome house, despite the fact that it is a wondrous mechanism. Our minds can roam the universe much faster than the speed of light. But the body must travel at a clumsy speed and be left far behind as the mind goes soaring in flights of fancy. After the resurrection, Christ received a glorified body that was able to accomplish those supernatural feats of transportation. Since Satan possessed certain powers in the spirit realm, he was able to escort Jesus to the pinnacle of the Temple to suggest a second temptation to Him. Again, it was the same temptation as in the Garden. "You shall be as gods." It was a temptation of the soul.

As the serpent offered Eve, and then Adam, a new realm of knowledge, so he offered the Lord a new realm of experience:

> "Then the devil took Him up into the holy city, set Him on the pinnacle of the temple, and said to Him, 'If You are the Son of God, throw Yourself down.' For it is written: 'He shall give His angels charge over you,' and, 'In their hands they shall bear you up, Lest you dash your foot against a stone.' Jesus said to him, 'It is written again, 'You shall not tempt the Lord your God'" (Matthew 4:5-7).

Jesus was to cast Himself down from the Temple, and gratify the gross desire of the crowd, just for the show of it. The idea was to do some sensational and startling miracle that would get their attention and enable Him to awe them into obedience. If by the power of God, His descent to the ground was stopped and He did not crash to instant death, the crowds would listen to Him as a superman from Heaven. Then, if He said, "I am the Messiah," the world would be at His feet. It was a plan to force the hand of God to reveal Christ's position as His Son in a spectacular way. It was to achieve a short-cut to power through a miraculous act.

The devil again addressed Jesus, "If you are the Son of God." The prince of the power of the air had just escorted Christ to the pinnacle of the Temple in the Holy City. Then the thought was, "You have been brought here safely; won't God also protect you in the short flight to the ground?"

In the temptation, Jesus was made to feel humiliated as the Son of man. Why should He not overthrow this bondage? Why should God's Son be forced to walk? The prince of the power of the air had demonstrated his power by the swift flight. Why shouldn't He, God's Son, show that He had a power as great, if not greater, than the devil's? Satan, in effect, was pointing a finger of scorn at the Godhead.

Nevertheless, Christ took the insult, and refused to be pushed into making a rash or gross display of the power of God. He accepted His human limitation and did not seek to copy the proud flight of Satan, He simply answered, "You shall not tempt the LORD your God" (Matthew 4:7).

Once, when Herod sought His life, certain Pharisees told the Lord to depart, "for Herod wants to kill You. And He said to them, Go, tell that fox, 'Behold, I cast out demons and perform cures today and tomorrow, and the third day I shall be perfected.' Nevertheless I must journey today, tomorrow, and the day following; for it cannot be that a prophet should perish outside of Jerusalem" (Luke 13:31-33).

Jesus declared that He must continue to endure until His mission was complete. He could not evade the perils and hardships to purchase comfort at the expense of the fulfillment of God's will.

There were several occasions when Jesus was tempted to use His power in a way inconsistent with His lowly position as the Son of man. At Nazareth, some of the citizens attempted to throw him over the brow of a cliff, but "He passing through the midst of them went his way." When they took up stones to stone him, "Jesus hid himself ... and so passed by." From this we may understand that He did not employ supernatural means to escape, but rather put His trust in the providence of God.

Satan never quit trying to tempt Christ in this matter. Even at the last hour of His life, the words were flung at Him, "Come down from the cross." Though Jesus could have done this as the Son of God, He could not do it as the Savior of men. After His resurrection, when He had cast off the restraints of His humiliation; He exercised quite freely those powers that the tempter tried to get Him to use as a display. Christ would not agree to the devil's proposal for Him to become a world's superman. He would not put on a theatrical display of His powers to win the awe and admiration of the fickle crowds. As Morris Stewart says in *The Temptations of Jesus:*

> "But Jesus left the great wealth that was His,
> in the grasp of His Father's hand; and He took
> nothing from its stove save with the sanction
> of His will and the bidding of His word ...
> But for Jesus to step from the Temple ledge
> would have been to dictate to Heaven instead
> of waiting its command. Such abandonment

of His dependence would have shifted the poise of His divinity which was steadied by the fingers of God; and His descent would have cast down the path of salvation from life to death and the shock of its fall have shaken the throne of God in all the Earth."

THE TEMPTATION TO RECEIVE THE KINGDOMS OF THIS WORLD

The first two temptations of Jesus appear to be almost trivial next to the third one. The first one was His refusal to use His power to make bread. The second one was the suggestion to trust God to save Him if He jumped. But totally different from the first two was the third temptation which confronted Christ:

"Again, the devil took Him up on an exceedingly high mountain, and showed Him all the kingdoms of the world and their glory. And he said to Him, 'All these things I will give You if You will fall down and worship me.' Then Jesus said to him, 'Away with you, Satan! For it is written, 'You shall worship the Lord your God, and Him only you shall serve'" (Matthew 4:8-10).

The devil took Jesus to a high mountain and showed Him the kingdoms of the world in a moment of time, and then said, "All these things will I give you, if you will fall down and worship me." Here was a change of strategy. The devil no longer challenged Who He was as God's Son. Now, Jesus was given a dazzling demonstration of Satan's temporal power. Satan, who was skilled in tempting, believed that the manhood of Christ outweighed His divinity. With blasphemous insolence, the devil paraded before the eyes of Jesus his tremendous power and the greatness and glory of his worldly kingdoms.

Since there is no mountain in the world that commands such a geographical view as the one mentioned, this scene was also a supernatural demonstration, performed on the part of Satan. In the spiritual realms, Christ was able to take in this incredible, panoramic view which transcended time and space.

The offer was obviously real. For in a profound sense, the kingdoms of this world belong to Satan. Adam originally had been given the dominion;

> "Then God said, 'Let Us make man in Our image, according to Our likeness; let them have dominion over the fish of the sea, over the birds of the air, and over the cattle, over all the earth and over every creeping thing that creeps on the earth'" (Genesis 1:26).

But Adam and Eve disobeyed God and obeyed Satan, transferring their allegiance to him. Satan now claims it, and the claim was not disputed by Christ. Indeed, all through the Scriptures, we find hints of the sovereignty of Satan. John the apostle says, "We know that we are of God, and the whole world lies under the sway of the wicked one" (1 John 5:19). In the Scofield Reference Bible, 'wickedness' is literally translated 'wicked one.'

The 10th chapter of Daniel clearly shows that the evil archangels of Satan dominate and control the great empires of the Earth.

It is true that in the days of Israel's kingdom, God had attempted to found a theocracy, and the throne of Judah was the throne of the Lord (1 Chronicles 29:23), but the effort at that time because it involved Israel's obedience hadn't achieved much success. When Christ went to the cross, He said to the unbelieving Jews, "This is your hour, and the power of darkness" (Luke 22:53).

God has never abandoned His plan to rule over the Earth, and in due time, the kingdoms of this world will become the kingdoms of the Lord Jesus Christ (Revelation 11:15). Yet, at the moment, the devil's boast of mastery was not unwarranted. He was king of the world, and not just a figurehead, endowed with only a shadowy rule. The power of the world was in his grasp, and he could dazzle the eyes of men. The temptation was an intensely real one.

Satan looked at Christ's coming onto the scene as an invasion of his own domain, and his whole kingdom was jeopardized by His Presence. He knew Christ's purpose was to incite men to revolt from Satan's power. Concerning this, Paul said, "… and that they may come to their senses and escape the snare of the devil, having been taken captive by him to do his will" (2 Timothy 2:26). Jesus had plans to build the Kingdom of Heaven right within the bounds of Satan's principality! And He said the "gates of hell" should not prevail against the Church He would build. The follower of Christ, indeed, has to wrestle against these diabolical powers:

> "For we do not wrestle against flesh and blood, but against principalities, against powers, against the rulers of the darkness of this age, against spiritual hosts of wickedness in the heavenly places" (Ephesians 6:12).

Apparently, Satan, realizing the grave danger he was facing, was willing to surrender his whole domain into the hands of Christ upon the sole condition that He bow down and worship him. It is a commentary on Satan, wise as he is, that he had hopes his offer would be accepted. It was dazzling, alluring, but he had not measured the steel in the One Who was "meek and lowly of heart," the One he tried to tempt. Christ gave the offer no consideration; He did not even think it over, nor did He weigh its possibilities. Indeed, His whole being revolted against the evil suggestion, and He answered the devil in the only way he could, saying, "Then Jesus said to him, 'Away with you, Satan! For it is written, 'You shall worship the LORD your God, and Him only you shall serve'" (Matthew 4:10). Christ's use of the Scriptures to defeat Satan is so consistent that the significance of it cannot be ignored. The Word of God has a force infinitely greater than the simple combination of sounds upon which that power is conveyed.

Satan's hold over mankind is based on catering to the material desires of obstinate, non believing men. Men hold on to this world's goods with strained hearts and a desperate grasp. Their attention is so absorbed in these temporal things that the treasures of Heaven have little or no attraction for them. Christ came to reverse this order, so instead of worshipping the things of Earth, men might desire to worship the things of Heaven. It was Satan's object to turn the Lord away from this purpose. Therefore, he led Him into the "sphere of Earth's power and glory" and invited Him to take all it contained and be content with just that.

But since Christ had subjected His own will entirely to that of the Father at the Jordan River, there was nothing in Him that responded to Satan's temptation. The Lord left ivory palaces to come to this world, giving up His heavenly riches that we, through His poverty, might become rich. Yet, He had a long, hard pull before Him to turn men from the attractions of this world to the riches of the one that is to come.

The temptation Jesus met in the wilderness would be experienced again and again. All Israel had a Messianic expectation. The throne of David was empty as far as they could see. If He would just occupy it, the nation was ready to back Him as a man. All that Christ had to do was speak the word. The nation was ready to make Him king during the early part of His ministry. Even His disciples expected Him to take the throne. Peter rebuked Him for His talk of the cross. Indeed, that disciple was ready to fight for Jesus with His sword. But that isn't the way it was supposed to be. Before Christ could rule over the Earth, He first had to rule over the hearts of men.

Later, the Medieval Church would fall for the very temptation Christ had rejected. It gave in to the riches and the wealth of this world; it laid claim to the temporal power over the kingdoms of Earth—the very thing the devil offered Christ and He rejected. The temporal power the Medieval Church attained certainly didn't bring blessings to the world.

The climax came when Satan said to Jesus, "Fall down and worship me." At that moment, Jesus turned His eyes from the tempter and said, "Get behind me." This final act of treason revolted Jesus to His depths. This appalling suggestion of disloyalty to His Father caused Him to turn to God to escape the grasp of the tremendous evil that had attacked Him. At that moment, the devil left, and the angels came. Christ, recovering from the torments of hell, accepted the fellowship of Heaven. As Morris Stewart says,

"And when Satan said, 'Fall down and worship me,' we see Jesus turn away in godly horror lest His fainting body should succumb and fall prone in the semblance of the unlawful homage! With the last strength of His manhood, He stretched out hands of appeal to God, and sent to heaven an urgent call that the arm of God would take and hold Him!"

Deep called to deep, and the angels came. It was not the angels which brought the deliverance of Jesus. Their chief ministry to Him was their company. They came not to help Him during the battle, but to minister to Him after the battle was won—a battle which Jesus fought and won single-handedly.

Chapter 20

THE CANA MIRACLE

It is significant that immediately after speaking with Nathanael, Jesus went to Cana of Galilee about 20 miles from Capernaum. This was the home of Nathanael (John 21:2). Is it possible that the meeting with Nathanael had something to do with the trip to Cana? Did Nathanael have some information about Jesus' mother, who may have been looking for Him? Did he know about the wedding which was about to take place? Surely, in so small a village as Cana, Nathanael would probably know both the bride and the groom.

It is generally believed that because of Mary's prominence in the story and her anxiety about the wedding arrangements, her knowledge of the family's resources, and the position she occupied in being able to address the servants, indicates a kinship to the family. Either the bride or the bridegroom may have been a near relative to Jesus. Since Cana is quite near to Nazareth, it is likely that Jesus knew the bride. And she may have wanted Him to be present at her wedding.

CHRIST'S STARTLING ANSWER TO HIS MOTHER

Mary, Jesus' mother said to Him, "They have no wine." Jesus replied in words that have been considered harsh, "Woman, what does your concern have to do with Me? My hour has not yet come" (John 2:4).

When the unclean spirit, addressed Christ in the synagogue, it used the same phrase, "What have we to do with You?" (Mark 1:24). The phrase in Greek is "ti emoi kai soi." This simply means, "What have we in common?"

Certainly the demons had nothing in common with Jesus. But in the case of Mary, we would at first think she and Jesus had everything in common, until we consider her request. The point of view of Jesus and that of His mother, Mary, on when His time had come were quite different.

However, with the rebuke the Lord did find a way to grant Mary's request. He turned the water into wine. This fruit of the vine was indeed a type of the blood He was to shed on the cross for mankind. But of this, He said, "My hour is not yet come," to fulfill that appointed purpose of His life. Still, in changing the water into wine, He would give the people a symbol of the covenant of His redeeming blood. Later, He would say, "Drink from it, all of you. For this is my blood of the new covenant, which is shed for many for the remission of sins" (Matthew 26:27, 28). So while the time had not yet come for the actual fulfillment of these things, He could and did grant them a miracle that evening which would be the type of His glorious redemption.

Having considered the event in its relation to Christ's making wine, we must look at the significance of the incident in its other aspects.

Christ's presence at the wedding shows us God wants His people to be joyful. The source of that joy, however, must be consistent with God's holiness and righteousness. Nothing can more totally destroy 'happiness than sin. It is important for the sinner to understand this. Religion would be a far more attractive thing to people if they learned it from Jesus' point of view.

However, Jesus' answer shows that Mary expected Him to do something. Mary believed that somehow Jesus would find a way to remedy the embarrassing predicament the family was in. The events of recent weeks could not have been hidden from her, and their importance suggested a possibility of power that she did not fully understand.

Not many weeks before, Satan had suggested to Jesus that He make bread out of stones. Jesus had refused to make bread at Satan's command. His mother had made a similar request, albeit for a far different motive. What should Jesus do?

Jesus decided the circumstances warranted that He do something. Had He been a guest of the high and mighty, it is probable He would not have performed the miracle of turning the water to wine. Nevertheless, He was careful to make certain His act was interpreted correctly.

His answer to His mother was also a reminder to her that there had come a change in their relation. She must no longer presume that things were the same as when He "came to Nazareth, and was subject unto them." He had a great mission to perform. There were things on His mind which she could neither understand nor share. It would be a hard lesson for her as a mother to learn.

Nor are we to think that the words, "Woman, what have I to do with you?" spoken by Jesus were severe. At that time, persons of the highest rank were addressed that way. The word "woman," which sounds harsh to us, was a form of address which Christ used to His mother when He spoke to her from the cross, "Woman, behold your son." Nor did Mary appear hurt or rebuffed by what He said at the wedding. She knew Him too well for that. She did not know what He would do, but she told the servants, "Whatever he says to you, do it."

We do not believe that when Jesus came to the wedding, He had no intention of performing a miracle. Jesus had bound Himself with human limitations. The problem He was confronted with was something that was unexpected; and He was being pressed to come to a sudden decision, just as we on occasions are forced to make unexpected decisions.

As Jesus waited for the leading of the Spirit, His course of action became plain. Although it was not the moment for the full revelation of His glory, God, Whose compassion can always be touched, recognized the need of the people and gave Jesus permission to perform His first miracle. But He must do it without any fanfare or notice.

Once the decision was made, Jesus gave instructions to the servants to not say anything to the guests or even to the governor of the feast, as to where the supply of wine came from—at least until the wedding was over. His mother, as we have seen, had given explicit command to the servants that they follow His instructions. Everything was to be done naturally and without undue display. The servants were to fill up the water pots with water and then draw it out and give it to the guests. The governor of the feast called the bridegroom, "And he said to him, 'Every man at the beginning sets out the good wine, and when the guests have well drunk, then the inferior. You have kept the good wine until now!'" John 2:10

In the miracle at Cana, we see foreshadowed the nature of the ministry of Jesus. His work was to be a work of transformation, ministry of blessing, a ministry of the supernatural. He did not dislike families coming together for fun and fellowship, nor did He have a sad countenance Himself. In fact, He was later to say of the Pharisees who fasted with long faces, "Do not be like the hypocrites with a sad countenance" (Matthew 6:16).

We see a difference between Jesus and His forerunner. John was solitary, unsocial, and stern in his denunciation of sin, so that he might get men to flee from it. The Messiah, by contrast, entered into men's lives to share their joys, their problems, their sorrows, and to give them victory over sin.

In His attendance at the wedding, Jesus set His seal on marriage as an institution ordained of God to promote the happiness and welfare of man. It is a sad thing that Jesus is not invited to all weddings. The marriage ceremony of the Church declares marriage to be a high and holy estate, signifying the supernatural union between Christ and the Church; therefore, it is not to be entered into lightly, but reverently, soberly, discreetly, and in the fear of God.

We are told in this miracle, Christ "manifested forth his glory; and his disciples believed on him" (John 2:11). Miracles were a part of His ministry, and they should have a definite place in the ministry of the Church. Yet, miracles are not for display or attention. They are a manifestation of God's compassion toward a suffering humanity. Christ never demonstrated miracles to satisfy curiosity, to dazzle the eyes of the crowd, to prove Himself to the unbeliever, or to excite mere wonder. He performed them to meet the needs of suffering humanity whom He came to heal and bless.

> "This beginning of signs Jesus did in Cana of Galilee, and manifested His glory; and His disciples believed in Him" (John 2:11).

According to the above verse, this was the first miracle Jesus performed. This indicates that the miracles recorded in the apocryphal books, alleged to have occurred in His boyhood days, were pure fiction.

Chapter 21

CLEANSING THE TEMPLE

After the wedding at Cana, Jesus and His mother and His brethren went down to Capernaum.

"After this He went down to Capernaum, He, His mother, His brothers, and His disciples; and they did not stay there many days" (John 2:12).

At this particular time, Jesus did not remain long in Capernaum, but decided to go to Jerusalem to be there at the time of the Passover celebration, as had probably been His custom since the first Passover of His boyhood.

The natural route southward would have been to walk around the lake and down the gorge made by the Jordan River. Three days of steady traveling would have brought Him and His disciples to the crest of the Mount of Olives. By the time He reached there, thousands of pilgrims would have been swarming about the mount and in the valley below.

Jesus' visit to Jerusalem at that time would have been different from any He had made previously. On other occasions, He had been a pilgrim, but this time, He came to the city—not to proclaim His place as the Messiah—but as a reformer. It was the capital of a nation where public opinion was formed, and if the people of Jerusalem received

Him, the city would be the natural center for His ministry. The officials and leaders of the nations could have the first opportunity to accept His ministry.

It was at this Passover that the words of Malachi were fulfilled which spoke of the coming, of both Christ and His forerunner. John the Baptist had already come, and then suddenly the Messiah presented Himself at the Temple:

> "Behold, I send My messenger, And he will prepare the way before Me. And the Lord, whom you seek, Will suddenly come to His temple, Even the Messenger of the covenant, in whom you delight. Behold, He is coming," Says the Lord of hosts. "But who can endure the day of His coming? And who can stand when He appears? For He is like a refiner's fire and like launderers' soap" (Malachi 3:1, 2).

Unfortunately, as we shall see, the Jews would not delight in Him, for Christ came as a refining fire. Power and privilege lay in the hands of an ecclesiastical group. They were very satisfied with things as they were and had no desire for change.

To Jesus, the Temple was a sacred place. It was a symbol of His Father's Presence, even at the age of 12, when in the Temple, He had felt that He "must be about his Father's business." But year-after-year, as He had come to Jerusalem for the Passover, He had seen the Temple destroyed by the money-changers, who exploited the worshippers who came to Jerusalem. The lust for money of the priests had turned the Temple into a great money-making machine.

As they made their way to the Temple, the pilgrims

had to pass through a large crowd of vendors, who were busy selling their wares in the streets. This trafficking near the Temple, while not altogether seemly, would perhaps be excusable. But the Court of the Gentiles, which was a part of the Temple, had become a stockyard filled with cattle and its accompanying stench and filth. This could not be overlooked or accepted. In the enclosure, there were men with wicker cages filled with doves, sitting under the shadow of the arcades. Finally, there were the money-changers. They performed the function of changing the various kinds at money of heathen governments—money defiled with heathen symbols and heathen inscriptions—into local currency. At one time, they had carried on their business outside of the Temple walls, but in time, the space inside the Court of the Gentiles had become too tempting for their greed, and they moved inside,

So, the place that should have been a house of prayer for all nations had been degraded into shambles and a busy bazaar. The lowing of the oxen and the bleating of the sheep, the cry of the huckster, the dink of the money, made the place a great Babel of confusion, disturbing the worshippers, as well as drowning out the prayers of the priests.

It was necessary, of course, to have cattle markets and moneychangers, but to bring all of this into the Temple grounds, where the people were waiting to worship, was a desecration of the Holy Place. It showed a lack of reverence.

However, on this day, there was a strange commotion at the gate. A young man, stern, and masterful, having an air of authority, came to the door of the Temple. In His hands was a scourge of cords, and after pausing a moment, He began driving out the sheep and oxen and those who attended them. Then going over to the money-changers, He overturned the tables of money, which were carefully stacked in piles, causing them to fall and the pieces to roll all over the floor. He did not overturn the tables of the dove-sellers, so the birds would not be injured, but to them he said, "Take these things away."

> "When He had made a whip of cords, He drove them all out of the temple, with the sheep and the oxen, and poured out the changers' money and overturned the tables. And He said to those who sold doves, 'Take these things away! Do not make My Father's house a house of merchandise!' Then His disciples remembered that it was written, 'Zeal for Your house has eaten Me up'" (John 2:15-17).

Certainly this was a startling turn of events! Who was this young man Who presumed to do such things? However, no one lifted a hand to stop Him. Soon the cattle and their drivers had disappeared. The money-changers stared angrily at the man Who had interfered with their profitable business and had "insulted" them. They looked around for someone to fight for their cause, but no one volunteered. There was something in the eyes of Jesus, which caused everybody to back up. Muttering dark threats, the money-changers gathered up their coins and wandered off.

The chief priests of the Temple were offended and dismayed. Their authority had been publicly challenged. It was something they could never forget nor forgive. When they had recovered from their astonishment, they came to Jesus. Although they didn't condemn what He had done, they self-righteously asked Him by what authority did He do these things:

> "So the Jews answered and said to Him, 'What sign do You show to us, since You do these things?' Jesus answered and said to them, 'Destroy this temple, and in three days I will raise it up.' Then the Jews said, 'It has taken forty-six years to build this temple, and will You raise it up in three days?' But He was speaking of the temple of His body. Therefore, when He had risen from the dead, His disciples remembered that He had said this to them; and they believed the Scripture and the word which Jesus had said" (John 2:18-22).

These words were obviously beyond their comprehension. "Destroy this temple, and in three days I will raise it up." Although they did not understand the meaning of this, it made a powerful impression upon them, which they never forgot. Why the very idea! It was 46 years since the Temple had been built. Herod the Great had lavished his resources on the Temple to gain favor with the Jews. 10,000 workmen had been employed to work and fashion the stones. 1,000 priests in sacred vests lay the stones, after they had been formed. The Temple with its colossal construction of marble, its costly mosaics, the magnificent sculptures, the embroidered veils, and the ornamentation of precious stones rivaled the Seven Wonders of the World. Now, this unknown stranger from the hills of Galilee had declared that if they destroyed it, He could raise it up again in three days!

The Jews might have realized there was a hidden

meaning behind those words, but it suited their purpose to take them literally to mean the Temple. Three years later, during the time of Christ's trial, they would quote Him on this more than any other statement He made. In doing so, they distorted what He had said to, "I will destroy this temple that is made with hands, and within three days I will build another made without hands" (Mark 14:58). Jesus, of course, had never used this expression, but the maddened Jews were aware that this version better suited their interests.

Yet, even His disciples did not fully understand what He meant at the time, nor did they realize until after the resurrection that He had spoken of the temple of His body. Up until then, there had been one Temple of the living God, the one which held the Shekinah glory. But now the Spirit of God was dwelling in a Temple made without hands. And this great truth was involved in the building of the mystical Body of Christ, the Church (Acts 7:45-48; 1 Corinthians 6:19).

It is likely the Jews had more insight into what Jesus really meant than they chose to let on. For when Jesus lay dead and buried in the tomb, they came to Pilate with the strange story saying, "Sir, we remember that that deceiver said, while he was yet alive, After three days I will rise again" (Matthew 27:63). It seems improbable that they had gotten this information from any other source than from this occasion. Since the disciples themselves had not believed that Jesus was going to die, they certainly would not have been the ones to volunteer this information.

Yet, while Jesus never said He would destroy the Temple, was not the worldly-minded priesthood doing this very thing? Were they not destroying its purpose and significance by allowing the Temple to be profaned and commercialized, so that God would have to allow it to be removed out of His sight, and a new Temple—the Temple called the Church—would have to grow up in its place?

There is something about this picture of Christ in the Temple which the artists have overlooked. Jesus was not always the meek lamb. There were times when He was angry. He became angry when the bigoted Jews sought to bring up their petty little rules to keep Him from healing a man on the Sabbath day. He exposed with fierce anger the hypocrisy of the Jews who held men back from seeking God and who "devoured widows' houses." He called them sepulchers, blind guides, and a generation of vipers! Men might mock Christ, might spit on Him and crucify Him, and He would show no personal resentment. He would have His disciples turn the other cheek to evil. But if the cheek of a helpless innocent was smitten, that was another matter.

The Book of John informs us that other miracles were performed while Jesus was in Jerusalem, although we are not told what they are (John 3:2; 4:45). But Jesus apparently saw there was not a deep enough work accomplished in the hearts of the people of that city so He could trust them. Jerusalem was not a place He could establish a sure foundation for His ministry. He would return to Galilee. But before He began His journey back, He was to have an unusual visitor, a man by the name of Nicodemus, a ruler of the Jews, who came to Him under cover at night.

Chapter 22

THE NIGHT VISITOR

One can imagine the excitement in Jerusalem that night after Jesus had cleansed the Temple. This Galilean prophet had challenged the chief authorities of the nation. Everyone was talking about what had happened. Those of the established order were hostile and critical. But there were those, even among the Pharisees who were impressed by the young man. It is also possible that John the Baptist's declaration about His being the Messiah had reached the ears of those in Jerusalem. The Baptist had a powerful influence throughout Judea.

Whatever the Pharisees were, they were alert to what might affect their own interests. When news came of John the Baptist's ministry in the wilderness, they immediately dispatched a deputy of priests and Levites to meet him and ask him whether he was Elijah or the Christ (John 1:19.27). It appears, therefore, that they sent Nicodemus to Jesus for the purpose of asking more about Him, and just what His claims were all about. They had already asked Him to show them a sign as proof of His authority (John 2:18), but the reply they had gotten was by no means satisfactory. Perhaps, Nicodemus could gain further information from Him.

Nicodemus seemed to be well-suited for such a delicate mission. He was a ruler of the Jews, a member of the Sanhedrin. Although, he was not a bold man, he was known as one who stood against injustice. While it is possible that Nicodemus was acting on behalf of the Jewish rulers, many believe Nicodemus made the visit without knowledge of the other members of the Sanhedrin. Whether he went as a messenger, or on his own accord, we know he went secretly, not wishing for the people of the city to know of His visit.

Where did this memorable interview of Nicodemus with Jesus take place? Probably on the Mt. of Olives, or its vicinity, since we have no record that Jesus spent the night within the city's gates. Nicodemus had to decide earlier in the evening where Jesus and His disciples were staying. Then, at nightfall, in the darkness, he went to see Him. Covered from head to foot with his cloak, he knocked at the door of the house where Jesus was staying. He was invited in and graciously received. Since the upper part of a house was often used for private conversations, it is probable they went up to the roof to talk. There, Nicodemus made known the purpose of his visit.

> "This man came to Jesus by night and said to Him, 'Rabbi, we know that You are a teacher come from God; for no one can do these signs that You do unless God is with him'" (John 3:2).

It is clear that Nicodemus recognized Jesus as a prophet, and had probably spoken to his colleagues in His favor. Later, he defended Christ at a time when it was dangerous for him to do so. Nicodemus acknowledged that Jesus was of God, although he probably was not prepared to accept Him yet as the Messiah. He said that some of the others of the Sanhedrin were of the same opinion; although, they had reservations about some of the things that He did, such as His act of cleansing the Temple.

Nicodemus recognized the miracles Jesus had performed. A miracle becomes the universal language that is understood by all. It is by miracles that the Gospel was to be introduced to the heathen and preached in all the world (Mark 16:15-18). The miracle was the sign of the Messiah, and of the approach of the Kingdom of God. Nicodemus wanted to hear about the Kingdom which the Messiah would establish. He expected, as the others did, that it would be a temporal kingdom, glorious, and prosperous. Every Israelite by birth would be a member of it. Nicodemus understood this.

Nicodemus might have asked other questions, but Jesus had this statement to make to him. "Most assuredly, I say to you, unless one is born again, he cannot see the kingdom of God" (John 3:3). We have only fragments of the conversation, but we do know that Jesus explained the Kingdom of God was not a kingdom of politics and earthly power. Something more was needed than Jewish birth to enter it. Men needed to be born-again, born of the Spirit of God. That was the only way they could enter into the Kingdom.

This declaration of Jesus amazed Nicodemus. He had known about the heathen needing conversion, but not Jews. The idea was abhorrent to this Pharisee's instincts. In a kind of querulous surprise, he chose to interpret the words of Jesus in an absurd physical sense. "How can a man be born when he is old? Can he enter a second time into his mother's womb, and be born?" (verse 4). Jesus did not pause to notice this kind of argument; He repeated, "Most assuredly, I say to you, unless one is born of water and the Spirit, he cannot enter the kingdom of God. That which is born of the flesh is flesh, and that which is born of the Spirit is spirit. Do not marvel that I said to you, 'You must be born again'" (verse 5-7).

Jesus explained that the work of the Spirit was as real as the wind that blew, although it was a mystery: "The wind blows where it wishes, and you hear the sound of it, but cannot tell where it comes from and where it goes. So is everyone who is born of the Spirit" (John 3:8).

Nicodemus was so puzzled by all this that he couldn't say anything else. Jesus half sorrowful and half reproachful went on to explain to him about spiritual things. He even divulged His mission to him—that He was to give his life so men might be saved.

> "For God so loved the world that He gave His only begotten Son, that whoever believes in Him should not perish but have everlasting life. For God did not send His Son into the world to condemn the world, but that the world through Him might be saved. He who believes in Him is not condemned; but he who does not believe is condemned already, because he has not believed in the name of the only begotten Son of God. And this is the condemnation, that the light has come into the world, and men loved darkness rather than light, because their deeds were evil. For everyone practicing evil hates the light and does not come to the light, lest his deeds should be exposed. But he who does the truth comes to the light, that his deeds may

be clearly seen, that they have been done in God" (John 3:16-21).

Nicodemus left the place a confused man. Yet, he felt compelled to believe in the young Man Who had given him such a memorable interview. Twice more we hear of Nicodemus. Each time, he acts with caution, but still takes the side of Jesus. Once, when the Jews were bent on violence, Nicodemus said, "Does our law condemn a man without a hearing?"

Shortly after this, Jesus left Jerusalem. Jerusalem was not the place to make His home. He departed out of the city and went down to the Jordan River. John had not yet been cast into prison, and he was baptizing in Aenon near Salem. We are told that the disciples of Jesus also began to baptize and make disciples. Why they baptized is not explained in the Gospels. We do know that as soon as John was put in prison the disciples ceased this type of ministry—until Christ gave them the Great Commission, after His resurrection.

It is obvious that earlier baptism was but a transitory phase of the opening ministry of Christ. Jesus probably did not consider it wise to make an abrupt change while John was still active. The baptism which He would authorize would be distinctly different from John's.

A certain Jew who seemed glad to sow disruption in John's camp said, "Rabbi, He who was with you beyond the Jordan, to whom you have testified—behold, He is baptizing, and all are coming to Him!" (John 3:26). John's answer is a credit to his greatness. He could not and would not enter into the petty rivalries of men. To him, God was the sole source of every good gift. He reminded his disciples that he had always said he was not the Christ, but only the friend of the

Bridegroom.

Even as Jesus prepared to leave Judah, word reached Him that John had been taken by Herod's soldiers (Matthew 4:12). In making his trip to Galilee, he decided to go through Samaria. He would never see John again during His earthly life. It was a new era in the ministry of Christ.

Chapter 23

THE WOMAN OF SAMARIA

"He left Judea and departed again to Galilee. But He needed to go through Samaria. So He came to a city of Samaria which is called Sychar, near the plot of ground that Jacob gave to his son Joseph. Now Jacob's well was there. Jesus therefore, being wearied from His journey, sat thus by the well. It was about the sixth hour. A woman of Samaria came to draw water. Jesus said to her, 'Give Me a drink.' For His disciples had gone away into the city to buy food. Then the woman of Samaria said to Him, 'How is it that You, being a Jew, ask a drink from me, a Samaritan woman?' For Jews have no dealings with Samaritans" (John 4:3-9).

At the time we are speaking about, most Jews had ceased taking the route through Samaria because of the bad feelings between the Jews and the Samaritans. These people of Samaria were of mixed blood, part heathen and part Israelite. At the time of the early captivities, they had been brought over by the Assyrian King to re-populate the country (2 Kings 17:26, 27). Their religion was a mixture of Judaism and paganism. The sacred record declares, "So these nations feared the Lord, yet served their carved images; also their children and their children's children have continued doing as their fathers did, even to this day" (2 Kings 17:41).

In the days of Nehemiah, they had volunteered their services to help build the walls of the city of Jerusalem; and since their services were refused, they had become the merciless enemies of the Jews.

Shortly after the birth of Christ, a new feud developed between the Samaritans and the Jews. The Samaritans had always refused to recognize the importance of Jerusalem and claimed that their sacred Mount Gerizim was the place to worship. But beyond this, the Samaritans minded their own business. Then, a serious incident occurred. During the days of the Passover, the custom of closing the gates of the city of Jerusalem at night was not observed because of the many visitors who had come long distances and had no place to lodge except outside the city walls. Some of the Samaritans, resolving to defile the Temple, brought in fragments of dead bodies and scattered them about the Temple area. Nothing could have angered the Jews more than this. From that time on, the Samaritans were excluded from the Temple grounds.

The incident resulted in a complete estrangement of the two peoples. They no longer had dealings with one another of any kind. Most Jews, when making the journey north to Galilee, did not take the shorter way through Samaria, but took the longer route up the Jordan valley. But Jesus decided to go on the old way. John records the statement that "he must go through Samaria."

Starting early in the morning, in order to secure as many hours of daylight as possible, He and His disciples left the Jordan area on their journey north, stopping for rest and refreshment at a well that was located near the town of Sychar in Samaria. This well was famous because it had been dug by the patriarch Jacob many centuries before. The well was a hundred feet deep, but its waters were unusually great, and the inhabitants of the city preferred the quality of its water over that which came from the springs of Mount Ebal. Jesus, being weary from His journey, sat down on the well under the shelter of an alcove which was built overhead. Since it was the noon hour, it was arranged for the disciples to continue on into the city to purchase the provisions they would need (John 4:8).

While Jesus was waiting for the disciples to return, His solitude was broken by the approach of a Samaritan woman. Turning around, He saw the woman coming to the well to draw water; her earthen vessel was gracefully poised on her head. The woman's appearance at this hour was unusual, for ordinarily the people of the East draw their water in the morning or the evening. The fact that she came at high noon indicated she was not on good terms with the women of the city. She was apparently an outcast of society, having been married five times, and at that time was having an affair with a man who was not her husband.

The Lord stopped her approach. Thirsty and fatigued Himself, and with no means of reaching the cool water that glimmered below, He said to her, "Give me a drink." The attire of Jesus and His accent were sufficient to show the woman that Jesus was a Jew. This startled her, and half in surprise and half in irony, she responded saying, "'How is it that You, being a Jew, ask a drink from me, a Samaritan woman?' For the Jews have no dealings with the Samaritans." Jesus responded saying, "If you knew the gift of God, and who it is who says to you, 'Give Me a drink,' you would have asked Him, and He would have given you living water." She pointed at the well, a hundred feet deep. He had no vessel to draw with, how then would it be possible for Him to draw water? Was He .greater than their father Jacob who had dug the well and drank of it? Jesus had met the same unimaginative dullness among the learned, but spiritually unperceptive. The woman could only think of common water, while He was speaking of the water of everlasting life that quenched one's thirst forever.

This seemed to be sheer absurdity to her, and even though the woman was puzzled by His words, and despite her own prejudices, she found herself beginning to have confidence in the stranger. So she said, "Sir, give me this water, that I may not thirst, nor come here to draw." In effect, if she could drink of this wonderful water, then it would not be necessary for her to come all the way from the village at the hot noon hour to draw water from this well.

At this moment, the Lord made what appeared to be a startling change of conversation. He asked her to go and call her husband and return. In the ways of the East, it was improper for Him to hold a conversation with a strange woman. But the purpose of His request was to awaken the conscience of the woman. For He could not give her the water of life until that was accomplished. Jesus' words forced her to answer that she had no husband, and the Lord, acknowledging her confession, brought out into the open her loose and sinful life.

"The woman answered and said, 'I have no husband.' Jesus said to her, 'You have well said, 'I have no husband,' for you have had five husbands, and the one whom you now have is not your husband; in that you spoke truly'" (John 4:17, 18).

Here we see the working of the gift of the word of knowledge. Christ had all omniscience, and the gift in its operation disclosed important information about the woman, which would be helpful in arousing her conscience. Jesus was not there to accuse and condemn her. However, it was necessary that her conscience be awakened before He could help her.

The woman was then convinced that Jesus was a prophet. Not eager to linger on the facts of her own history, her mind leaped to the great question that not only bothered the ideals of her people, but was the basis of the fierce controversy between her race and the Jews. It was the age-old question which has been fought over thousands of times, "Which church is the true Church?"

Because of this golden opportunity to speak to a prophet, she thought this might be a good time to settle the question whether Gerizim, the place where Joshua had uttered the blessings, or Jerusalem, where Solomon had built the Temple, was the place where men should worship? Her question received an answer, but one that was different from what the woman expected:

"'Our fathers worshiped on this mountain, and you Jews say that in Jerusalem is the place where one ought to worship.' Jesus said to her, 'Woman, believe Me, the hour is coming when you will neither on this mountain, nor in Jerusalem, worship the Father. You worship what you do not know; we know what we worship, for salvation is of the Jews. But the hour is coming, and now is, when the true worshipers will worship the Father in spirit and truth; for the Father is seeking such to worship Him. God is Spirit, and those who worship Him must worship in spirit and truth'" (John 4:20-24).

The Jews were unquestionably right in their contention that Jerusalem was the place where God had chosen to put His Name. Compared to Judaism, the worship of Samaria was considered a hybrid and defective. Jesus skillfully avoided the controversial issue and carried the matter beyond the temporal aspect by saying the time had come when true worshippers might worship God at any place and at any time.

The woman was deeply moved, but how could she change her whole belief on the words of a passing stranger? She merely sighed and said, "I know that Messiah is coming" (who is called Christ). "When He comes, He will tell us all things" (John 4:25). Then in sudden and startling revelation, Jesus chose to reveal to this outcast the secret of His identity and the reason for His coming into the world! He said, "I who speak to you am He" (John 4:26).

At this moment, the disciples had returned with the provisions they had purchased at the village. They stood surprised as they listened to Jesus conversing with the Samaritan woman. Ordinarily, a Jew might not talk to a woman on the street, even if she were his own wife or daughter. In the Vinaya a Bhikshu of Buddhism, a man is not only forbidden to speak to a woman, but he may not hold out his hand to his own mother if she were drowning. The disciples, therefore, marveled that the Master would converse with this Samaritan woman. Yet, they had become accustomed to His strange and unexpected ways, so they did not object to Him or make a comment on His conversation with her.

The woman herself gave the disciples no attention. Overwhelmed by the words she had heard, she hurried away, forgetting to take her water pot. After producing the provisions they had brought, the disciples invited Jesus to partake. But all hunger had been satisfied in His exaltation of winning a soul. He merely said, "... 'I have food to eat of which you do not know" (John 4:32). Here was the explanation of the words He had spoken when the evil one tempted him, "... man shall not live by bread alone; but man lives by every word that proceeds from the mouth of the LORD" (Deuteronomy 8:3).

The disciples still did not know what He was referring to, and they asked each other, if someone had brought Him food while they were away. Patiently, the Lord explained what He meant. He pointed to the people of the city of Sychar who were now coming out to Him because of the Samaritan woman's testimony, "Come, see a Man who told me all things that I ever did. Could this be the Christ?" (John 4:29).

Jesus told His disciples not to say to themselves that there were four months yet before the harvest, but to look at the fields already white unto harvest. Jesus stated that while He sowed in sorrow, they would be joyful reapers of the harvest in the time to come.

Now this woman (who incidentally was the first woman to preach the Gospel in the Christian dispensation) in the joy of her discovery, forgot that she was banished and scorned from society, and went boldly to the people and told them she had found the Messiah. Her words apparently made a remarkable stir. It should also be remembered that a few months before, the whole region had been moved by the preaching of John the Baptist. The people had probably heard John's announcement of the Messiah's coming. Therefore, upon hearing the words of the woman that a wondrous prophet had come to their neighborhood, they ran out to meet Him.

When Jesus saw the people rushing toward Him, He longed to bless them. It was a welcome contrast to the poor reception He had received in Jerusalem. When He saw the hunger in their hearts, He no doubt was saddened at the limitations of His mission that confined His ministry to that of Israel. It must have been hard to refrain from putting in the sickle, then and there, as He longed for the day when the river of His grace could break all bounds and stream out to a thirsty world. But it was only His to sow; later the disciples would reap.

> "I sent you to reap that for which you have
> not labored; others have labored, and you
> have entered into their labors" (John 4:38).

In these words, Jesus congratulated the disciples—for this high ministry was reserved for them and all those who followed them.

However, the ministry to these people was so great that Jesus consented to stay with them for two days. Although He performed no miracles there, the people received Him joyfully and believed He was the Christ, the Savior of the world.

"And many more believed because of His own word. Then they said to the woman, 'Now we believe, not because of what you said, for we ourselves have heard Him and we know that this is indeed the Christ, the Savior of the world'" (John 4:41, 42).

Those two days that Jesus stayed there brought abundant fruit, and the results were first fruits of the great Gentile harvest to come. No doubt, it was the teaching in these two days that played a large part in the rich harvest of souls, which took place a few years later when Philip went down to Samaria and preached Christ to them (Acts 8). Jesus might have stayed longer in Samaria, and other cities in that vicinity might have received Him with just as much enthusiasm. But a public demonstration in His favor in Samaria at this time would surely have prejudiced His future work in the Jewish culture; so He told them goodbye and turned His footsteps toward Galilee.

Chapter 24

THE VISIT AT NAZARETH AND CANA

"So He came to Nazareth, where He had been brought up. And as His custom was, He went into the synagogue on the Sabbath day, and stood up to read. And He was handed the book of the prophet Isaiah. And when He had opened the book, He found the place where it was written: 'The Spirit of the Lord is upon Me, Because He has anointed Me To preach the gospel to the poor; He has sent Me to heal the brokenhearted, To proclaim liberty to the captives And recovery of sight to the blind, To set at liberty those who are oppressed; To proclaim the acceptable year of the Lord.' Then He closed the book, and gave it back to the attendant and sat down. And the eyes of all who were in the synagogue were fixed on Him. And He began to say to them, 'Today this Scripture is fulfilled in your hearing'" (Luke 4:16-21).

Jesus and His disciples continued their journey northward until they reached Galilee. It appears that He stayed there only a short time, and then went on to Nazareth.

He was well received in Galilee, for some of the people had been in Jerusalem at the Passover Feast, and they had seen the miracles Jesus had performed there. Upon returning to Capernaum, they spread His fame abroad (John 4:45).

Christ was becoming known as a "wonder-worker" before He had an opportunity to preach to them the Gospel of the Kingdom. People wanted healing for their bodies before healing for their souls. He did not desire to become an object of their wonderment. He decided, therefore, before He settled down in Galilee, He would first go to His home town of Nazareth. Leaving His disciples behind, so they could catch up on their fishing, He made the seven-hour journey.

In the years Jesus spent in Nazareth, it was His custom to attend the synagogue on each Sabbath. Upon the next Sabbath day, He went with the others there to worship. Since He had previously been a reader in the synagogue, they brought out the scroll and gave it to Him to read. He took it and unrolled it until He came to the Book of Isaiah, chapter 61. Then the whole congregation stood to their feet while He read. Jesus did not read the whole passage, but stopped with the words, "the day of vengeance of our God." That part of the prophecy was not to be fulfilled at that time. This was not the day of vengeance, but "the acceptable year of the Lord."

Jesus went on to explain to the people that no prophet is acceptable in his own country. He reminded them that miracles were not limited to a geographical area, and He gave them examples of the healing of Naaman the Syrian, and the multiplying of the meal and oil for the widow at Sarepta; both incidents were with Gentiles.

As He continued, it appeared to the people at Nazareth

that He was saying they were no better than Gentiles and lepers. This struck hard at their racial pride. It was intolerable for a mere carpenter, who grew up in their village, to talk to them in this way. Their anger burst into a flame. Rising up, some of the more vengeful citizens probably demanded an apology for His words, and securing none, "... thrust Him out of the city; and they led Him to the brow of the hill on which their city was built, that they might throw Him down over the cliff" (Luke 4:29).

His hour, however, had not yet come; and suddenly Jesus asserted His mastery. "Then passing through the midst of them, He went His way" (Luke 4:30). It was not exactly a miracle, but it was a demonstration of His personal power. Something about Him awed them. Under the spell of His Presence, the mob, which had intended to hurt Him, involuntarily bowed before Him.

There would be other times when the Jews would take up stones to kill Him, but somehow, each time, they would fail to carry out their plan. It was this same power that prevented the officers from arresting Jesus after they had been given a charge to do so by the Sanhedrin. It was this dominion of His Spirit that caused the soldiers to fall backward when they came to take Him after Judas betrayed Him.

But was there no boyhood friend in Nazareth to stand by Him? It didn't seem so. There were friends, however, in Cana of Galilee, only a few miles away. That was the village where He had performed His first miracle—turning the water into wine. At Cana, He would probably stay at the home of Nathanael, one of His first disciples. Yes, at Cana, He would find a friendly reception waiting for Him. The little maiden whose wedding He had honored by His

Presence would be glad for His visit there. Those who were present at the wedding feast would all want to see Him. No doubt, there was a great indignation at Cana when the news reached them of how rudely He had been treated by the citizens of Nazareth. The people of Cana had little use for those of Nazareth. Nathanael's response to Philip's news about the One who came from there was, "... 'Can anything good come out of Nazareth?'" (John 1:46).

THE HEALING OF THE NOBLEMAN'S SON

Jesus had not been in Cana long when a visitor from Herod's Court, hearing of His arrival, came to Him. He asked Jesus to come at once to Capernaum to heal his son. Not all of Herod's court had shown the spirit of Herodias. We know that Manaen, the foster-brother of Herod, was a believer later on in life, and indeed a prophet (Acts 13:1).

We also know that Joanna, the wife of Chuza, Herod's steward, was among the women who ministered to Jesus of their substance (Luke 8:3). It has been considered with some probability that the nobleman was none other than Chuza himself.

> "So Jesus came again to Cana of Galilee where He had made the water wine. And there was a certain nobleman whose son was sick at Capernaum. When he heard that Jesus had come out of Judea into Galilee, he went to Him and implored Him to come down and heal his son, for he was at the point of death. Then Jesus said to him, 'Unless you people see signs and wonders, you will by no means believe.' The nobleman said to Him, 'Sir,

come down before my child dies!' Jesus said to him, 'Go your way; your son lives.' So the man believed the word that Jesus spoke to him, and he went his way" (John 4:46-50).

It was at one o'clock in the afternoon when the nobleman arrived. This man was in serious trouble. His only son was lying sick of a deadly fever in Capernaum. The fame of Jesus' miracles at Jerusalem, as well as those performed already in Galilee, had inspired the father with a desperate hope. He left the bedside of his dying child and searched until he located Jesus in Cana. Now he implored Him to come and heal his son.

Every minister who prays for the sick has many kinds of people to deal with. Some are desperate; they can think of nothing but the fact that their loved one faces death. They have to be shown that "healing is the children's bread," and that it is appropriated by faith.

Therefore, Jesus said unto him, "... 'Unless you people see signs and wonders, you will by no means believe" (John 4:48). That was Herod's case. He had a sort of superstitious belief in the supernatural. When he heard of Jesus' ministry, he was sure that He was John the Baptist raised from the dead (Matthew 14:1, 2). Later, when Jesus was on trial, Herod wanted Him to perform a miracle for him. If Jesus had done that, Herod would have probably released Him. Jesus, however, would perform no signs to gratify the gross curiosity of the monarch.

Nevertheless, the nobleman's passionate mission caused Jesus to yield to his request, which illustrates how actions will move the heart of God. The nobleman had more desperation than real faith, but even that desperation gave way to faith for healing. Jesus told the nobleman his son would live.

It appears Jesus' words calmed the anxieties of the father; for instead of going directly to Capernaum, he slept somewhere that night while on the road. He could have gotten back within five or six hours, but he believed the words of Jesus. The following day, while still on the way, he met his servants who brought him the wondrous news that his son was recovering. The father asked them when he began to mend. The servants replied that it was at the seventh hour of the previous day, which was at the same hour that Jesus spoke the word (John 4:51-53).

There is great truth in this incident. Not all sick people have faith for an instant miracle. But if they will only believe the word that is spoken, they will, just as the nobleman's son did, begin to mend from that very hour.

Chapter 25

THE DEMONIAC IN THE SYNAGOGUE

From Cana, Jesus went to Capernaum on the sea of Galilee, making the trip soon after the nobleman's son was healed. There has been some dispute as to where Capernaum was located, but it is generally believed that it was at the northwest corner of the Sea of Galilee. The lake is some thirteen miles long and eight miles wide, and shaped somewhat like a harp. It lies 682 feet below the level of the Mediterranean Sea, and basks in tropical heat. The water is crystal clear and filled with edible fish. In the Lord's day, the surface of the lake was dotted with the boats of fishermen, some of whom were Andrew and Peter and James and John. On its banks were thriving cities, Tiberias, Bethsaida, Chorazin, Capernaum, Magdala, and others. Capernaum means Village of Nahum, and tradition claims it was the burial place of the prophet.

Capernaum was a city of unusual prosperity. First of all, it was the principal center of the fishing industry. A suburb of the town was given to the salting of fish, which were packed in kegs and exported. South of the city is a fertile plain which brought forth figs, grapes, olives and nuts in luxurious abundance.

One other important circumstance contributed to Capernaum's prosperity, and that was the fact that several of the great trade routes met at this point. Caravans from the East and West, as well as from the North and South, crossed near Capernaum. This heavy stream of traffic made the city a great trade center. It was, therefore, more than a provincial town in Jesus' day; it was, in fact, fast becoming a cosmopolitan city. Capernaum was well adapted and situated for the purposes of the Lord's ministry. Nowhere else could He have secured such an extensive hearing, except perhaps at Jerusalem—as we have already noted, only reluctantly responded to His revolutionary teaching.

It will be noted presently, the great number of sick people who were brought to Christ for healing, while He was in Galilee. Not far from Capernaum, at Tiberias, there were hot springs where many sick people gathered. The nobleman, no doubt, let it be known in Tiberias how his son was healed. The news that this distinguished family had professed faith in Jesus would spread rapidly, and it is not surprising that the sick gathering around these spots would seek to have Christ lay hands upon them for healing.

THE MEETING IN THE SYNAGOGUE

"Then they went into Capernaum, and immediately on the Sabbath He entered the synagogue and taught. And they were astonished at His teaching, for He taught them as one having authority, and not as the scribes. Now there was a man in their synagogue with an unclean spirit. And he cried out, saying, 'Let us alone! What have we to do with You, Jesus of Nazareth? Did You come to destroy us? I know who You are—the Holy One of God!' But Jesus rebuked him, saying, 'Be quiet, and come out of him!' And when the unclean spirit had convulsed him and cried out with a loud voice, he came out of him. Then they were all amazed, so that they questioned among themselves, saying, 'What is this? What new doctrine is this? For with authority He commands even the unclean spirits, and they obey Him'" (Mark 1:21-27).

Christ's disciples, as we have noted, seem not to have been with Him at Nazareth and Cana, with the possible exception of Nathanael who lived in Cana. Apparently, they remained in their homes while He went on to Nazareth. We find them at Capernaum and active in their occupations when the Lord returned.

Jesus stayed at the home of Peter for a time, but later it appears He had His own house. Perhaps someone healed through His ministry asked Him to use it for the time (Mark 2:1, 2). Regardless of who owned the house, it apparently suffered damage, when four men broke open the roof to let a palsied man down for healing (Mark 2:1-4).

After establishing His headquarters in Capernaum, Jesus began to regularly attend the local synagogue, where He was often invited to speak (Luke 4:31). The structure was of white limestone, some 60 feet wide and 80 feet long, being one of the finest synagogues in the land. It had been built by a wealthy centurion who was a friend of the Jewish people (Luke 7:4, 5). The synagogue was later destroyed, perhaps by an earthquake, and built again, only to experience another devastation later on. But the stones are still there today, and the site is considered one of the best, authenticated places in Israel.

There was a women's gallery in the synagogue which was supported by stone pillars. The women and girls did not enter the lower part of the building to reach this gallery, but ascended an outside stairway of stone.

On the day Jesus made His first appearance in the synagogue at Capernaum, we can trace the order of events. The morning service would have been at nine o'clock. Shortly before that hour, people from every part of the city could have been seen making their way to the new white synagogue. Farmers and fishermen came with their families. Zebedee arrived with his wife and their full-grown sons, James and John. Andrew came with Peter and his family. Perhaps Jesus walked along with them. Jairus, the ruler of the synagogue, was there with his wife and daughter. It is not improbable that "the nobleman whose son was sick at Capernaum" and whom Jesus healed was present. Many people had heard that the stranger who had been performing wonderful miracles was in town and was expected at the synagogue. By nine o'clock the place was packed to the doors.

The service began. The chief minister rose to begin prayers. The whole congregation bowed their heads. When prayers were over, one of the rolls was taken out of the ark, and a rabbi or prominent person began to read. After that, the chief minister looked toward the visitor sitting next to Peter, and told Him that if He had a word of exhortation to come forward and speak. Jesus accepted the invitation and went to the front and sat in the chair of the rabbi. Every eye was fixed on Him as He began to speak. People had heard many rumors concerning Him. Who was He? What was His teaching? As Jesus began to speak, it was not in the dull conventional tone of the scribes. His words went forth with power and authority.

We do not have a record of the actual words Jesus spoke that day. But it is probable that His message was along similar lines to that which He preached on the Mount of Beatitudes. The reaction of the people to the sermon was nearly the same as that which occurred when He came down from the Mount (Matthew 7:28, 29; Mark 1:27).

It was not the intention of Jesus for the people to think that He was coming to overthrow the Law. He said, "Do not think that I came to destroy the Law or the Prophets. I did not come to destroy but to fulfill" (Matthew 5:17). He showed that He was lifting the Law to a higher and more honorable plane. The following is probably an example of what He said:

> "You have heard that it was said to those of old, 'You shall not murder, and whoever murders will be in danger of the judgment.' But I say to you that whoever is angry with his brother without a cause shall be in danger of the judgment. And whoever says to his brother, 'Raca!' shall be in danger of the council. But whoever says, 'You fool!' shall be in danger of hell fire" (Matthew 5:21, 22).

> "You have heard that it was said to those of old, 'You shall not commit adultery.' But I say to you that whoever looks at a woman to lust for her has already committed adultery with her in his heart" (Matthew 5:27, 28).

In saying this, Jesus took the people far above the letter of the Old Law, telling them to "... 'love your enemies, bless those who curse you, do good to those who hate you, and pray for those who spitefully use you and persecute you …" (Matthew 5:44).

Suddenly, while Jesus was in the midst of His message, there was a wild disturbance. A demon-possessed man slipped into the congregation. Apparently, this unfortunate person was not violent, except at times. However, when the evil spirit was in charge, it would throw him into a spasm. Demons are very sensitive to the Presence of Divine power, as anyone who has had experience in casting out these evil spirits knows. We can understand that the Presence of Christ would be quickly felt in the spirit world. Demons writhe in agony when the power of the Holy Spirit is manifested in their vicinity. The evil spirit realized that his own security was threatened, and he cried out "…saying, 'Let us alone! What have we to do with You, Jesus of Nazareth? Did You come to destroy us? I know who You are—the Holy One of God!'" (Mark 1:24).

We notice that some who write on the life of Christ doubt the existence of evil spirits. David Smith in The Days of His Flesh says:

"The idea is of course simply a fantastic notion of a dark-age unskilled in natural science, and it was nothing strange that people in the New Testament should have entertained it. But it is disconcerting that it seems to have been entertained by Jesus, also. He would address the supposed demon, rebuking it and commanding it to come out of the man! That He should thus share the limitation of His age is at first blush somewhat of a shock of faith;

yet, even if it be allowed, there is perhaps no real occasion for disquietude. When the Lord of Glory came down to Earth, He assumed the nature of the children of men, being made at every point like unto his brethren, and it might be accepted as a welcome evidence of the reality of the Incarnation if He were found to have shared the scientific and metaphysical conceptions of His contemporaries."

This weird opinion about demons is a pitiful one, written as it is by one who evidently has had no practical knowledge of the reality of the spirit world. The activities of demon forces in the Earth today have become so widespread that to deny their existence can only mark a professed Christian as a person of incredible ignorance. The above "explanation" is a miserable attempt to make Christ a "nut-case," who fell in with the delusions of His time.

As the people of Capernaum listened to the speaker with silent astonishment, hanging on to His words with deep reverent admiration, the demon in the man, disturbed by the Presence of Christ, cried out in fear. Perhaps the evil spirit hoped to break up the meeting and bring discredit upon the speaker.

Many times, I have personally witnessed demons distressed by the Presence of an anointed minister. They may rave against him, demanding to be left alone. But Jesus recognized the source of the disturbance and spoke to the evil spirit, commanding it to come out of the man. Immediately, the demoniac fell to the floor in a fearful position, screaming and convulsing. But it was soon all over, for the man got up, wonderfully healed and in his right mind.

It was a thrilling moment for the congregation. The ruler of the synagogue, as well as the other officials, had been transfixed by this strange occurrence. They had seen the man, his face twisted and distorted, collapsing and writhing on the pavement. They heard the shriek of the baffled and tormented devil. But the man was now in his right mind and could talk to people with a normal conversation. The demoniac's deliverance was so remarkable that it commanded the astonishment and admiration of the entire audience.

THE HEALING OF PETER'S MOTHER-IN-LAW

The news of what happened spread like wildfire throughout the community. People from a distance went back to tell other friends. By evening the whole region had heard about it. Meanwhile, Jesus returned to Peter's house with James and John.

> "Now as soon as they had come out of the synagogue, they entered the house of Simon and Andrew, with James and John. But Simon's wife's mother lay sick with a fever, and they told Him about her at once. So He came and took her by the hand and lifted her up, and immediately the fever left her. And she served them" (Mark 1:29-31).

Peter lived with his wife and her mother in a little house by the seashore. When Jesus and the group reached the door of the home, they were met by Peter's wife, who had distressing news. The mother-in-law, who had been feeling badly enough to not attend the synagogue services, had become ill with a raging fever. Peter witnessed the miracle at the synagogue and lost no time in requesting Jesus to come into the sick woman's room. Jesus complied. After speaking to the mother, He took her by the hand and lifted her up. It should be noted that Jesus did not pray for the afflicted one. He exercised His authority and she was made whole. Luke 4:39 declares, "So He stood over her and rebuked the fever, and it left her. And immediately she arose and served them." The woman at once felt the flow of strength into her body, and at the same moment, the fever left.

Obeying the command to arise, she got up out of bed and began to help prepare the dinner. "She arose and ministered unto them." Faith is an act. The act of Peter's mother-in-law may well be copied by other sick people. When they receive healing, their gratefulness should overflow as service to the Lord.

The Lord then enjoyed a few hours of relaxation. It was the Sabbath day and the rules of traveling about on that day were very strict. Nevertheless, when the sun was set and the Sabbath was over, there was great excitement in the city of Capernaum. The eager multitude began to press about the doors of Peter's home, bringing with them their sick and diseased.

> "When evening had come, they brought to Him many who were demon-possessed. And He cast out the spirits with a word, and healed all who were sick, that it might be fulfilled which was spoken by Isaiah the prophet, saying: 'He Himself took our infirmities and bore our sicknesses'" (Matthew 8:16, 17).

What a strange scene it was. Only a few steps away was the Sea of Galilee, one of the most beautiful bodies of water in the world, reflecting the glow of the evening sunset. But all around the door were the hideous results of sin—not necessarily the sin of the individual, but the sin of the race. There was no sickness before the fall of man. How many times have we watched similar heart-rending scenes of a multitude of sick people who have come to a meeting where people are ministered to for healing? How sad is the sight—cripples, mentally handicapped, those with Down's syndrome, paralytics, the demon-possessed, others wasting away with an incurable disease.

Unfortunately, there are some who believe and tell others that they are suffering for the glory of God. Peter, who saw Jesus heal that day, knew better. When he preached his sermon at the house of Cornelius, the apostle explained that sickness owed its origin to Satan, not God. He said that Jesus "went about doing good, and healing all that were oppressed of the devil."

> "... how God anointed Jesus of Nazareth with the Holy Spirit and with power, who went about doing good and healing all who were oppressed by the devil, for God was with Him" (Acts 10:38).

Jesus ministered to the sick and the diseased. Tortured souls were brought to Him. The evil spirits repeated the words of the one in the synagogue. They cried out saying, "... 'You are the Christ, the Son of God!" (Luke 4:41). They had known Jesus in the ages before, when they were holy beings. Rejected of God, their corrupted natures were beyond repair. To come into the Presence of Christ was unspeakable torture, and they cried out in their anguish.

Jesus could do nothing for these evil spirits. They were beyond mercy, and it was His duty to close their mouths, so they wouldn't call attention to His deity before He was ready. He "commanded them not to speak." What a warning to sinners who carelessly ignore the call of Christ, Who stands at the door of their heart knocking. For the time must come when they, too, if they reject His call, will be forever outside the pale of mercy, with the demons and lost spirits.

Jesus was touched with the infirmities of the afflicted, and laboring into the night, He ministered until every sick person had received deliverance. Matthew makes a significant remark. He says that Jesus healed these people "... that it might be fulfilled which was spoken by Isaiah the prophet, saying: 'He Himself took our infirmities and bore our sicknesses'" (Matthew 8:17). The meaning is unmistakable. Jesus took our sicknesses upon Himself, even as He did our sins. Divine healing is in the atonement! Because Christ took our sicknesses on the Cross, we don't need to carry them again!

Healing is the children's bread, and deliverance of the sick was also a part of Christ's ministry. It expressed God's compassion for the afflicted and the suffering. It also opened a great door, for it brought the people to Him.

Early the next day, long before sunrise, Jesus arose from His bed and without disturbing the rest of the household, departed to a solitary place. He needed communion with His Heavenly Father at that important moment.

"Now in the morning, having risen a long while before daylight, He went out and departed to a solitary place; and there He prayed. And Simon and those who were with Him searched for Him. When they found Him, they said to Him, 'Everyone is looking for You.' But He said to them, 'Let us go into the next towns, that I may preach there also, because for this purpose I have come forth.' And He was preaching in their synagogues throughout all Galilee, and casting out demons" (Mark 1:35-39).

When daybreak came and Peter and the other disciples got up, they found that people were already gathering at the door, but Jesus was nowhere to be found.

What a crowd there must have been that morning on the street in front of Peter's house. No wonder when he and James and John finally found Jesus they said, "… 'Everyone is looking for You'" (Mark 1:37). Jesus replied that it was necessary for Him to go to the other cities in the area—although He may have yielded to ministering to the multitude before He and His disciples departed.

Chapter 26

THE HEALING OF THE LEPER

"So it was, as the multitude pressed about Him to hear the word of God, that He stood by the Lake of Gennesaret, and saw two boats standing by the lake; but the fishermen had gone from them and were washing their nets. Then He got into one of the boats, which was Simon's, and asked him to put out a little from the land. And He sat down and taught the multitudes from the boat. When He had stopped speaking, He said to Simon, 'Launch out into the deep and let down your nets for a catch.' But Simon answered and said to Him, 'Master, we have toiled all night and caught nothing; nevertheless at Your word I will let down the net.' And when they had done this, they caught a great number of fish, and their net was breaking. So they signaled to their partners in the other boat to come and help them. And they came and filled both the boats, so that they began to sink. When Simon Peter saw it, he fell down at Jesus' knees, saying, 'Depart from me, for I am a sinful man, O Lord!' For he and all who were with him were astonished at the catch of fish which they had taken; and so also were James and John, the sons of Zebedee, who were partners with Simon. And Jesus said to Simon, 'Do not be afraid. From now on you will catch men.' So when they had brought their boats to land, they forsook all and followed Him" (Luke 5:1-11)

Everywhere Jesus went the people followed, hanging on to every syllable He spoke and trying to get within reach for Him to touch them for healing. As the crowds got closer and closer, He saw a boat that was nearby. The fishermen weren't in the boat; they were cleaning their nets. Jesus asked them to push the boat out a little from the land so that He might use it as a pulpit. Then as the people congregated along the shore, Jesus began to teach them the Word of God. When He had finished, Jesus turned to Simon (Peter) and told them to go back out to fish one more time. Peter reminded the Lord that they had toiled all night and had caught nothing. However, he quickly added, he would let down the net and try again because the Master had said to do it.

When they brought up the net, there were so many fish that the net began to break! They motioned for their partners, James and John, to come to their assistance, and soon they filled both boats with fish until they were actually about to sink.

When they got the boats to the shore, Peter was moved by the miracle. What did he do? Did he give thanks to the Lord for the great catch? No. He was no longer interested in the fish. Now his whole focus was on the Man Who had given him the command to go back out. It was then he recognized he was a sinful man. As Peter was convicted of being a sinner, he cried out saying, "Depart from me; for I am a sinful man, O Lord." Yet, this was the last thing Peter wanted—for the Lord to actually depart from him.

Mankind's hearts all react differently to the Gospel! One of the thieves on the cross mocked the Lord, calling Him an impostor. But the other thief was deeply repentant, and even rebuked the first thief. He realized they had done wrong and deserved to be there, while Christ was an innocent man and deserved nothing of the kind. This repentant soul turned to Jesus and said, "Lord, remember me when You come into Your kingdom." One thief went to the region of lost spirits, the other to paradise (Luke 23:42, 43).

Herod wanted Jesus to perform a miracle to gratify his curiosity. There was no thought on his part of taking Christ as his Savior. On the other hand, the miracle of catching all the fish brought Peter to the truth about his sinfulness. Today, miracles still have this dual effect, depending upon the individual. Some consider them as mere wonders to excite curiosity. Others see the hand of God in the miracle and are brought to the point of deep conviction of their sins. But the words from Jesus to Peter were not those of self-reproach, but of great gentleness. He said, "... 'Do not be afraid. From now on you will catch men'" (Luke 5:10). It was Christ's call to Peter to leave everything behind and launch out into full-time ministry.

THE HEALING OF THE LEPER

We should note at this point a difference of opinion among Bible scholars as to the exact chronological order of some of the events which transpired at this particular period of time in our Lord's ministry. One such instance is the healing of the leper. However, we believe the exact sequence in which the miracle occurred is of no great significance. It is enough to know it happened at this particular time when Jesus was making a tour of the Galilean cities.

The Lord had just come from the seashore where He had been teaching the multitude and entered a town—probably Bethsaida or Chorazin. At this moment, He was met by a most forlorn creature—a man who was afflicted with leprosy, a skin disease. Once someone was diagnosed with leprosy, they were doomed to a living death, cast out from the presence of others. For the rest of his life he would have to make his living as a beggar. Only death could relieve his misery.

Then news came to him of the Man from Nazareth. He heard of people with incurable afflictions who had been healed by Jesus. A wild hope sprang up from within him, but how could he meet Jesus? Because he was a leper, he was not allowed to mingle among the crowd. He could not go into the town. People would flee in horror if he approached them. Even the rabbis would throw stones at him if he came near them. When they saw a leper, the Pharisees would cry, "Away to your own place, so you don't pollute others!"

Leprosy carries a fearful and tragic fate, once the disease gets settled in the blood. But the wild hope would not leave this beggar. He would watch for the moment when Jesus was separated from the rest of the people; then he would go up to Him and make his desperate appeal. And that is what he did. He cried out in a pleading voice, "… 'Lord, if You are willing, You can make me clean'" (Luke 5:12). And to his overflowing joy, the Lord put forth His hand without a moment's hesitation. He touched the leper and said, "… 'I am willing; be cleansed'" (Luke 5:13).

Here we see Christ's expression of God's will concerning sickness and disease. Some, in their ignorance of the Scriptures, have taught that it is not God's will to heal. Thousands of sick and afflicted have gone through life suffering because they have been told that God has sent the sickness upon them for some mysterious reason. Yet, Jesus taught that sickness was of the devil (Luke 13:11, 16). The apostles taught that Jesus healed those who were oppressed of the devil (Acts 10:38). The Scriptures teach that sickness is part of the curse (Deuteronomy 28), and Jesus Christ was revealed to redeem men from the curse (Galatians 3:13).

Jesus Christ not only healed the leper, proving that it is God's will to do so, but He plainly said, "I am willing; be cleansed." The fact is if sickness were the will of God, every physician who attempts to cure would be violating the Divine will and every hospital would be a house of rebellion.

Yet, according to the Law, He contracted ceremonial pollution because it was considered a dangerous thing for Jesus to reach out and touch the man. In pronouncing the man clean, He had trespassed upon the authority of the priest, and had given the rulers a place to accuse Him of violating the Law. As has been said, it was a glorious violation of the letter of the Law, but it was at the same time a glorious illustration of the spirit of the Law, which declares that mercy is better than sacrifice. Christ was not polluted by touching the leper. Instead, the whole body of the leper was healed and cleansed by His hand. So it is that Christ touching man's sinful nature cleansed it; yet, at the same time, He remained without sin.

Jesus, even while He healed the people, must fulfill the Law by perfect obedience. The miracle had not been witnessed by the multitude. He told the man to say nothing to anyone, but to go and show himself to the priest. The man was to offer the things commanded by the Law of Moses and to secure the certification that he was clean.

The rites pertaining to the priestly cleaning of the leper are fully described in Leviticus, chapters 13-14. The priest took the leper outside the town and performed an elaborate ceremony before pronouncing him clean. The man made an offering, shaved off his hair, bathed, and remained seven days out of his house. The ceremony was so elaborate and occupied a considerable period of time so that there would be no dispute over his actual cleansing.

Christ told the leper to show himself to the priest for a witness. For one thing, Jesus wanted to give the religious authorities of the nation evidence that His mission was of God. On the other hand, He asked the leper to say nothing to the people.

He healed the leper because of His compassion for him, but considered it advisable that nothing be said about the matter. He did not want to put such accent on miracles that men would be carried away by the spectacular.

Unfortunately, the leper in his joy of being delivered overlooked this request. Failure to understand that obedience is better than sacrifice, the man, instead of carrying out the Lord's instructions, began to publish the news of his cleansing to everyone who would listen. As a consequence, "… Jesus could no longer openly enter the city, but was outside in deserted places; and they came to Him from every direction" (Mark 1:45). Even so, we are told that the people still came from everywhere to see Him.

Chapter 27

HEALING THE CENTURION'S SERVANT

While Jesus was carrying on His ministry in the various cities of Galilee, He preached a sermon which is known as the Sermon on the Mount, on a hill north of Capernaum. In bringing His sermon to a conclusion, Jesus made some searching remarks that must have given His hearers serious thought:

> "'Not everyone who says to Me, 'Lord, Lord,' shall enter the kingdom of heaven, but he who does the will of My Father in heaven. Many will say to Me in that day, 'Lord, Lord, have we not prophesied in Your name, cast out demons in Your name, and done many wonders in Your name?' And then I will declare to them, 'I never knew you; depart from Me, you who practice lawlessness!'"(Matthew 7:21-23)

Unless the people suppose that supernatural demonstrations were always proof of holiness, or even of the person's right relationship with God, Jesus pointed out that on the Day of Judgment there would be some who would come to Him and say that they had prophesied in His name and cast out devils and did many wonderful works, but He would have to tell them to depart from Him, for they were workers of iniquity.

Many have raised questions about this subject. And there are those who don't believe it could be so, but since Jesus spoke the words it must be true. We know that such cases exist because of the testimony of the many acts of a man who stood only a few feet from Jesus, listening to all He said. His name was Judas Iscariot.

We have every reason to believe that Judas healed the sick and cast out devils as the other disciples did. Acts 1:17 specifically declares that Judas "had obtained a part of this ministry." Jesus gave the sign of true discipleship, saying, "Therefore by their fruits you will know them" (Matthew 7:20).

HEALING THE CENTURION'S SERVANT

Now we are told that following His Sermon on the Mount, the Lord returned to Capernaum. Upon entering the city, He was met by certain Jewish elders, who informed Him about the servant of a certain centurion who was ready to die.

> "Now when He concluded all His sayings in the hearing of the people, He entered Capernaum. And a certain centurion's servant, who was dear to him, was sick and ready to die. So when he heard about Jesus, he sent elders of the Jews to Him, pleading with Him to come and heal his servant" (Luke 7:1-3).

There are those who take exception to the accuracy of the story at this point, because of a trivial variation between the Luke and Matthew narratives. This is one of their claims that is supposed to provide proof against the verbal inspiration of the Scriptures. They point out that Luke says that the elders of the Jews brought the message to Jesus. In Matthew 8:5, it declares it was the centurion who personally came to Him.

Those who find a contradiction here simply want to fight over words. Because there may be some variations in the Scriptures proves there was no collusion of witnesses in the writing of the Gospels. In the same chapter, it speaks of Jesus' healing the multitude at evening (Matthew 8:16). Luke 4:40 says this took place when the sun was setting. Of course, we know that the sun does not set in the technical sense—it's actually because the Earth rotates on its axis which causes the effect. However, doesn't everyone still know what is meant?

A lawyer writes a legal document that spells out every technicality. God knew that the Bible would be more easily understood if it were written as it is, rather than as a legal or a scientific document. Words are skeletons of the thought. For example, John 4:1 says:

"Therefore, when the Lord knew that the Pharisees had heard that Jesus made and baptized more disciples than John."

This verse states that Jesus baptized. Was this true? In the sense that Jesus permitted His disciples to do it, it was true. But that He actually performed the act Himself, technically, was not true, as the next verse states. "... (though Jesus Himself did not baptize, but His disciples) ..." (John

4:2).

The present instance is a similar case. The Matthew account tells about the centurion's request—for it was his request—but the Luke account goes into detail and explains that the centurion did not actually go personally, but sent certain elders of the Jews as his messengers. It also explains why the centurion had not gone himself (Luke 7:7). But we are ahead of our story. Let us return to the elders who met Jesus as He entered the city of Capernaum.

The news of Jesus' return to Capernaum had brought joy to the heart of this officer who was not a Jew himself. He was a centurion of Herod's army who had probably heard of the miracle of the healing of the nobleman's son. Perhaps he had also been present in the synagogue on the Sabbath when Jesus had healed the demoniac. The centurion had reverence for the Jewish faith, for he had built for the people this beautiful synagogue and won their gratitude.

There is another circumstance which shows the centurion to have been an unusually kind and gracious man. He treated his servants not as slaves as was common in those days, but almost as members of his family. The text says that a "… servant, who was dear to him, was sick and ready to die" (Luke 7:2). So when the news went through the town that Jesus had returned, the centurion immediately called for some of the Jewish elders to ask Jesus to come and heal his servant.

The elders were indebted to the centurion for his benevolence in building them a place of worship. For this reason, they felt they had to respond to his request. It was still early in the ministry of Christ, and the rulers of the Jews had not yet taken a public stand against Him. There are some who believe that these Jews didn't approve the centurion's purpose and only agreed to the request because they did not wish to offend their benefactor. However, we hardly think this view is correct, for apparently the ministry of Christ at this time had deeply impressed the people of Capernaum. One of the rulers of the synagogue was Jairus, who soon after had to seek the services of Jesus to heal his daughter from a fatal illness.

At any rate, those elders who were assigned met Jesus as He was entering into Capernaum. They informed Him about the centurion and to strengthen their petition, they said, "... that the one for whom He should do this was deserving, 'for he loves our nation, and has built us a synagogue'" (Luke 7:4, 5).

Jesus made no comment about this extraordinary explanation as to why He should heal the centurion's servant. Nevertheless, He consented to go with them. It is true that by works men show forth their faith, but works are not a basis for receiving the gift of God, which is entirely by grace. No effort from mankind, regardless of how big or small, can possibly purchase God's blessings.

It is not uncommon even today to hear people seeking healing or salvation on a similar basis. There are those who think God should answer their petition because they have been a Sunday school teacher, or have given to the poor, or performed other good works. No one is healed, or for that matter, saved by their good works. However, Christ in His condescension overlooked their faulty understanding of the ways of God. Since He could not commend their theological views, He said nothing. In His own spirit, Jesus felt the centurion was ready to receive His blessing, although not for the reason mentioned. And so He said, "... 'I will come and heal him'" (Matthew 8:7).

Now the centurion would likely have been horrified if he had heard the plea which the elders made on his behalf. It seems the delegation had scarcely left his house before he had misgivings. The soldier, although perhaps not well versed in the Scriptures, seemed to have an intuitive understanding of what was right and proper.

It occurred to him that he, a centurion engaged in commanding a band of Roman soldiers, was not worthy that Jesus should come under his roof.

> "Then Jesus went with them. And when He was already not far from the house, the centurion sent friends to Him, saying to Him, 'Lord, do not trouble Yourself, for I am not worthy that You should enter under my roof. Therefore I did not even think myself worthy to come to You. But say the word, and my servant will be healed. For I also am a man placed under authority, having soldiers under me. And I say to one, 'Go,' and he goes; and to another, 'Come,' and he comes; and to my servant, 'Do this,' and he does it'" (Luke 7:6-8).

The centurion had faith. Being under the direct authority of Herod, and familiar with those of Herod's court, he undoubtedly knew about the nobleman's son—how Jesus had said the word and the boy was healed. His reasoning was that although he had only 100 men under him and limited authority, he could speak the word and his command would be obeyed. Therefore, if Christ was Lord over all, did He not have the power to issue a command and it would also be obeyed? Let Jesus speak the word and ministering angels would carry out His orders.

Jesus regarded this man's statement as a manifestation of faith—faith that was greater than any He had ever found in Israel. After telling the centurion's messengers the servant was healed, Jesus made a most extraordinary remark:

> "And I say to you that many will come from east and west, and sit down with Abraham, Isaac, and Jacob in the kingdom of heaven. But the sons of the kingdom will be cast out into outer darkness. There will be weeping and gnashing of teeth" (Matthew 8:11, 12).

In these words, Jesus foresaw the self-righteous Jews rejecting the message of repentance and being cast away into the outer darkness; while on the other hand, Gentiles from the east and the west would come and sit down with Abraham, Isaac, and Jacob in the Kingdom of Heaven.

This statement from Jesus was obviously disturbing to the ears of the Jews. They conceded that the centurion who had built them a synagogue was worthy of some consideration, but to declare that Gentiles would be on the same plane as Abraham, Isaac, and Jacob, was to them a totally unorthodox statement. It served to put them on the alert to watch Jesus carefully for any further statements of this nature.

Chapter 28

RAISING THE SON OF THE WIDOW OF NAIN

When the messengers of the centurion returned to the house, they found the servant was made completely well. It was impossible that this miracle, which occurred in such a prominent home, should not come to the attention of the whole city. Jesus could not stay long in Capernaum, so the next day, Jesus set out on the trip to the little city of Nain. He could not escape the people, for as He and His disciples made their way, "many people" followed Him.

The distance from Capernaum to Nain is about 25 miles. It lies on the west slope of Little Hermon, which is not far from Endor, where the witch who was visited by Saul once lived. They left early in the morning and sailed to the southern part of the lake. Then they were able to walk the rest of the way. They probably reached their destination sometime in the afternoon.

A person standing on an elevated position near the city of Nain that day would have noted an interesting circumstance. There was a procession in the city that was making its mournful way toward the city gate, and another that was following Jesus; both groups were moving in such a way that they would meet as they reached the gate. The procession moving out of the city was coming from a funeral that was making its way to some ancient burial caves. These caves may still be pointed out today; they are located about a mile from the city.

A funeral is always a sad scene, but this procession was sadder than usual because the young man being carried out was the "only son of his mother, and she was a widow." His dead body was placed upon a wicker form. Even at a distance, the wails of the mourners could be heard. The Jews, as was their custom at funerals, expressed their anguish for the poor widow in sorrowful cries.

The followers of Jesus stood aside to let the processional pass by. The broken-hearted mother stumbled along. She had no eyes for the Man Who stood watching the sorrowful sight. The light had gone out of her life, and she was quietly sobbing out her grief.

Jesus looked upon this tortured woman, and her grief moved His heart. The sight of her sorrow appealed to Him. Pausing only to say to the mother, "Weep not," He approached the dead lad. As He touched the platform, something about His Presence caused the pallbearers to stand still. Then He spoke to the dead and said, "Young man, I say to you, arise" (Luke 7:14). These words of authority went out into the spirit world, calling the departed soul back into the body.

It was a moment of breathless drama. For a few seconds, no one moved. The mourners ceased their wailing. The watchers were motionless from the strange scene. Then it happened! As if awakened from a deep sleep, the lad sat up and began to speak. What a dramatic moment it was as Jesus delivered the youth to his mother! Tears of grief were suddenly turned into tears of uncontrollable joy. It was a rehearsal for the resurrection day when loved ones will be brought together again. Jesus taught about this great truth of life beyond the grave:

> "Do not marvel at this; for the hour is coming in which all who are in the graves will hear His voice and come forth—those who have done good, to the resurrection of life, and those who have done evil, to the resurrection of condemnation" (John 5:28, 29).

What about the audience? What indescribable awe must have settled upon them! Death is the veil which conceals from human vision that which goes on beyond the grave. Yet that veil had parted at the words from the Man of Nazareth!

> "Then fear came upon all, and they glorified God, saying, 'A great prophet has risen up among us;' and 'God has visited His people.' And this report about Him went throughout all Judea and all the surrounding region" (Luke 7:16, 17).

Several years ago, I personally saw a young boy, who had been killed in an accident, brought back to life through the prayer of faith. It was a scene that baffled description. I can clearly understand something about the tremendous emotional experience the people must have had that day as they witnessed this amazing scene of the widow's son being brought back to life.

Chapter 29

SIMON, SON OF JONAH

The hometown of Peter was Bethsaida, which was probably only a short distance from Capernaum (John 1:44). His father Jonah, named him "Simon." There are many Simons in the New Testament: Simon the Pharisee, Simon of Cyrene, Simon the Zealot, Simon the brother of Jesus, and others. During a Maccabean revolt, a high priest by the name of Simon had become a national hero. It is likely Peter was named after him.

Jesus took note of the headstrong spirit of Simon when He said, "Most assuredly, I say to you, when you were younger, you girded yourself and walked where you wished; but when you are old, you will stretch out your hands, and another will gird you and carry you where you do not wish" (John 21:18). In other words, he went where he wished.

As a fisherman's son, Simon would have spent much time on the Sea of Galilee. Peter learned to swim, to set a sail, and to pull the oars. Certainly he spent much time in the boat of his father and of other fishermen, as they made their living by fishing.

The Sea of Galilee was a rich fishing-ground, and the demand for fish in this busy commercial metropolis was good. Bread and fish were the staple foods of the nation. Besides this, a great quantity of fish was pickled and sent abroad in the export trade.

Peter owned his own boat which was large enough to accommodate the Lord and all 12 of the disciples. Since a dragnet required two ships to tow it, he and his brother Andrew had entered into a partnership with James and John and their father, Zebedee. They would go out a distance to sea, and then row to shore gathering up the fish in their net as they came back. When they got near to shore, they would have to jump into the sea to maneuver the net to land. Some of the fish had sharp spines which cut the net, and thus they had the task of mending the nets after each expedition.

Peter was far from a model Jew. He was a rough man, and even after he became a disciple of Jesus, once under strong temptation, he began to curse and swear (Matthew 26:74; Mark 14:71). How shall we assess the character of Peter except to say that he was very human? Goodhearted and generous, he was impetuous and prone to rebuke others, even the Lord on one occasion.

Given to impulse, he once boasted readiness to go to prison and even to death for Jesus. Yet, with all his faults, there was much good in Peter. Jesus saw in him a diamond that just needed some polishing.

Simon, as well as others, looked forward to the day when the hated Roman legions would be driven from their land. Even as we look forward today to the Second Coming of Christ, so did the people of Peter's day look forward to the First Coming.

The ideas that people had about the coming Kingdom were often fantastic and farfetched. When the Messiah came, the Earth would yawn and swallow up the heathen. Jews would live to be 1,000 years of age and would have 1,000 children. The Galileans hoped on, expecting that in their lifetime, they would see the coming of the Messiah. Their hopes were to be realized even sooner than they thought.

A prophet was to arise in Israel whose message aroused the attention of the nation. This man was John the Baptist. Elsewhere we have described this prophet's ministry, and in the next chapter we shall take note of some of the disciples he made, which included Peter and his brother Andrew.

Chapter 30

THE APPEARANCE OF THE FORERUNNER

It was in the 15th year of Tiberius Caesar that a rumor went through Galilee that a great prophet had risen and was even preaching at that time at the Jordan River. He was a man who was clothed in rough garments, but his voice carried a note of authority. Large numbers of people were coming out of Judea to hear him. His theme was "Repent, for the kingdom of heaven is at hand!" (Matthew 3:2).

John the Baptist, upon a person's confession of their sins, baptized them in the Jordan River. The fame of the prophet spread abroad and multitudes flocked from the cities to hear him. Peter and his brother, Andrew, were among those who decided to go and hear the prophet. When they arrived, they found a large number of people camped out around the village of Bethabara.

John told him to confess his sins, and then when he believed Peter was a true convert he baptized him in the river. The young fisherman felt something had happened in his life when he was baptized, and ever afterward he emphasized water baptism. On the Day of Pentecost when the multitude asked him, "Men and brethren, what shall we do?" he told them to "Repent, and be baptized every one of you in the name of Jesus."

Peter and Andrew apparently continued to stay with

John. John spoke of One Who was to come after him, and Who would baptize them with the Holy Ghost and fire.

"I indeed baptize you with water unto repentance, but He who is coming after me is mightier than I, whose sandals I am not worthy to carry. He will baptize you with the Holy Spirit and fire. His winnowing fan is in His hand, and He will thoroughly clean out His threshing floor, and gather His wheat into the barn; but He will burn up the chaff with unquenchable fire" (Matthew 3:11, 12).

Who could this be, but the Messiah—the One they had dreamed of, the One for whom prayers were made in the meetings in the synagogue for His speedy appearance. John said this One was already in their midst, but that He had not yet been revealed! (John 1:26).

Then one day, while Peter was absent, Andrew heard John say, "Behold the Lamb of God." Andrew looked, and there was the 'Man of whom the Baptist spoke before him! Andrew watched the Man and was fascinated by Him. Surely this was the Messiah! He rushed off to find his brother Peter and said to him, "… 'We have found the Messiah'" (which is translated, the Christ)" (John 1:41).

Andrew and Peter knew nothing about Him. He had grown up in Nazareth only a few miles away, but they had never heard of Him. Jesus had appeared to John about six weeks before and had been baptized by him. At that time John had seen the Holy Spirit descending upon Him like a dove. But the Baptist had no opportunity at the time to introduce Him to his disciples. By the time the service was over, Jesus had disappeared.

But now Andrew had gotten his brother to return with him to see Jesus. As Peter stood facing Jesus, He said, "… 'You are Simon the son of Jonah. You shall be called Cephas' (which is translated, A Stone)" (John 1:42). We are given no further information about the conversation which followed. Subsequent events show that Peter was as impressed as his brother Andrew had been. Later, when the call came to Peter to follow Jesus, he was ready.

Jesus soon came to Capernaum on His way to a wedding at Cana of Galilee. After the wedding, He stayed a few days in Capernaum. Then, He left to celebrate the Passover at Jerusalem.

One day, pilgrims who had visited Jerusalem during the Passover began to return, and they brought back strange reports. Jesus was making quite a sensation in the city. The rulers there, however, were not enthusiastic about Him. They did not like the way He went into the Temple and drove out the animals and the money-changers.

About that time there came startling news that John had been cast into prison by Herod because he preached against his adulterous marriage with Herodias. Once Jesus heard this, He came back to Galilee, which was in the very heart of Herod's dominion. Later, Herod beheaded John. The superstitious king heard of the miracles Jesus was performing and hastily concluded that He was John the Baptist … risen from the dead. For the time being, he had no intention of interfering with the ministry of this new preacher.

THE CALL OF PETER AND ANDREW

"And Jesus, walking by the Sea of Galilee,

saw two brothers, Simon called Peter, and Andrew his brother, casting a net into the sea; for they were fishermen. Then He said to them, 'Follow Me, and I will make you fishers of men.' They immediately left their nets and followed Him" (Matthew 4:18-20).

Early one morning while Peter and Andrew were casting their nets into the sea, they looked up and their hearts leaped with joy. The One Who stood before them was none other than the Master, the One Whom they believed in their hearts to be the Messiah. At His word they immediately left their nets and their boat and followed Him. Going along the shore a little further, they came to where their partners, James and John, were mending their nets with Zebedee, their father. The same words were spoken by Jesus to them, and they also joined the party with Peter and Andrew. The call was irresistible.

In a way, it was a daring act on the part of the four men, for they supposed the Messiah was to gather men about Him to revolt against Herod. Herod was wary about any new leaders rising up, and beheaded John for alleged conduct that supposedly jeopardized the interests of his kingdom. However, his superstitious belief that Jesus was John raised from the dead would prevent him from taking any action against the work that Jesus was doing.

The choice they made that day, or any of the others who chose to follow Jesus, led them down a path they could have had no concept of. Peter, nonetheless, invited the Lord into his house, and thereafter whenever He was in Capernaum, He was the honored guest.

Peter himself was later to claim that they had "left all" to follow Him (Mark 10:28).

Chapter 31

THE CALL OF THE OTHER APOSTLES

Andrew was Peter's brother. He is scarcely more than a name, being completely overshadowed by his famous brother, Peter. He also was a fisherman who shared his brother's house in Capernaum. Peter, James, and John became the inner circle of the apostles. Andrew "... did not attain to the first three" (2 Samuel 23:19). Yet, on occasion, he joined the others so that he might ask Jesus questions concerning the things to come (Mark 13:3).

The Book of John does give us a closer look at Andrew than the synoptic gospels. Andrew, in nearly all instances he's mentioned in acts as an intermediary. When news reached Capernaum of John the Baptist's preaching, Andrew and his brother, Peter, and the two Zebedee sons decided to hear the prophet. Arriving at the meeting place, they listened earnestly to the Baptist as he preached repentance and foretold of the coming of the Messiah to Israel, as mentioned in the previous chapter. Apparently they were very impressed by the Baptist's preaching, and they lingered on, hoping that the Messiah would appear.

Then, one day, Jesus did come, and the Baptist proclaimed Him saying, "Behold the Lamb of God, which takes away the sin of the world!" None of the four was present on the day Jesus was baptized by John. But the next time, the Man walked by, John the Baptist cried out, "Behold the Lamb of God!" (John 1:35, 36). Andrew heard the words and a thrill of excitement went through him. The Apostle John volunteers no more information, but the two disciples of John the Baptist began to follow Jesus.

Jesus realized He was being followed, so He turned to them and asked, "… 'What do you seek?'" (John 1:37). The sound of His voice must have encouraged them. It was not, "Who do you seek?" It was, "What do you seek?" Some, for example, followed Jesus for healing, and some never returned to give God thanks. Others followed Him for the loaves and fishes.

However, these men asked, "…. 'Rabbi … where are You staying?'" (John 1:37). Jesus encouraged them even further and said, "Come and see." What kind of place did they find when they arrived? It could hardly have been more than a place in the wilderness, far from human habitation. Later on, Jesus said, "… the Son of Man has nowhere to lay His head" (Luke 9:58).

On the day when John the Baptist pointed Jesus out, Peter was absent. It was up to Andrew not to lose sight of Him. Peter would have had plenty to say if he had missed out on the experience of meeting the One John had talked about! Although Andrew was not as bold as Peter, he decided that he had to find out where Jesus was staying. Then he would know where to bring Peter when he found him. In the meantime, the conversation Andrew had with Jesus was enough to convince him that Jesus was indeed the Messiah. It is to the credit of Andrew that they did not allow the golden opportunity to slip through their fingers, but followed it up when they saw Jesus. It was a decision from which both Andrew and his brother, Peter, as well as the Zebedee brethren, would reap eternal benefits.

We are to see Andrew again at the time of the feeding of the 5,000. When the question came up about how the vast multitude could be fed, Andrew anticipated the situation and brought forth the information that the only one who had brought any food with him was a lad with five barley loaves and two fishes. "One of His disciples, Andrew, Simon Peter's brother, said to Him, 'There is a lad here who has five barley loaves and two small fish, but what are they among so many?'" (John 6:8, 9).

It turned out to be, to Andrew's surprise, a useful piece of information. Jesus took the five loaves and two fishes, blessed them and broke them, and there was more than enough to feed the whole multitude.

Another brief view of Andrew is found in John 12:21, when certain Greeks desired to see Jesus. Philip brought the word to Andrew and together they went to Him. It was then that Jesus shared with them about how He must die, but that in His death He would bring forth much fruit. Indeed! His death would result in the salvation of the Gentiles, even some of those certain Greeks.

NATHANAEL AND PHILIP

"Now Philip was from Bethsaida, the city of Andrew and Peter. Philip found Nathanael and said to him, 'We have found Him of whom Moses in the law, and also the prophets, wrote—Jesus of Nazareth, the son of Joseph.' And Nathanael said to him, 'Can anything good come out of Nazareth?'

Philip said to him, 'Come and see.' Jesus saw Nathanael coming toward Him, and said of him, 'Behold, an Israelite indeed, in whom is no deceit!' Nathanael said to Him, 'How do You know me?' Jesus answered and said to him, 'Before Philip called you, when you were under the fig tree, I saw you.' Nathanael answered and said to Him, 'Rabbi, You are the Son of God! You are the King of Israel!' Jesus answered and said to him, 'Because I said to you, 'I saw you under the fig tree,' do you believe? You will see greater things than these.' And He said to him, 'Most assuredly, I say to you, hereafter you shall see heaven open, and the angels of God ascending and descending upon the Son of Man'" (John 1:44-51).

The following day after Andrew brought Peter to Christ, Jesus went forth and found Philip, who came from Bethsaida, the same city where Andrew and Peter had been brought up. Philip, just like Andrew, believed that Jesus was the Messiah, and he went to find his friend, Nathanael and brought him to Jesus. It is puzzling, in light of the lengthy interview Jesus had with Nathanael, that he should drop out of the Gospel narrative. His name is not seen in any of the lists of the apostles. Yet, he does appear again in John 21:2, after the resurrection of Christ, with several of the other apostles. It is conjectured that Nathanael is to be identified with Bartholomew whose name follows immediately after that of Philip on the lists.

When Philip was drawn to Christ, his first act was to

find his friend Nathanael. He then joyously communicated with him that he and his other friends had found the Messiah of whom Moses in the Law and the prophets had written—Jesus of Nazareth. Upon receiving this information, he replied, "Can anything good come out of Nazareth?" Here we see the influence of rivalries between the adjacent towns. Cana was near Nazareth, and neither of the villages had a good opinion of the other. Nathanael was indeed looking for the coming of the Messiah; however, the idea that He might have come out of Nazareth shocked him.

Although Cana is near Nazareth, and Nathanael and Jesus probably knew a number of the same people, it does not appear that Nathanael had met Jesus personally prior to that particular meeting. It is likely, however, that Nathanael and Philip knew Joseph, for Philip spoke of Him as "the son of Joseph." This isn't hard to understand because at that time Jesus was known as the son of Joseph, and the supernatural conception was still a sacred secret that was known by only a few. But it was not the lineage which troubled Nathanael. It was the place of His residence. It seems that the people of Nazareth were of a mediocre quality. Their rude treatment of Jesus when He tried to minister in His hometown bears witness of this. Cana was close enough to Nazareth for Nathanael to have had some first-hand knowledge of the people. In general, the Jews did not expect the Messiah to come out of Galilee (John 7:52).

Philip did not argue the question with Nathanael, but simply said, "Come and see." Nathanael's problem was common to the whole Jewish nation. Christ's origin was too humble for them to accept. Their pre-conceived ideas were a constant barrier that prevented them from recognizing the Messiah when He came. Although Nathanael was perplexed, his mind was not closed on the matter. He quickly accepted Philip's invitation to see Jesus.

When Nathanael approached the Lord, he was met by the strange salutation, "Behold, an Israelite indeed, in whom is no deceit!" The first Israelite, Jacob, had been full of guile. The Jews of that day were notorious for their guile. The hypocrisies of the Pharisees, by which they succeeded in voiding the Word of God through the traditions of men, had become a part of their very nature. They revealed their guile by posing compromising dilemmas before Jesus under the guise of seeking truth, hoping all the while that they might somehow trap Him.

But Nathanael was free from such deceit, and Jesus looked into his heart and knew what was there. Nathanael was startled that Jesus seemed to read his innermost thoughts, and he could only exclaim, "How do You know me?" (John 1:48). Jesus gave him a straightforward answer:

"Before Philip called you, when you were under the fig tree, I saw you." (John 1:48). Since Jesus in His human body was not omniscient, we know that the gift of the word of knowledge was operating at this moment. Nathanael realized that Jesus had acquired this knowledge supernaturally. The young man had deliberately sought a place of concealment where he could meditate and pray. He knew he had been followed there by Jesus in Spirit, and this was enough to convince Nathanael that He was more than a man. With forthrightness he made his confession, "Rabbi, You are the Son of God! You are the King of Israel!" (John 1:49).

Jesus' reply to his confession was still surprising. He told Nathanael that he would see greater things than these. "And He said to him, 'Most assuredly, I say to you, hereafter you shall see heaven open, and the angels of God ascending and descending upon the Son of Man'" (John 1:51). Jacob's vision formed a background of the statement of the Lord. New truth was brought out. The ladder became a person. Christ is the ladder, the means of communication between Earth and Heaven. Nothing was mentioned about Heaven being opened for Jacob. But it was to be opened for Nathanael and his companions.

"Blessed are the pure in heart; for they shall see God." So the guileless Nathanael was to be able to see Heaven open and the harmony restored between God and mankind.

One-by-one, Christ added various disciples to His group, until He had a total of 12, each of a different temperament than the other, but each one was fiercely loyal to their Master. The one who would defect was Judas Iscariot, the official treasurer of the group. That story will be told later.

Chapter 32

CHRIST STILLS THE STORM

The mid-Galilean ministry of Jesus was marked by the beginning of His use of the parable, an unusual method of teaching. At this time, His fame had spread abroad and great multitudes were being drawn to hear Him. Men had used the parable before in teaching, but Christ's parables were unique and unparalleled in their range of areas. Nothing, which approached their depth and power, their brevity and manifold application, had ever appeared in the entire literature of mankind before or since.

It is not our purpose at the present moment to enter into a detailed exposition of the parables. (These will be discussed in another volume.) We, today, not only have the parables in written form, but also Christ's explanation of some of them. But it was not so easy for those who heard them spoken for the first time to understand them. Even the disciples failed to catch their significance, and when they were alone with Jesus they asked Him for their true meanings.

The day He spoke these first parables of the Kingdom came to an end, He desired to have some solitude and a time of rest. He called His disciples to prepare the ship, so that they might go over to the other side.

Before He could get away, an interruption occurred. As anyone who has handled large crowds at a gospel meeting knows, when the service is over there is always a number of people who come forward with special questions or problems. One may need help for this, while another may need something else. It is not unusual for some to want to stay to be a part of the ministering team. It is hardly surprising, therefore, that at the close of this great service by the seashore that certain ones should come to Jesus and request to become members of His band:

> "Then a certain scribe came and said to Him, 'Teacher, I will follow You wherever You go.' And Jesus said to him, 'Foxes have holes and birds of the air have nests, but the Son of Man has nowhere to lay His head.' Then another of His disciples said to Him, 'Lord, let me first go and bury my father.' But Jesus said to him, 'Follow Me, and let the dead bury their own dead'" (Matthew 8:19-22).

The first was a scribe, who said, "Teacher, I will follow You wherever You go." He probably thought that his official rank would make him an acceptable addition to the group. The man had witnessed the growth of popular enthusiasm, and he may have thought that joining the group would have a lucrative outcome. Jesus quickly disillusioned him on his thinking, declaring that whereas the foxes had holes and the birds of the air had nests, the Son of Man had nowhere to lay His head.

The second man who approached Him was already a disciple, but he had some matters that needed attending. His father had died. There had to be a period of mourning, and the business of the settlement of the estate had to be addressed. He would follow Jesus as soon as these things had been resolved. How many, even since then, have received the call of God on their lives and have allowed such temporal matters to delay them until their hour of opportunity has passed? Time waits for no man. Jesus encouraged the man, saying, "Follow me, and let the dead bury their own dead."

The third one had a similar case. He also wanted to follow Jesus, but he had to first say goodbye to his friends. Too often this apparently innocent act has resulted in fatal effects. A young man is convinced that Jesus has called him, but he confides his intentions to someone who is against the idea. Now, reasonable arguments could be brought against his plans. Warnings might be given that the enterprise could fail and come to nothing. The spirit of fear intervenes, and the result is that individual's outlook becomes altered. Jesus said, "No one, having put his hand to the plow, and looking back, is fit for the kingdom of God"(Luke 9:62).

CHRIST STILLS THE STORM

"And a great windstorm arose, and the waves beat into the boat, so that it was already filling. But He was in the stern, asleep on a pillow. And they awoke Him and said to Him, 'Teacher, do You not care that we are perishing?' When He arose and rebuked the wind, and said to the sea, 'Peace, be still!' And the wind ceased and there was a great calm" (Mark 4:37-39).

With these interruptions over, the disciples lifted anchor and set sail in their ship toward the eastern side of the lake. After they had gotten out a little way, Jesus laid down in the rear of the boat to get some much-needed rest. Soon, He was fast asleep.

About the time they reached the middle of the lake, they became conscious of a brisk wind which was steadily increasing in strength. The Sea of Galilee is especially noted for its storms that burst with a sudden fury upon the surface of its waters. With scarcely a moment's notice, the ship began to be tossed about in a most dangerous way. The disciples let down their sails. Peter used all of his skill at the helm to keep the boat from being swamped. Again and again, the ship was half buried under the foam of the breakers. Now, the disciples are doing everything they can to bail the water out of the boat.

Then, things took a turn for the worse. The storm produced large billows which broke over into the boat itself, causing it to be so filled with water that it began to sink.

It is a matter of controversy as to just how much control Satan has over the natural elements and to what extent he is responsible for storms of this nature. Certainly, the devil does not possess unlimited power, nor can he put the people of God in physical jeopardy at will. Otherwise, he would certainly use those powers without restraint. No doubt, there was a combination of circumstances involved. We do know Satan is "the prince of the power of the air" and has limited power over the natural elements. He was able to send the fire, or lightning, which destroyed Job's flocks (Job 1:12, 16). He also sent the cyclone or windstorm which destroyed the house where his children were banqueting (Job 1:18, 19). Nothing would suit the destructive purposes of Satan better than for the ship which carried Jesus and the apostles to go down with all of them on board.

It appeared to the disciples that such a fate was highly

probable. Despite their desperate efforts, they saw their boat becoming filled with water. Seized with panic, they turned to Christ, Who was in the rear of the ship still sleeping. They woke Him with the cry, "Teacher, do You not care that we are perishing?"

Here, indeed, was a crisis to test a man's stamina. To be awakened suddenly and find one's self in a ship about to go down is enough to try the courage of any man. The disciples were no weaklings. They knew the ways of the sea. They were hardy fishermen whose courage and know-how could take them through a storm at sea, as well as any man, if human skill alone could accomplish it.

But not for a moment was the Spirit of the Lord ruffled. Without a single indication of alarm, He got up and took command of the situation. He rebuked the wind. Did His rebuke indicate that there was an intelligence behind the storm? The majestic Christ stood there only a moment until the pent-up fury of the wind relaxed and the giant waves began to subside. In a matter of minutes the sea became as a mirror and "there was a great calm." For a moment we can assume that the disciples were fully occupied in bailing out the water which had gotten into the ship. Then they turned with faces filled with wonder, exchanging glances with one another and realizing that God was standing before them, clothed in human flesh.

They had in their terror accused Him of not caring for them. But instead of apologizing for neglecting them, Jesus said, "Why are you so fearful? How is it that you have no faith?" (Mark 4:40). If we take these words literally, we are compelled to come to one conclusion: Christ's philosophy of life envisions mankind putting themselves completely into the hands of God, and because of that commitment, they will be perfectly safe from all harm. Not that anyone who is committed to Him should tempt God. Jesus would not cast Himself down from the pinnacle of the Temple to prove the reality of that Divine protection. Men should use all proper precautions in their business of living. Even in the Mosaic Law, those who built a house were commanded to put battlements around the roof to guard against anyone's falling off the edge.

Even when all possible problems are anticipated, there is always the danger of the unexpected and unforeseen. That is where Divine providence comes in. Jesus was implying that men who put themselves fully under the protection of God need to have no fear of the unexpected—they are God's, and He will take care of His own.

Therefore, neither men nor devils could harm Christ nor frustrate His mission before His time had come. So why then should His disciples fear the storm or be afraid the boat would sink? No boat was ever made that could sink, if Christ was in it! Those who cry in despair because they think their ship is going down need to have no fear. All they have to make sure of is that Christ is in their ship!

The significance of Christ's words appeared to be lost on the disciples. They were saying to each other, "Who can this be, that even the winds and the sea obey Him?" (Matthew 8:27). Nevertheless, these very human disciples made the right choice to obtain the faith that Jesus had. They chose to live where faith was. They walked and talked with Jesus. They saw His miracles; they listened to the words of Him, and about Him it was said "No man ever spoke like this Man!" (John 7:46). They saw Him heal the sick, raise the dead, and cast out devils. They learned how He did it, and the day came that they no longer marveled, but those who saw their works in turn marveled. When Peter and John healed the lame man at the Beautiful Gate, it was the rulers of the Jews that were amazed; and we are told that they perceived that they had been with Jesus.

> "Now when they saw the boldness of Peter and John, and perceived that they were uneducated and untrained men, they marveled. And they realized that they had been with Jesus" (Acts 4:13).

Some would cast doubt on this remarkable intervention of nature and say that what was meant was that Jesus calmed "His terrified companions, and that the hurricane, from natural causes sank as rapidly as it had arisen." Of this, Dean Farrar in his Life of Christ declares:

> "I reply, that if this were the only miracle in the life of Christ; if the Gospels were the loose, exaggerated, inaccurate, credulous narratives which such an interpretation would suppose; if there were something antecedently incredible in the supernatural; if there were in the spiritual world no transcendent facts which lie far beyond the comprehension of those who would bid us see nothing in the universe but the action of material laws; if there were no providences of God during these nineteen centuries to attest the work and the Divinity of Christ— then indeed there would be no difficulty in such an interpretation. But if we believe that God rules; if we believe that Christ rose; if

we have reason to hold, among the deepest convictions of our being, the certainty that God has not delegated His sovereignty or His providence to the final, unintelligent, pitiless, inevitable working of material forces; if we see on every page of the Evangelists the quiet simplicity of truthful and faithful witnesses; if we see in every year of succeeding history, and in every experience of individual life, a confirmation of the testimony which they delivered— then we shall neither clutch at rationalistic interpretations, nor be much troubled if others adopt them. He who believes, he who knows, the efficacy of prayer, in what other men may regard as the inevitable certainties or blindly-directed accidents of life-he who has felt how the voice of a Savior, heard across the long generations, can calm wilder storms than ever buffeted into fury the bosom of the inland Lake—he who sees in the person of his Redeemer a fact more stupendous and more majestic than all those observed sequences which men endow with an imaginary omnipotence, and worship under the name of Law—to him, at least, there will be neither difficulty nor hesitation in supposing that Christ, on board that half-wrecked fishing-boat, did utter His mandate, and that the wind and the sea obeyed; that His word was indeed more potent among the cosmic forces than miles of agitated water, or leagues of rushing air."

Chapter 33

LEGION OF THE DAMNED

"Then they came to the other side of the sea, to the country of the Gadarenes. And when He had come out of the boat, immediately there met Him out of the tombs a man with an unclean spirit, who had his dwelling among the tombs; and no one could bind him, not even with chains, because he had often been bound with shackles and chains. And the chains had been pulled apart by him, and the shackles broken in pieces; neither could anyone tame him. And always, night and day, he was in the mountains and in the tombs, crying out and cutting himself with stones. When he saw Jesus from afar, he ran and worshiped Him. And he cried out with a loud voice and said, 'What have I to do with You, Jesus, Son of the Most High God? I implore You by God that You do not torment me'" (Mark 5:1-7).

When Christ and His disciples reached the other side of the Sea of Galilee, they did not find the rest they had anticipated. They were met by a demonstration of fury which rivaled anything they had encountered on the sea. There in the country of the Gadarenes, the mountains rose up sharply from the surface of the water. Near the shore was located an old cemetery where people lay buried. The hills, too rainy for ordinary human habitation, were not, completely unoccupied. Nearby was a herd of swine. In the distance was the city of Gadara.

Two men afflicted with a raging madness inhabited this rocky desolation. They wandered to and fro through the tombs and rocks and came out to meet the group. One of the men appeared to be more dangerous and aggressive. The other kept at a distance and did not take an active part in the unfolding drama. The fiercer of the two began to cry out against Jesus, indicating that he was a lunatic of the most violent kind. Since he was so dangerous to society, many attempts had been made to bind him with strong chains. But when the symptoms of his mania came upon him, he became possessed of such superhuman force that the chains and bonds fell away. All attempts to hold him failed, and he had been abandoned to his lunacy. Driven from mankind, wearing no clothes, this raving maniac had been forced to wander in his torment, while night and day he cut himself on the rocks and his voice rang out with wild, demented yells. His only companionship was this other demented man who was hovering about some distance away.

When the man possessed with the demons approached Christ, there was a great change in his attitude. The demons recognized the One Who had mastery over them. Apparently, they took a humiliating attitude, hoping in their desperation that Christ would not send them away into the deep. Here we have one of the few Scriptural examples of a colliding between a holy person and evil spirits. The demon possessed man fell before Jesus in an attitude of worship and cried with a loud voice:

> "... 'What have I to do with You, Jesus, Son
> of the Most High God? I implore You by God
> that You do not torment me'" (Mark 5:7).

It is doubtful that the man himself had any knowledge of what he was saying. The demons had such control over his mind that they completely dominated his personality. Such persons, when delivered, rarely have a recollection of the events which occurred during the period of their obsession. Demons know they are damned spirits beyond the hope of redemption. It is a torment and agony to them to be brought into the presence of a holy being, and thereby, be reminded of their lost condition, the coming bliss of the righteous, and the awful prospect of their future doom. So what did they have in common with Christ, and why should He come to torment them before their time? (Matthew 8:29).

The fact is that demons have no right to possess a human being who is made in the image of God. Nevertheless, it is also true that if men, through sinful acts go outside the boundaries of God's Divine protective power, demons are always on the alert to take advantage of the situation that has been given to them. Indeed, Jesus pointed out on another occasion that if the man who was delivered continued to wander outside the realm of Divine protection, the exorcised demon would sooner or later return, and seeing the house "swept and garnished," would take unto himself seven other spirits and the last state of the man would be worse than the first.

> "When an unclean spirit goes out of a man,
> he goes through dry places, seeking rest;

and finding none, he says, 'I will return to my house from which I came.' And when he comes, he finds it swept and put in order. Then he goes and takes with him seven other spirits more wicked than himself, and they enter and dwell there; and the last state of that man is worse than the first" (Luke 11:24-26).

The demons, therefore, were contesting a point of law as to whether or not they had the right to remain in the man. Jesus overruled their objection and said, "Come out of the man, unclean spirit!" (Mark 5:8). Having established the fact that the demons would have to come out, He perceived there were a large number of them present. It is not uncommon after one or more demons are cast out for others to hide away in the victim, hoping to escape detection by pretending to have departed. Subsequent events show that such persons are not fully delivered. On this occasion, Jesus demanded that the demons tell Him their name, to disclose information concerning their number.

The leader of the demons responded saying, "My name is Legion: for we are many." The name "legion" was adopted from the Romans, whose armies were composed of legions, which consisted of 6,000 men. This does not necessarily mean that there were exactly 6,000 devils in the man, but it does indicate a great number. Jesus knew that the whole colony should be eliminated from these victims.

This brings up a question involved in the study of demonology and the spirit world. The question is, how many demons can inhabit a single human body at the same time? In certain instances, we are told that a person was possessed with as many as seven devils. Mary Magdalene had seven devils cast out of her (Luke 8:2). One thing is clear—spirit and matter can occupy the same space at the same time. No scientific instruments can measure or analyze spirits, but they make their presence known through a human body. Evil spirits can operate through the body of a spiritualist medium. They can speak and carry on intelligent communication, even as the demons were doing through this lunatic. They are the source of all sorts of phenomena, such as causing objects to fly about; they can produce knockings, simulate voices, accomplish levitation, etc. But they must have a physical body to manifest themselves to be in the physical realm.

The words of Jesus imply that demons crave embodiment in a human body, which indicates that they are disembodied spirits. When they are cast out, they "walk through dry places, seeking rest; and finding none ..." They cannot rest until they find and inhabit a human body. Once they enter, they are to a degree able to control it and to share the sensations and appetites of the body. Demons appear willing to share their habitation with other demons, since the increased number apparently gives them almost absolute control over their victim (Luke 11:24-26).

This is the reason for the demons' apprehension at being cast out. They feared that Jesus, for some reason, might cast them into the bottomless pit or the abyss:

"And they begged Him that He would not command them to go out into the abyss" (Luke 8:31).

We do not have record that Jesus cast any demons into the pit. The devils themselves contended that the time of their punishment had not yet come (Matthew 8:29). This was probably true. Satan and his evil spirits will be incarcerated in the bottomless pit at the end of the age, at which time they will no longer be able to deceive the nations until the thousand years are finished (Revelation 20:1-3).

We also know that some fallen angels and demon spirits are already in confinement. Jude 6 and Revelation 9:1-3 make this clear. On the other hand, it is certainly true that many demons are free to roam the Earth. This gives rise to the question as to whether or not, if demons should disobey the restrictions God has set for them, it might be lawful to take their liberty from them. In other words, the demons seemed to recognize if they did not subject themselves to Christ's authority, He might bind them and cast them into the abyss, which was a place they exceedingly feared.

Actually, the demons wished to remain in the country of the Gadarenes. The people in that region were given to ungodly living, and there would be a better chance for them to find further victims whose bodies they might inhabit. So their second plea was that He "... would not send them out of the country" (Mark 5:10). Not being refused, and there being a large herd of 2,000 swine nearby, all the devils besought Him saying, "... 'Send us to the swine, that we may enter into them'" (Mark 5:12). Why did the demons make such a request and hope that it would be granted?

The children of Israel had been given charge by the Mosaic Law not to eat swine flesh. In Jesus' day, the time had not yet come when God lifted this ceremonial prohibition (Acts 10:9-16), which would typify the cleansing of the Gentiles (Acts 11:1-18). The people of the Gadarenes were deliberately violating the Law of Moses by raising and selling large numbers of hogs, and obviously, they were making swine's flesh available for general consumption.

Since the owners of these swine were disobeying the

Law of Moses, could Christ forbid their request and actually protect the property of these lawbreakers? Actually, Jesus would not interfere with them for good or ill will. Neither would He exercise His power to protect their illicit business. If the devils wished to enter the swine, it was up to them.

In the beginning, demons may seem to have unusual power; and upon leaving the man they moved like a gigantic swarm of invisible bats upon the herd of swine. How many of the demons immediately succeeded in entering the swine is not known, but the sum result was that the herd became wild and unmanageable. (It has been aptly said that the hogs were different from some people. They couldn't live with the demons.) In their panic, the great herd "ran violently down a steep place into the sea," and perished. It would appear doubtful that the demons had anticipated this result or taken into account what would happen if the swine, now driven into a frenzy in this precipitous location, panicked.

The narrative at this point ceases to follow the activities of the baffled demons. Disembodied, they probably began the restless search for fresh victims. Some very profound results followed as a result of the incident. The man, who a few moments before was a raging maniac, suddenly became quiet and calm and was in his right mind. Apparently, he at once realized he was naked. As long as the man was possessed of the devil, he would wear no clothes. Once he was delivered, he wanted his nakedness covered. Perhaps one of the disciples had an extra garment in the boat. At any rate, the man was soon clothed and began to talk in a normal way with Jesus and the disciples.

It can be understood that the event had a startling effect upon the herdsmen. They witnessed their swine stampeding violently down the mountainside and drowning in the waters below. Far from being able to quiet them, they barely managed to get out of their way in time to escape with their own lives. Anything of such a violent and unexpected nature must have had a cause. What was it? They were not long in arriving at the truth. The lunatic who had terrorized the whole countryside with his wild gestures and fierce cries was sitting at the feet of Jesus, clothed and carrying on an intelligent conversation.

Realizing that a vast amount of property had been destroyed and that they were accountable to their masters, the keepers fled to the city, telling everyone they saw what had happened. Ordinarily, such a wondrous miracle would have caused joy and thanksgiving, but in this case, men's pocketbooks had been affected. The loss of such a great number of swine, jeopardizing the industry that many of the people depended upon, overruled every other consideration.

The reaction of the Gadarenes, who came out to see what had happened, was different from that in other places. It is not said that they disbelieved in the deliverance of the lunatic, or said that it was not accomplished by the power of God. But their precious swine had perished, their industry was threatened, and consequently their livelihood was at stake. Jesus might be a great prophet; He might be the Messiah, but they could not afford to accept what would cost them so much. As the demons wanted to be left alone, so did the Gadarenes. Mankind is always given free choice as to whether or not they will serve Christ. When the day comes for Christ to be their Judge, they will not have a choice (Matthew 25).

Jesus turned away. He, Himself, had warned His disciples not to give that which was holy unto dogs, neither to cast their pearls before swine, "Lest they trample them under their feet, and turn and tear you to pieces." These people loved their sins and their swine, preferring them to Christ. Therefore, they asked Him to leave them alone, and this He sadly agreed to do.

Yet, Jesus did not altogether leave the people to their doom. He knew that there were some who did not agree with what the majority had done. There were some precious souls who would have accepted Him if He had remained there. Was the blindness of those who thought only of their swine going to deprive all of the others with a chance of salvation? No, Jesus would give those who wanted an opportunity to reconsider their decision.

Previously, in Galilee, when a great miracle had been performed, Jesus had silence for reasons mentioned. But in this case, there was no need for that here, for Jesus would never personally return to the Gadarenes.

The people had prayed that Jesus would depart and He complied with their request. But the man who had been healed "... begged Him that he might be with Him. However, Jesus did not permit him ..." (Mark 5:18, 19). Instead, He had a task for him to perform.

> "However, Jesus did not permit him, but said to him, 'Go home to your friends, and tell them what great things the Lord has done for you, and how He has had compassion on you'" (Mark 5:19).

The man was disappointed that he could not go with Jesus, but he who was once possessed of devils, faithfully obeyed the Lord's request. He returned to the people and began to publish in all the cities of Decapolis what great things Christ had done for him. Those of that region had hoped Jesus would go away and let them forget. But with this man who had once been demented, whom no prison chains could hold, nor man could tame, going up and down the country telling people of the great things that God had done for him, how could they forget?

There is one last word that we might say concerning the people of Gadara. The day was to come (A.D. 67) when Vespasian and Titus would enter that region, massacring the inhabitants and burning to the ground the city of Gadara (Josephus B. J. III 7, 1). It was as Jesus said of Jerusalem, "... you did not know the time of your visitation" (Luke 19:44). The man in whom the legion of the damned dwelt became a great missionary for Christ, but the people of that region, who turned Christ away, lived to join the damned.

Chapter 34

RAISING JAIRUS' DAUGHTER
AND OTHER MIRACLES

So Jesus and His disciples retraced their journey back across the Sea of Galilee. What marvelous events had transpired in the short time of just 24 hours! But other remarkable miracles would take place that day before the sun would set. The return to Capernaum was without incident; but when the sail of their ship was observed in the distance, crowds at once began gathering on the shore. Some who had witnessed the curing of the lunatic had hurried back to carry the news of what had happened. At any rate, when Jesus reached the shore there was a vast multitude waiting to meet Him.

THE PARALYTIC HEALED AFTER BEING
LET DOWN FROM THE ROOF

"Now it happened on a certain day, as He was teaching, that there were Pharisees and teachers of the law sitting by, who had come out of every town of Galilee, Judea, and Jerusalem. And the power of the Lord was present to heal them. Then behold, men brought on a bed a man who was paralyzed, whom they sought to bring in and lay before Him. And when they could not find how they might bring him in, because of the crowd, they went up on the housetop and let him down with his bed through the tiling into the midst before Jesus. When He saw their faith, He said to him, 'Man, your sins are forgiven you'" (Luke 5:17-20).

Jesus went directly to a house and began to teach. He probably sat near the doorway while the crowd pressed as close as possible to Him from every side. After He had taught for a while, He began to minister to some of the people for healing, for we are told that the "power of the Lord was present to heal them." There is such a thing as an atmosphere of faith which makes it easy for people to get healed. The very opposite condition had prevailed during His second visit to Nazareth. He could do no mighty work there because of their unbelief (Mark 6:5).

When a man on a cot was brought into the courtyard, the place was so full of people that there was no way for those who brought him to get near to the Lord. The sick man was in a desperate condition, paralyzed with the palsy. The four tried to get him to Jesus, but could find no way of doing it directly. However, they were determined men, and they made their way up onto the roof of the outer stairway (Luke 5:19). By removing a few tiles, they made an opening and lowered the man on his cot to a place close to where Jesus was sitting. The palsied man had nothing to say; he was probably embarrassed by the manner in which his friends had brought him into the Presence of Jesus.

But the Lord, looking around, appeared to be pleased

by their faith, instead of rebuking them for tearing up the roof of the house.

> "When He saw their faith, He said to him, 'Man, your sins are forgiven you'" (Luke 5:20).

The fact that the words, "their faith," is used is highly significant. The poor paralytic probably was so shaken up by being brought into the building in such an unorthodox fashion that he manifested no active faith in his healing. But Jesus showed that it is possible for others to supply the needed faith when the sick person is unable to exercise it for himself. So He said to the paralytic, "Man, your sins are forgiven you."

The Lord knew there were Pharisees and doctors of the law present. Some of them were emissaries from Jerusalem, and He realized that His word about forgiving the man's sins had made an unfavorable impression upon them. He observed the exchange of glances and looks of disapproval on their countenances as they whispered among themselves, "Who can forgive sins, but God alone?"

> "But when Jesus perceived their thoughts, He answered and said to them, 'Why are you reasoning in your hearts? Which is easier, to say, 'Your sins are forgiven you,' or to say, 'Rise up and walk'? But that you may know that the Son of Man has power on earth to forgive sins"—He said to the man who was paralyzed, 'I say to you, arise, take up your bed, and go to your house'" (Luke 5:22-24).

Anyone can say, "Your sins are forgiven you," and who can say whether he is telling the truth? But when one says to a paralytic, "Arise and walk," and he walks, the person who speaks, obviously, must have authority. If God gave Him power to do the first, was that not enough evidence that He had given Him power to do the other? But obstinacy is a peculiar trait and subsequent events were to show that the Pharisees would not accept the explanation. As the old saying goes, "He that is persuaded against his will is of the same opinion still."

Nonetheless, although the doctors of the Law opposed the work of Jesus in healing the paralytic, the rest of His audience, when they saw what was happening, began praising and glorifying God. Strength surged into the paralyzed limbs, and at the same time, peace came to the man's soul. He arose, lifted his cot, and carried it triumphantly out through the doorway, while the people made way for him. As he disappeared, he was still shouting praises to God. The people who witnessed this extraordinary miracle began to speak exclamations of astonishment mixed with awe, and said, "We have seen strange things today." They had never seen it in this fashion.

THE CALL OF MATTHEW (MATTHEW 9:9)

As most Bible readers know, the Gospel narrative does not by any means give a complete record of all the things that Jesus did, nor does it always present them necessarily in the order in which they occurred (John 21:25). We do know, however, that it was about this same time when Jesus gave the call to Matthew, whom He saw sitting at the receipt of customs. Apparently, the Lord, after healing the man of the palsy, had gone back to the seashore where He could more conveniently minister to the people. Matthew's office was located nearby, and when Jesus passed that way He said to Matthew, "Follow me." At once the man got up and followed Him. Years afterward, Matthew would write the Gospel that bears his name.

A little later that day, Jesus went to the home of Matthew who had prepared a feast for Him and had invited many of his own personal friends. We won't linger over this event, but it would be safe to say that certain scribes and Pharisees were closely observing those who attended the feast. Christ's cordiality to the sinners present caused them misgivings. But as for the people, they were more and more convinced that Jesus was the great prophet who should come into the world. Unfortunately, they, as well as Christ's own disciples, shared the illusion that the Messiah, after a brief period of preaching, would begin to set up a visible earthly kingdom.

HEALING THE WOMAN WITH THE ISSUE OF BLOOD

"So it was, when Jesus returned, that the multitude welcomed Him, for they were all waiting for Him. And behold, there came a man named Jairus, and he was a ruler of the synagogue. And he fell down at Jesus' feet and begged Him to come to his house, for he had an only daughter about twelve years of age, and she was dying. But as He went, the multitudes thronged Him. Now a woman, having a flow of blood for twelve years, who had spent all her livelihood on physicians and could not be healed by any, came from behind and touched the border of His garment. And immediately her flow of blood stopped" (Luke 8:40-44).

The feast at Matthew's house had scarcely come to a conclusion when one of the most prominent men of the city came to Jesus with a most urgent personal request. It was none other than the ruler of the synagogue, and the one who probably invited Jesus to speak on the day He healed the demoniac. It is also very likely that he was among those who were deputized to come to Jesus to plead the case of the centurion for the healing of his servant. If this is true, it would explain his faith in Jesus, who he believed could save the life of his daughter that lay dying.

Falling at the feet of Christ, he informed Jesus that his young daughter—his only daughter—lay at the point of death. If Jesus would just come and lay His hand upon her, she would live. It is possible that Jesus had seen the little girl when she came with her father to the synagogue on one of the days He had preached there. At any rate, Jesus touched by the appeal, went with him, with a large crowd following.

But there was another woman in the crowd. One day, news had reached her of people who had been healed of incurable diseases by the Great Physician. Probably from modesty, she hesitated to reveal to Jesus the particular kind of affliction she had been suffering from. It occurred to her that if she could only get near Him and touch the hem of His garment, she would be made whole. Therefore, she made her way through the crowd, repeating to herself, "If I can only touch the hem of His clothes, I will be made whole."

Suddenly, she reached up and grabbed a hold of His hem. Even as she drew her hand back, she felt the power of God go through her disease-wracked body, making her completely whole!

She shrank back; her act was quite unnoticed by the crowd, but not by Jesus. He perceived immediately that virtue had flowed out from Him. He turned quickly and said, "Who touched me?" Jesus could have discovered the woman, but He preferred for her to come forward and make herself known. Peter said, "Master, the multitudes throng and press You, and You say, 'Who touched Me?'" (Luke 8:45).

But Jesus was insistent, and His eyes wandered from face to face, looking at the people to distinguish between those who were curiosity-seekers and the one who had the touch of faith. Then His glance fell upon the poor woman, who saw that she could not hide. She came forward and fell at His feet, telling Him the truth. Perhaps she feared His anger, for the Law declared that anyone who was touched by a person so afflicted was made ceremoniously unclean until evening (Leviticus 15:19).

It is sad to note the pitiful attempts of some who try to explain the operation of the Gifts of the Spirit from a purely psychological basis. As Jesus said to the Sadducees, "You are mistaken, not knowing the Scriptures nor the power of God" (Matthew 22:29). We who have witnessed the Gifts of the Spirit in operation have observed similar manifestations of the word of knowledge and discerning of spirits many times. When those given to unbelief and ignorance have finally wrecked their lives because of unbelief, we shall see that the Word of God has stood the test, and those whose faith is in its truth shall never come to shame.

If the poor woman who had been healed had any

apprehension of the Lord's displeasure, those fears were quickly dismissed. Her touch could not pollute Him, but instead, it cleansed her. Far from being upset, the Lord's gracious words spoke peace to her troubled life. He said, "Daughter, be of good cheer; your faith has made you well. Go in peace" (Luke 8:48).

The fact that healing virtue is a tangible thing which can be transmitted through pieces of cloth, such as aprons and handkerchiefs, is no fluke, as seen in the case of Paul. After cloths had touched his body, he sent them out to the sick and they were healed; even evil spirits went out of those possessed by them:

> "Now God worked unusual miracles by the hands of Paul, so that even handkerchiefs or aprons were brought from his body to the sick, and the diseases left them and the evil spirits went out of them" (Acts 19:11, 12).

RAISING JAIRUS' DAUGHTER

> "While He was still speaking, someone came from the ruler of the synagogue's house, saying to him, 'Your daughter is dead. Do not trouble the Teacher.' But when Jesus heard it, He answered him, saying, 'Do not be afraid; only believe, and she will be made well.' When He came into the house, He permitted no one to go in except Peter, James, and John, and the father and mother of the girl. Now all wept and mourned for her; but He said, 'Do not weep; she is not dead, but sleeping.' And they ridiculed Him, knowing that she was

dead. But He put them all outside, took her by the hand and called, saying, 'Little girl, arise.' Then her spirit returned, and she arose immediately. And He commanded that she be given something to eat. And her parents were astonished, but He charged them to tell no one what had happened" (Luke 8:49-56).

The incident with the woman and the issue of blood, which had just occurred, caused a brief delay, and though it must have profoundly impressed the people who were following Jesus, to Jairus, who knew his daughter was gasping her last breaths, it must have caused deep anguish. It was only a few minute's interruption, but it seemed like hours to the father. And then, as the company started on its way again, a messenger reached Jairus saying, "Your daughter is dead. Do not trouble the Teacher." It was too late after all!

How those words must have stung the father's heart. If Jesus had only gotten there a little sooner, his child would have lived. But it was too late. Although the message was not addressed to Jesus, He overheard it, and knowing the anguish of the father, He said, "Do not be afraid; only believe, and she will be made well." At such a time, faith grasps at the impossible and the words of Jesus must have been reassuring.

As the company drew near the house, they could hear the hired mourners and minstrels as they beat their breasts and set up their wailing chants. When Jesus arrived, He sought to still them by saying, "Do not weep; she is not dead, but sleeping." The professional mourners thought this was a poor joke, and they ceased their mercenary wails only long enough to give Him a laugh. Jesus did not prolong the unprofitable conversation, but ordered them to be put out of the house and commanded that none other should enter except Peter, James, John, and the parents.

There was a reason for this. The kind of spiritual atmosphere produced by a mixed crowd—especially if it is one of unbelief—has much to do with the effectiveness of the working of the gifts of healing and miracles. A curiosity-seeking audience is far from a help, when one has to minister to serious cases.

Having put the crowd out, Jesus took the hand of the little girl. He spoke two words, "Talitha cumi" which means, "Maid, arise." Then suddenly, out of eternity, the spirit of the girl returned, and she got up and walked before them. Amazement took hold of the parents, so that they scarcely knew what to say. Who can describe the wild emotions of joy that thrilled them when they saw what had happened! Jesus calmly told them to give their daughter some nourishment. Here is a simple lesson for those who teach Divine healing— Rest, proper food, and care of the body is important if one is to maintain health after receiving healing. If the girl had not been fed and received proper nourishment, she might have had a relapse. On the other hand, the person who receives healing is not to be treated as an invalid. It is good for those who have been healed to get up from their bed and walk. Faith is an act; faith and works must function as one.

While we are discussing the subject of raising the dead, we may note that those Jesus raised were comparatively young people with most of their lives before them. It is ordinarily the will of God for people to live out their days in this world—for as it has been said, "Earth is a school to prepare us for glory." Divine providence so designed Earth for that purpose. Nevertheless, there is nothing immortal about the temple of clay that we live in. The human body in its physical state, with its frailties and weaknesses, is not designed for immortality. There comes a time when we must put off this tabernacle so we might receive a glorified body like that of Christ's.

Jesus cautioned the ruler of the synagogue to say nothing to the crowd outside. Hiding the miracle would be impossible, for neighbors would soon learn about it. But it seemed to be a consistent policy with Jesus that He never wanted to prove His power to unbelievers. He had performed more than enough miracles to prove His Divinity, and it was important that mankind hear and heed His mission before He gave them more. It is a terrible thing for a person to get hardened to an acceptance of miracles before he has been moved to repentance. For there is little left to move him.

HEALING THE TWO BLIND MEN

As Jesus slipped out of the house, He gave no word to the wondering crowd, who stood about the door waiting to hear what was happening inside. They would have to get their information from others. The Lord now hastened homeward. But as He went, two blind men posted themselves in His path. Realizing that He could not allow a healing line to be found outside the house of Jairus, which might continue through the night, He hurried on.

The blind men, nonetheless, were persistent. They followed Him, probably guided by some friend, crying in a loud voice, "Son of David, have mercy on us!" (Matthew 9:27). "Son of David" was a Messianic title, but Christ never accepted it, except in the sense of His mother's lineage

(Matthew 22:41-46). Although Jesus went on without pausing, the blind men managed to follow Him to His house. They were at His door begging Him for admittance, and He could not turn them away.

However, before the Lord healed them, He paused to give them certain instructions. One of the mistakes of some who minister healing is that they often fail to give their listeners proper instructions. Consequently, many who receive deliverance, also lose it (Luke 11:24-26). Jesus, however, in His perfect understanding of the human heart, always went directly to the root of the trouble. Perhaps in this case He would say something to draw out their faith. It is one thing to be desperate for healing; it is another thing to have faith. The two circumstances are not exactly the same, although there is such a thing as desperate faith.

The two blind men were desperate enough. They were so determined to get their healing that they had overcome all obstacles and had pressed their way until they were in His Presence. Was it just a hope on their part, or did they really believe He was able to give them their sight? That was the question Jesus wanted to know. Sometimes, when people are asked this question, the note of hesitancy is apparent in their voice. They are relying altogether on the other person's faith. In such case, their request for healing is premature. They need to listen to teaching until faith springs up in their hearts. "So then faith comes by hearing, and hearing by the word of God" (Romans 10:17).

The desperation of the blind men evidently caused them to have faith. And in a chorus they answered, "Yes, Lord." Then Jesus touched their eyes saying, "According to your faith let it be to you." Jesus showed that mankind's faith was an essential element of healing—that He was not just a miracle man, wandering around performing wonders, but that people receive healing, according to the faith they exercise. So when Jesus had spoken the words, their eyes came open. Then, as they looked, the first thing they saw was the kind compassionate eyes of the One Who had healed them.

Jesus foresaw what would happen if word of this miracle went out. Popular excitement was steadily rising. News of the girl who had been raised from the dead would soon spread. Therefore, He strictly commanded the blind men to not say anything about receiving their sight. But they paid no attention to His command. They did not pause to consider that obedience is better than sacrifice. There is such a thing as service which doesn't honor Christ, but only hinders His purpose, and it results in harm, instead of good. So they went out from the Presence of Jesus to tell the story far and wide, with the very result that Christ anticipated.

Chapter 35

THE DISCIPLES ARE COMMANDED TO HEAL THE SICK

"Then Jesus went about all the cities and villages, teaching in their synagogues, preaching the gospel of the kingdom, and healing every sickness and every disease among the people. But when He saw the multitudes, He was moved with compassion for them, because they were weary and scattered, like sheep having no shepherd" (Matthew 9:35, 36).

So great were the multitudes that came to hear the preaching of Jesus, that He saw the time had come for Him to make a change. Until this time, the Twelve had followed Him on all occasions. But it was time for them to launch out on their own. There were two reasons for this. One was that the day was not far off when the Lord would be taken from them. The other was that by dividing up the work, more could be accomplished. As Jesus looked out on the fields and saw the multitudes without a shepherd, He turned to the disciples and said, "Therefore, pray the Lord of the harvest to send out laborers into His harvest" (Matthew 9:38). He not only saw the people of the regions where He had been ministering, but He saw the field as the whole world. Soon He would be saying to His followers, "… 'Go into all the world and preach the gospel to every creature'" (Mark 16:15).

The men around Him came from humble stations in life, but they were the ones that would be given the work of the Christian Church. They were to be great, but their greatness was to come from Christ alone. It was the magnitude of His character that made them fit for the gigantic task. In the beginning, they were rude and carnal, but Christ patiently taught them, ridding them of their earthly illusions concerning the coming Kingdom. He had made their training His most constant work. They saw all He did and heard all He said. Often, He took them aside to give them some special teaching. Gradually, He stamped His own image upon them.

The time had come for them to be sent forth on their first preaching mission, and He called them unto Himself:

> "And when He had called His twelve disciples to Him, He gave them power over unclean spirits, to cast them out, and to heal all kinds of sickness and all kinds of disease" (Matthew 10:1).

It was an ordination service, in which He would give them final instructions before sending them out two-by-two. Although it is not explicitly stated, the order of the apostles as they were sent out was probably as is listed in Matthew 10:2:

1. Peter and Andrew
2. James and John
3. Philip and Bartholomew (Nathanael)
4. Thomas and Matthew

5. James and Lebbaeus (Thaddaeus)
(James is also called Cleopas, Lebbaeus
was also called Judas)
6. Simon and Judas Iscariot

THE INSTRUCTIONS GIVEN TO THE TWELVE

1. They were to limit their ministry to Israel. They were not to go to Samaria nor to any city of the Gentiles (verses 5-6).

2. They were to go forth in the ministry of deliverance, the same ministry that Jesus had demonstrated:

"And as you go, preach, saying, 'The kingdom of heaven is at hand.' Heal the sick, cleanse the lepers, raise the dead, cast out demons. Freely you have received, freely give" (Matthew 10:7, 8).

This remarkable commission to minister to the sick was given at the head of the list of His instructions, and shows the importance of this ministry.

3. They were to take nothing with them; neither money in their purses nor scrip to buy food. Nor were they to take two coats, nor an extra pair of shoes. "… 'for a worker is worthy of his food'" (Matthew 10:10).

There were several reasons why Jesus gave these instructions. First, when God calls a man to the ministry, He wants him to learn to depend entirely upon Him. Second, the disciples were on an urgent errand; He did not want them to waste any time in making unnecessary preparations. Jesus had spent many months preparing them spiritually, but He did not wish them to burden themselves on their preaching tour with unnecessary baggage. Third, Jesus pointed out that the "workman was worthy of his food." Another translation says, "They are worthy of their hire." They were going to bless the people, heal them, and give them the Good News of the Kingdom. They were worthy to receive in return for those things which were necessary.

They were not beggars in any sense of the word; those who entertained them would receive a rich reward (Matthew 10:40-42). When they arrived in a city, they were to inquire who was worthy, and then stay at that place. They were not to move from house to house. In other words, they were not to waste their time in social visits. While they were under a man's roof they were to be gracious and considerate, finding no fault with the food or the accommodations.

They were to bless the house where they were guests, saying, "Peace to you." Sometimes they would be ill-received and their message would be rejected. They were then to depart, after first solemnly protesting against that city, and shaking off the dust of their feet as a witness against it:

> "And whoever will not receive you nor hear your words, when you depart from that house or city, shake off the dust from your feet" (Matthew 10:14).

We should note that at the end of His ministry, Christ changed His instructions about them not taking a purse. At the present time, He wished to show His disciples that regardless of what circumstances they might meet, God would always take care of His own when they were on His business. However, the Lord did not want people to get the idea that His plan for the ministry was that it should be supported in strange and mysterious ways. Nor did He wish to deprive the people of the blessing that comes from giving and supporting the ministry. At that time, there was a common purse for the group. Later, when Christ's time was about to come, He reminded them that although He had told them they were not to take a purse, they were now to carry one (Luke 22:36).

Next, Jesus gave them a warning: "Behold, I send you out as sheep in the midst of wolves. Therefore be wise as serpents and harmless as doves" (Matthew 10:16). They were warned against recklessness. Certainly, the minister needs wisdom in facing the forces of evil that seek to entrap him. Wisdom was to be the first gift of the Spirit (1 Corinthians 12:8). Indeed, God has promised this to all who ask for it (James 1:5, 6). Many, because they have lacked that wisdom, have had their ministry end in calamity.

The disciples were not to invite danger openly. If it seemed as if physical force were about to be used on them, they were to leave at once and go to the next city. As it turned out, during their lifetime, some were taken before magistrates and even governors or kings. If and when that happened, they were not to depend upon their human wisdom, but on the wisdom given by the Holy Ghost:

"But when they deliver you up, do not worry
about how or what you should speak. For it

will be given to you in that hour what you
should speak; for it is not you who speak, but
the Spirit of your Father who speaks in you"
(Matthew 10:19, 20).

It is obvious that the instructions Jesus gave
to the disciples went beyond their immediate mission.
Prophetically, it was projected into the years and centuries
ahead, when many of their successors would give their lives
as martyrs. Especially it referred to the age of persecution of
the second and third centuries, when believers "… will be
hated by all for My name's sake" (Matthew 10:22).

The 23rd verse is of singular importance, for Christ
leaps ahead in time to the very end of the age, when the
messengers of the Kingdom would complete the work of
the disciples. The preaching of the Gospel would practically
cease in Israel after about 66 A.D., when the Jewish-Roman
wars began. The dispersion of Israel would follow and last
for many centuries. Then as the age would draw to an end,
God would gather His people again into their land—yet in
unbelief.

Then, the task would be to try to take the Gospel
message of truth, the Messianic message, to them again. The
workers would have to finish the task in a hurry, for the work
would scarcely be completed before the coming of the Son
of man:

"When they persecute you in this city, flee
to another. For assuredly, I say to you, you
will not have gone through the cities of Israel
before the Son of Man comes" (Matthew
10:23).

Truly, the evangelization of Israel is one of the most urgent tasks confronting the Church today.

When the Lord had finished giving His instructions, He sent them out two by two, and then He went His way, also to preach and teach in the cities of Galilee. He probably did not stay long in Galilee, for it's about this time that John informs us that Jesus made a visit to Jerusalem to attend a feast, and He went alone.

As Dean Farrar brings out in his Excursus VIII, this feast probably was the Feast of Purim, which was one that occurred about a month before the Feast of the Passover. It was not a Passover Feast, since John always mentions those feasts by name (John 2:13; 6:4; 11:55). And if this were a Passover Feast, then John omitted a whole year of Christ's ministry (John 6:4). All and all, we are most certain that this was the Feast of Purim.

The Feast of Purim was a saturnalia of Judaism. It was without divine authority, and had its roots in the vindictive and provincial feelings of the nation. It was unconnected with religious service. Why Jesus departed for Jerusalem at this time is not explained, but nothing is said that He went merely to attend the feast. He may have gone up to Jerusalem to be present at the later Passover Feast. He would leave early in order to avoid the publicity and the dangerous excitement involved in joining the caravans that traveled at that time. The opportunity obviously presented itself at the time when His disciples were engaged in their missionary work. However, Jesus did not remain for the Feast of the Passover, and the events of the next chapter reveal the reason why He did not.

Chapter 36

THE POOL OF BETHESDA

"After this there was a feast of the Jews, and Jesus went up to Jerusalem. Now there is in Jerusalem by the Sheep Gate a pool, which is called in Hebrew, Bethesda, having five porches. In these lay a great multitude of sick people, blind, lame, paralyzed, waiting for the moving of the water. For an angel went down at a certain time into the pool and stirred up the water; then whoever stepped in first, after the stirring of the water, was made well of whatever disease he had. Now a certain man was there who had an infirmity thirty-eight years. When Jesus saw him lying there, and knew that he already had been in that condition a long time, He said to him, 'Do you want to be made well?' The sick man answered Him, 'Sir, I have no man to put me into the pool when the water is stirred up; but while I am coming, another steps down before me.' Jesus said to him, 'Rise, take up your bed and walk.' And immediately the man was made well, took up his bed, and walked. And that day was the Sabbath" (John 5:1-9).

Over one year of Christ's ministry was completed, and the time of the Passover came around again. As we have seen, Jesus probably had been in Jerusalem for some weeks. During His visit He was kept under close surveillance. The emissaries of the Sanhedrin had brought back a report of His doings in Galilee, and it was a heavy indictment. He had spent time with sinners, they said; He claimed power to forgive sins, and showed laxity in the matter of keeping the Sabbath. Moreover, in their opinion He had been guilty of blasphemy. They were soon to find fault against Him in Jerusalem.

In Jerusalem, near the Sheep Gate there was a pool known by the name of Bethesda, which was claimed to have remarkable properties. A multitude of sick people—victims of being blind, deaf, lame, and every manner of disease—gathered around this pool. It was said that at certain times an angel went down into the water and troubled it. Whoever then went down first, after the troubling of the water, "was made whole of whatsoever disease he had."

Many scholars believe that the evidence against the genuineness of this passage is strong, since it is omitted in so many manuscripts. Of this, Dean Farrar in his Life of Christ makes the following remarks which may be of interest to the reader:

> "The weight of evidence both external and internal against the genuineness of John 5:3-4 is overwhelming. It is omitted by not a few of the weightiest MSS, and versions (B. D. the Cureton Syriac). In others in which it does occur it is obelisked as dubious. This abounds in various readings, showing that there is something suspicious about it. It contains in

the short compass of a few lines, no less than seven words not found with a different sense. It relates a most startling fact, one wholly unlike anything else in Scripture, one not alluded to by a single other writer, Jewish or heathen, and one which, had there been the slightest ground for believing in its truth, would certainly not have been passed over in silence by Josephus. Its insertion (to explain the word in verse 7) is easily accounted for; its omission; had it been in the original text, is quite inconceivable. Accordingly, it is rejected from the text by the best editors as a spurious gloss, 'and indeed there is no earlier trace of its existence than an allusion to it in Tertullian (De Bapt. 5). (Ob. cire. A.D. 220)."

While it is possible the verse could have been interjected, we do not believe the proof is absolute. We leave it to the reader to draw his own conclusions.

Among the sufferers lying some distance from the water was one in an especially pitiful condition, who had been a paralytic for 38 years. He had come to the pool either by crawling there, or by whatever means he found available. Being left there unaided, and as the motion of the water occurred at irregular intervals, others less feeble were always able to get into the water before him.

Jesus looked on the man with deep pity. It is obvious that his whole life had been one of frustration and despair. He was a beaten man—a soul for whom no man cared. Still, he held a slender hope. Who knows, some day someone could take pity on him, and when the water was troubled might assist him into the pool first.

To attract the man's attention, Jesus asked, "Do you want to be made well?" This man had been hopeless for so long that the words hardly stirred him. Now, thinking that this stranger might be kind enough to help him get into the water when the moving again took place, he explained the sad story of his long frustration.

It is notable that Jesus had nothing to say, either for or against the pool. Jesus' ministry was not negative, but positive. He spoke a word of command, "Rise, take up your bed and walk." His voice carried such a weight of authority that the man involuntarily made an effort to get up. And as he did, to his unspeakable joy, he found the dead muscles responding! After 38 years of lying on a cot, he suddenly found he could walk.

It is a strange commentary on the multitude of sufferers, that the man was able to do so without attracting their attention. But they had their gaze so focused on the pool, watching for the water to move, that even the commotion caused by the man picking up his cot failed to get their attention. Surely, they represent many today whose focus is also on physical remedies. We would not speak against these things or the physicians who serve to alleviate mankind's suffering. Jesus never spoke against them. Nonetheless, the average physician will be as ready as anyone to admit that there are many diseases medical science cannot cure. Some people go from one operation to another—one doctor to another—and they are so intent in trying to find a cure that they miss out on what the Great Physician has already prepared for them.

The people at the pool evidently failed to notice the man's healing or they would have clamored for Jesus to heal them, as well. But the ecclesiastics took quick note of the situation. Not that they noticed he had been healed, for these hireling shepherds did not recognize the man as a paralytic. They apparently cared little about the sick and broken of their flock. But the matter that angered them was that the man was carrying his cot on the Sabbath day. This they considered a flagrant violation of the Sabbath. The man answered saying, "... 'He who made me well said to me, 'Take up your bed and walk'" (John 5:11).

As the inner life of a professor of religion becomes dead, the more he becomes attached to formalism and the observance of petty rules. The Sabbath was made for man, but the Jews had changed it around until it seemed that man was made for the Sabbath. The observance of the Sabbath had practically become a custom, hedged with innumerable unimportant and senseless restrictions. The great provisions of the Mosaic Law of mercy and judgment were passed by.

These heresy-hunters already half-suspecting that this Jesus, Who had come from Galilee, was the source of the miracle, began to question the man as to who it was that told him to take up his bed and walk. They didn't ask him who had healed him. They purposely ignored this fact, but interrogated him as to who told him to take up his bed. The breach of their law was their sole concern.

They believed they had a clear-cut case of someone violating the Law. Didn't a man, during the days when the children of Israel wandered in the wilderness, get stoned for gathering sticks on the Sabbath days? And didn't Jeremiah say, "Thus says the LORD: 'Take heed to yourselves, and bear no burden on the Sabbath day, nor bring it in by the gates of Jerusalem ..." (Jeremiah 17:21)?

But the reason for these injunctions was the one

of mercy intended to protect the oppressed from a life of constant toil. If it had not been for the institution of the seventh day as a day of rest, the greed of employers would have demanded the working man to labor without ceasing.

Now, when a man who had been healed wished to carry home his pallet, why should the commandment be interpreted to force the man to leave behind his bed, which was probably the only thing he possessed? Where is that fellow who told you to carry your cot?" Their voices rose with indignation. But the man could not tell, for Jesus had already gone away.

After a while, the man went to the Temple. This would seem to be in his favor. It would appear that he had gone there to give God thanks. While in the Temple, Jesus saw him and gave him a word of warning, "See, you have been made well. Sin no more, lest a worse thing come upon you" (John 5:14). Jesus said nothing to embarrass him among the crowd, but He looked for him and brought to his remembrance his sin—a sin that might have been the cause of his affliction in the first place. The man had to forsake it.

There are those who would tell us that if a man is truly healed by God, the affliction cannot come back on him. Such statements are in total difference with the Scriptures. Not only may the affliction return, if a man fails to go on with God or falls back into sin, but an even worse thing may come upon him. Surely, some are in need of biblical teaching if they are to understand God's way of healing.

It is at this point that we are confronted with a rather peculiar circumstance. The man went and told the Jewish authorities that Jesus had healed him. This resulted in the Jews wanting to kill Jesus.

Dean Farrar makes some interesting remarks on this

in his *Life of Christ:*

> "Perhaps the warning had been given because Christ read the worthless nature of the man; at any rate, there is something at first sight peculiarly revolting in the 15th verse. The man went and told the Jewish authorities that it was Jesus who had made him whole. It is barely possible, though most unlikely, that he may have meant to magnify the name of One Who had wrought such a mighty work; but as he must have been well aware of the angry feelings of the Jews—as we hear no word of his gratitude, no word of glorifying God—as too, it must have been clear to him that Jesus in working the miracle had been touched by compassion only, and had been anxious to shun publicity —it must be confessed that the prima facie view of the man's conduct is that it was an act of contemptible delation—a piece of pitiful self-protection at the expense of his benefactor—an almost inconceivable compound of feeble sycophancy and base ingratitude. Apparently, the warning of Jesus had been deeply necessary, as if we judge the man aright, it was wholly unavailing.

For the consequences were disastrous. They changed, in fact, the entire tenor of Christ's remaining life. Untouched by the evidence of tender compassion, unmoved by the display of miraculous power, the Jewish inquisitors were up in arms to defend their favorite piece of legalism. "They began to persecute Jesus because He did such things on the

Sabbath day."

If the man did this deliberately, he was a monster of ingratitude, one who would betray his benefactor in order to clear himself from the charge of Sabbath-breaking. However, it is more likely that he testified of a miracle of mercy in gladness of heart supposing it would evoke their wonder and admiration. Then too, his presence in the Temple would indicate he had gone there as a repentant sinner to give thanks to God and to vow to lead a new life. It is unlikely that the man, having been in the condition he was, had any knowledge of the Jews hatred of Christ. What he did, therefore, would seem to be a simple act of good faith.

At any rate, the result of the miracle was that the Jews came to Jesus, angrily charging Him with violating the Sabbath day. In answer to their charge, Jesus delivered the wonderful discourse recorded in the fifth chapter of John. He said, "My Father has been working until now, and I have been working" (John 5:17). God had worked through the creative week and rested on the seventh day (Gen. 2:1, 2). So, man's disobedience disturbed the Sabbath paradise, and forced God to resume His work in the redeeming of a race that had fallen into sin.

Where this conversation took place, we are not told. It can't be determined whether it was delivered in the Temple, before the Sanhedrin, or before some committee of the Jews, except that some of the chief rabbis and priests were present. They were ready to instruct Him and set Him right on the Sabbath day. But it was He Who did the instructing. For when they mentioned the Sabbath He declared He was emulating His Father, thus "making himself equal with God." They were horror-stricken. In their eyes, He was not only guilty of Sabbath-breaking, but also of blasphemy. This crime was worthy of death. But Christ, instead of backing down, only amplified His claim. As Son of God, He stood in a unique relation to the Father.

This message is one of the most remarkable of the Gospels. We cannot go into it in detail, but we give a brief synopsis of its important truths:

1. There is a distinction of persons in the Godhead. "Then Jesus answered and said to them, 'Most assuredly, I say to you, the Son can do nothing of Himself, but what He sees the Father do; for whatever He does, the Son also does in like manner'" (John 5:19). "For the Father judges no one, but has committed all judgment to the Son ..." (John 5:22). Although a distinction of persons is made, one does not act independently of the other. There is a perfect unity of action, even as there is a perfect unity of nature.

2. Christ reveals man's duty. "... that all should honor the Son just as they honor the Father. He who does not honor the Son does not honor the Father who sent Him" (John 5:23). Jesus went further than making known His position as the Messiah, for the Jews generally did not expect a Divine Messiah. He revealed His Divinity.

3. Christ attests His deity with a four-fold witness:
   (a) By John who bare witness of Him (John 5:33-35).

(b) By His miracles (verse 36).

(c) By the Father (verses 37-38). This was a witness that John the Baptist saw, but not the Jews.

(d) By the Scriptures (verses 39-47).

Through these witnesses, God had provided the means so that all men might know the true Messiah, the Son of God, in Whom is life eternal.

But Jesus charged that their great error was in failing to believe the witness of the Word of God. True, the Jews gave the Scriptures superstitious reverence. They counted the very letters in them. Why then could they not believe them? What was standing in their way?

Surely, this was an important question. Today, we witness the amazing manner in which the prophets foretold all things about the Messiah—of His birth in Bethlehem, of His humanity and divinity, of His mission and ministry. They all were told beforehand, even that His coming would be in humility and condescension. The 53rd chapter of Isaiah plainly showed this fact. The prophet Daniel even gave the time that the Messiah would appear—69 weeks of years after the commandment went forth to rebuild Jerusalem (Daniel 9:24-27).

Why then couldn't they believe? They were intelligent men in temporal matters; why were they so grossly blind in spiritual things?

Jesus gives the answer: It was because of their pride. "How can you believe, who receive honor from one another, and do not seek the honor that comes from the only God?" (John 5:44). Their pride made them see a different kind of Messiah—one who would throw off the yoke of the Romans and make the Jews a worldly power, and one who would bring great prosperity. They wanted a Messiah who would defeat Israel's enemies and usher in a golden age. This pride made it constitutionally impossible for the Jews to accept such a Messiah as Jesus, Who came in meekness and lowliness of heart.

So, they rejected Him Who came in His Father's Name, and instead, they became open victims of every false Messiah that appeared on the scene. A century later, they would accept Bar-Cachebas, whose fanaticism resulted in the final destruction of the Jewish nation. In all, some 60 false Messiahs have appeared—each in his own name. The most wicked and deceptive of them all will appear just before the days of the Great Tribulation. Jesus referred to him when he said, "I have come in My Father's name, and you do not receive Me; if another comes in his own name, him you will receive" (John 5:43).

THE RESURRECTION OF THE DEAD

At the same time, Jesus gave another revelation—the truth of the resurrection of the dead. The Old Testament hints at it, makes allusions to it, but Christ was the One Who brought to light the glorious truth of immortality and of life beyond the grave. He did not speak of the Christians' future existence as that of disembodied spirits—but that their bodies should be raised from the graves and glorified:

"Do not marvel at this; for the hour is coming in which all who are in the graves will hear His voice and come forth—those who have done good, to the resurrection of life, and those who have done evil, to the resurrection of condemnation" (John 5:28, 29).

Jesus was by no means a universalist. Not all would share the resurrection of life. There was also a resurrection of judgment. Those who did evil would have their part in the resurrection of damnation.

How could a man have a part in the resurrection of life? He could have apart by listening to the voice of the Son of Man. All were spiritually dead, but if they listened to His voice in this world, they would pass from death unto life:

"Most assuredly, I say to you, he who hears My word and believes in Him who sent Me has everlasting life, and shall not come into judgment, but has passed from death into life. Most assuredly, I say to you, the hour is coming, and now is, when the dead will hear the voice of the Son of God; and those who hear will live. (John 5:24, 25).

What a sermon it was! In Galilee, Jesus had suppressed the revelation concerning Himself—that the truth might come gradually to those who heard His words. But at Jerusalem, where the decisions of the nation were being made, where His appearances would be briefer and His mighty works fewer in number, He revealed His identity and mission in its fullness. Unfortunately, it was to be rejected. Yet, at the moment, the Jews could do nothing. They could only gnash their teeth in rage, and wait for an opportunity to pass the death sentence. Under these circumstances, it was useless for Jesus to remain in Jerusalem. He returned to Galilee with a clear vision of what the end would be. He would continue His work, but now, He was racing against time, when the conspirators would come, take Him, and condemn Him to death.

Chapter 37

FEEDING THE FIVE THOUSAND

"Then the apostles gathered to Jesus and told Him all things, both what they had done and what they had taught. And He said to them, "Come aside by yourselves to a deserted place and rest a while." For there were many coming and going, and they did not even have time to eat" (Mark 6:30, 31).

When Jesus returned to Galilee, the disciples "gathered to Jesus" to give Him a report of all that had taken place during their preaching mission. It must have been an exciting story, although the details are not given to us. However, we are told later about the Seventy who were sent out, and afterwards returned with joy, saying that even the devils were subject to the Name of Christ. The Twelve who were closer to the Lord must have had a glowing report of their victories, as well, although it was dampened by the sad news of John the Baptist's death, an event that had just occurred.

Jesus considered the time opportune to take a few days of rest before they continued their activities. People were coming and going steadily; the sick were being brought for healing; others were asking questions. We are told that the group even had no opportunity to eat. So at Jesus' direction, they took a boat over the sea to a desert place near the city of Bethsaida-Julia. In noting these words of Jesus, we are made aware of the importance of regular times of rest. If Jesus and His disciples required seasons of relaxation, certainly all Christian workers need such periods of rest. Many have developed neurotic symptoms simply because they neglect the obvious requirements of the physical body.

After they arrived at the eastern shore near Bethsaida-Julia (named in honor of Julia, the beautiful but infamous daughter of Emperor Augustus), Jesus and His disciples found a fertile and well-watered plain which was located on the far side of town. Since it was springtime, just before the Passover (John 6:4), the grass formed a soft green carpet. Here, they hoped to find a quiet retreat where they could rest a few days.

But Christ was unable to hide Himself from the people. His departure had been observed, and a vast crowd set out from Capernaum and they walked around the edge of the lake to join Him on the other side. After some time, for it took a considerable while to detour around the lake, the disciples saw a large group making their way toward them. Jesus should have departed as soon as he saw them, but He would not disappoint them. Some had come from a great distance, bringing their sick for healing. He could not leave them.

Jesus forgot about the plans for rest that day, and gave the people a kindly welcome. After healing their sick, He began to teach them many things (Mark 6:34). The multitude listened with much interest, forgetting that there was such a thing as mealtime. But as the day was beginning to end, the disciples came to Jesus and said, "This is a deserted place, and already the hour is late. Send them away, that they may go into the surrounding country and villages and buy themselves bread; for they have nothing to eat" (Mark 6:35, 36).

It is a commentary on the eagerness of the people to hear the Master—that they had taken off so suddenly to not even have paused to purchase or prepare any food to take along. Some had actually outrun the boat and arrived in the area before Jesus and the disciples did! But with darkness approaching, the disciples became apprehensive that there might be trouble from the people fainting from hunger, since they were a long way from shelter or supplies of any kind.

Jesus turned to Philip, one of His disciples, and said to him, "Where shall we buy bread, that these may eat?" (John 6:5) Philip was a man who thought for himself. He had accepted Christ as the Messiah because he had studied the prophecies and saw that they were fulfilled in Him (John 1:45). Philip was computing what it would take to feed the multitude. He said, "Two hundred Denari worth of bread is not sufficient for them, that every one of them may have a little" (John 6:7). A penny, or denarius, was approximately a shilling, equivalent to a fair day's wage. A denarius would have fed approximately 25 people, but would have provided each person of the multitude just a mouthful.

Andrew came up with a suggestion. "There is a lad here, which has five barley loaves, and two small fishes; but what are they among so many?" (John 6:9). Somewhere in the crowd he had found a little boy who wanted to see and hear Jesus so much that he had come along with the adults. But he had more foresight than they had. He had remembered to take a lunch with him. And though he might have eaten it himself, he offered to share it with Andrew, and in doing so he immortalized himself in the Bible story.

Jesus did not turn down the lad's contribution. Some think the Church could make great missionary gains if only the rich could be persuaded to give large sums. But it is a truth that the money which blesses the Kingdom of God should be given out of sacrifice or devotion to God. He can bless the little and multiply it in His own way.

The Lord now stated, much to the amazement of the disciples, to feed the people. But first, He gave some instructions. The disciples were to make the multitude to sit down on the grass in groups of fifties and hundreds. This was a sensible arrangement which prevented confusion and at the same time assured them that no one would be overlooked. Jesus then blessed the food, and breaking it, gave it to the disciples for distribution to the people. As He continued to break it, the few loaves and fishes became an insurmountable supply.

One thing the disciples had with them was baskets. These were retrieved from the boat and used to distribute the food. To show that it is not God's will to waste anything, Jesus commanded the disciples to gather up the fragments when the meal was concluded. And when this was done, there were 12 basketfuls. Each disciple came back with his basket loaded!

There are some things about this incident which need to be noted. Christ did not ordinarily use His supernatural powers to produce that type of miracle. He fed the multitude because He had compassion on them (Matthew 15:32). But events that followed indicate that He had a further purpose in the miracle. The news that His cousin, John the Baptist, had just given His life for the cause, reminded Him of His own approaching death. He had taken His disciples to the desert so He might have some time to instruct them and give them a true conception of the purpose of His coming into the world. But the multitude had descended upon Him and interfered with His plans.

As the people came and stood about Him, He had formed His decision to perform this miracle. The Passover, we are told, was close (John 6:4). This was the sacred feast in which the children of Israel ate unleavened bread. As Paul has stated in his writings, He, Christ, was the world's Passover (1 Corinthians 5:7).

A year later, after the miracle of the loaves and fishes, Jesus would become that Passover, and on its eve, He would break bread with the disciples. He would take the bread, bless it, break it, and give it to the disciples saying, "… 'Take, eat: this is my body'" (Mark 14:22). This did Jesus also when He blessed the bread, broke it and fed the multitude. There was, therefore, a greater purpose behind the miracle of the loaves than just satisfying the physical hunger of the people. Actually, Jesus was preparing the multitude for the Bread-of-Life message He would deliver to them the next day in Capernaum when He would say:

> "I am that bread of life" (John 6:48). "I am the living bread which came down from heaven. If anyone eats of this bread, he will live forever; and the bread that I shall give is My flesh, which I shall give for the life of the world" (John 6:51).

In witnessing the miracle of the loaves and the fishes, the hearts of the people would be prepared for the truth that Christ was the Bread of Life, which if any man would eat of Him, He would give him eternal life. The miracle at Bethsaida was, therefore, actually a prophecy of the sacrament of the communion.

The remarkable event produced a profound impression on the multitude. It was exactly in accordance with what they had in mind. They were convinced that Jesus was the prophet that Moses foretold of (Deuteronomy 18:15-18).

"Then those men, when they had seen the sign that Jesus did, said, 'This is truly the Prophet who is to come into the world'" (John 6:14).

The moment seemed ripe to the leaders of the people. The Passover was at hand. Why should they not take Jesus to Jerusalem and in a triumphant procession there proclaim Him king? He would be hailed everywhere as the Messiah, for whom the nation had hoped for, for 1,500 long years. Jesus saw them whispering among themselves. He perceived their undisguised admiration. Yet if they took Him by force and proclaimed Him king, it would have upset the entire purpose for which He came into the world. His own disciples seemed to share in the excitement.

The situation called for instant action. Jesus immediately commanded His disciples to get into their ship and go before Him to Capernaum (Matthew 14:22). Then, the leaders could further pursue their purpose to make Him king. He dispersed the multitude, perhaps reminding them that they had to leave quickly or be caught in the darkness of nightfall. He then departed to the mountain to pray.

Chapter 38

THE MIRACLE OF CHRIST WALKING ON THE WATER

"And when He had sent the multitudes away, He went up on the mountain by Himself to pray. Now when evening came, He was alone there. But the boat was now in the middle of the sea, tossed by the waves, for the wind was contrary. Now in the fourth watch of the night Jesus went to them, walking on the sea. And when the disciples saw Him walking on the sea, they were troubled, saying, 'It is a ghost!' And they cried out for fear. But immediately Jesus spoke to them, saying, 'Be of good cheer! It is I; do not be afraid.' And Peter answered Him and said, 'Lord, if it is You, command me to come to You on the water.' So He said, 'Come.' And when Peter had come down out of the boat, he walked on the water to go to Jesus. But when he saw that the wind was boisterous, he was afraid; and beginning to sink he cried out, saying, 'Lord, save me!' And immediately Jesus stretched out His hand and caught him, and said to him, 'O you of little faith, why did you doubt?' And when they got into the boat, the wind ceased. Then those who were in the boat came and worshiped Him, saying, 'Truly You are the Son of God'" (Matthew 14:23-33).

After the miracle of feeding the multitude, Jesus went up to the mountain to pray and be by Himself. The Lord spent hours in prayer that night. As Jesus prayed alone on the mountain, a violent wind arose and swept down through the barren hills. Satan knows how to strike one blow after another and to confuse the person who is trying to do the will of God. Jesus knew what the wind meant: it meant that His disciples, who had started across the sea at His command, would run into real trouble.

When the first light of dawn appeared, Jesus looked out and saw the disciples' ship in the midst of the sea, being roughly tossed by the waves. The disciples did not start on their trip as soon as they should have, hoping that Jesus would come to them. When at last darkness fell, they started out without Him. They hadn't gone far when the wind increased. They had to take the sail down and use the oars. If you are familiar with the sea, you know it is possible to make a little headway in a small boat against a strong wind. However, this was now the fourth watch of the night, and they were still in the midst of the sea, making no progress.

There is a parallel here that we should note. Satan had presented Jesus with three temptations in the wilderness. These same three courses of action were presented again, but the circumstances were altered. In the wilderness the devil had suggested to Jesus that He make bread to satisfy His hunger. But Jesus refused to use His miraculous power for the gratification of His own personal needs. Nevertheless, when the eager multitude forgot to take any bread with them and now needed food, He made sufficient food to satisfy over 5,000 and had 12 basketfuls left over.

Second, Satan had offered Christ the kingdoms of this world and the glory of them, if He would fall down and worship him. Jesus spurned the offer. In this case, the people, after they had been fed the loaves and fishes, wanted to make Him king (John 6:15). But it was not the time, nor the place. This offer did not come from the heavenly Father, and Jesus would have none of it. He would indeed become Israel's King in due time—not of a temporal kingdom, but of one whose subjects would have life eternal. It was to be the very next day that Jesus would present His claims as the Bread of Heaven, which if any man would eat, would cause him to live forever (John 6:58).

Satan, in his third temptation, had proposed that Jesus should cast Himself down from the pinnacle of the Temple (Luke 4:9-12). He also refused this proposition. He would not shake the people with works and wonders. But when His disciples were in the midst of the lake in mortal jeopardy, He would perform an even greater miracle. He would overrule the law of gravity and walk out on the water to come to the assistance of His faithful group, who had risked their lives to obey His command. Why did He do it? Because He was the One Who commanded the disciples to make the trip. We may come up against serious dangers in obeying Christ, but if we do not throw away our confidence, God will move both Heaven and Earth on our behalf, if need be, to come to our aid.

As Jesus got closer to the disciples, the waves were still high, and it was just getting light. The disciples did not see Him approaching until He was almost upon them.

According to Mark, He "would have passed by them." But as they looked up, they saw a Figure with a fluttering robe, treading upon the ridges of the waves. In the semi-light they could not see clearly. This is what made them think they were seeing a ghost. At this point, they cried out in fear. But the voice they heard reassured them. He said, "Be of good cheer! It is I; do not be afraid" (Matthew 14:27). The familiar voice of the Master Who meant so much to them made them lose their fear. Peter recovered from his momentary fright, and asked, "Lord, if it is You, command me to come to You on the water" (Matthew 14:28).

Earlier, in his walk with the Lord, he had said, "... 'Depart from me' ..." (Luke 5:8), but now he just could not wait for the Lord to come to him. When Jesus said, "Come," Peter was over the side of the ship into the troubled waters, while the other disciples, content to be observers, looked on. As long as Peter kept his eyes on Jesus, he was safe. Most sermons dealing with this event emphasize Peter's sinking, but the fact is that as long as his gaze was on Jesus, Peter walked on the water.

Unfortunately, when his attention was put on the waves and the rough wind, fear came into his heart. Why had he attempted to walk on the water? Why had he been so reckless as to try to do what only Jesus could do? And as Peter let himself become afraid, he began to sink.

This is an extremely important truth for all who seek deliverance. As long as they keep their eyes upon Christ and His promise, they will have victory. But if they, like Peter, look at the water and the waves—meaning they look at their symptoms or listen to their feelings—they will also go down. Let us then decide to not look at conditions, but at the promise that Christ has given. It can never fail.

There are those who would tell us that if God really performs a miracle, it can never be lost. They point to an individual who has lost their healing and declare that this is proof that they were never healed in the first place. Because if they had truly been healed, then they would not have become sick again. What mankind may think, and what is fact, are often a long way a part. The truth is that we receive by faith, and we walk by faith. Doubts can well cause us to lose what God has already done for us. When Peter walked on the water, it was a miracle. Yet, when he took his eyes off of Christ and looked at the waves of the storm, he began to sink.

One thing Peter did do in the nick of time. When he ran out of his own faith, he depended upon the faith of Christ. Jesus once, said to them, "Have the faith of God." When natural faith fails, we may depend upon the supernatural faith of Christ. Here we see the difference between natural faith and supernatural faith. Peter started walking on the water on the strength of his own natural faith, and it would have been sufficient, if he had kept it. In his moment of peril, he cried out, "Lord, save me." So Jesus stretched out His hand and drew him up out of the water. Together, they made their way back to the boat.

This is a picture of the two phases of a Christian life. The first phase is that of the Christian who has been redeemed, but who walks to a considerable extent in the flesh. He still has confidence in his natural abilities and would seek to accomplish spiritual things in his own strength. But as he continues to walk in his Christian faith, sooner or later, he will meet a crisis which is beyond his own ability to solve. When his own faith fails, he at last in desperation will cry out as Peter did, "Lord, save me." The Lord, in His mercy, will reach down a hand and lift him up. Together the two can walk through life victoriously over the threatened waves. The trust must be in Christ, instead of one's own natural abilities.

SUPERNATURAL TRANSPORTATION

When Jesus and Peter got into the ship, we are told that the wind ceased. But that was not all. There was still one more miracle that morning. John says, "... and immediately the boat was at the land where they were going." (John 6:21). The 19th verse informs us that when the Lord met the disciples, they had rowed 25 or 30 furlongs, which is a distance of three or four miles—just half-way across the lake. Since the Sea of Galilee is seven or eight miles wide, the disciples were, at the time Jesus entered the ship, in the very middle of the sea (see Matthew 14:24). Yet, the ship was immediately at land! When the waves subsided, and they looked toward land, they saw the familiar shoreline where they had so often drawn up their boats.

The miracle of transportation had taken place. Here we see faith not only overruling the law of gravity, but superseding the laws regarding physical matter, making possible instantaneous transportation. The events of this night involved both the gift of faith and the working of miracles.

Will such occurrences as this (or that of the transportation of Philip—Acts 8:26-40—when he was supernaturally taken to Azotus, which was 40 or 50 miles away) take place again in these last days? No doubt they will. However, such happenings were rare, even in Bible days, and they will be uncommon when they happen now. Jesus could have been transported from place to place by the Spirit, if He had chosen for it to be that way. Even so, not until after the resurrection, do we have record of these types of miracle's happening, and even then, it was only once or twice in His ministry. On this occasion, His disciples, exhausted from battling the wind and waves through the long hours of the night, needed to reach shore so they could get rest and sleep.

It would be amusing, if it were not so tragic, to note the pathetic attempts some use to explain what happened on this occasion by using purely natural grounds. It is alleged by some, that under the stress of the storm, the boat had gotten close to land so that what the disciples really saw was Jesus, not walking on the water, but on the shore! This attempt to dismiss the miracle in this fashion borders on the ridiculous.

The whole ministry of Christ was a series of supernatural occurrences, and no one can do away with His miracles without doing away with Christ, Himself. But mankind would have to reach up and take the stars out of the Heavens before he could do this.

Chapter 39

MESSAGE ON THE BREAD OF LIFE

We are told that not all of the people who had followed Jesus to the place where the miracle of the loaves and fishes had taken place returned home that evening. Despite the fact that the Lord had dismissed them, they lingered on in the little plain of Bethsaida-Julia, so they might follow the movements of Christ and share in the triumphs that they thought were to take place. Evidently, they laid down on the grassy green and slept through the night. When morning came, they waited for Him to come down the hill where He had gone to pray. When they saw that He did not appear, they finally decided to return to the other side in the boats that came over from Tiberias.

When they arrived in Capernaum, they were surprised to see that Jesus had already arrived. How did He get there? They asked, "Rabbi, when did You come here?" Jesus didn't explain the miracle of Him walking on the water. It did not concern them, and He did not wish to claim their allegiance on the basis of these miracles.

The truth was that these people were already convinced of Jesus as their Messiah. The miracle, which had now taken place the day before, had fully strengthened their conviction. But their conception was that of a different kind of Messiah than who Jesus really was. It was a current expectation that the Messiah, when He came, would feed them manna as Moses did in the wilderness (John 6:30, 31). The miracle of the loaves and the fishes had seemed to prove to them that their anticipations were correct. Why then did Jesus elude them and go away to the mountain when they were ready to claim Him asking? The people wanted an answer to that.

It so happened on that day, there was a service in the synagogue (John 6:59). Jairus, whose daughter He had raised from the dead, had charge of the synagogue and would have given Jesus full freedom to preach in it. Therefore, the Lord led the people there where He could teach and preach to them. And as was the custom in the synagogue, they could ask Him questions. However, it was here that He shared with them that He had not come at this time to be an earthly king to set up a temporal kingdom. He had to remove the false ideal of His mission.

> "Jesus answered them and said, 'Most assuredly, I say to you, you seek Me, not because you saw the signs, but because you ate of the loaves and were filled. Do not labor for the food which perishes, but for the food which endures to everlasting life, which the Son of Man will give you, because God the Father has set His seal on Him'" (John 6:26, 27).

Jesus went to the heart of the matter. The people wanted Him to be their king because He had fed them with loaves and fishes. This has been a fateful error of others besides the Jews. People become totally absorbed in the physical needs of the present, to the total disregard of the future. They dedicate their lives to gathering wealth with no thought for eternity. Therefore, He told them not to labor for that which perishes, but to labor for that which would endure into everlasting life, which He, the Son of Man, would give to them.

The people were touched and a little ashamed. The Lord had read their hearts correctly. So they queried, "What are we to do that we may work the works of God?" Jesus then answered that the work of God was to believe on Him Whom God had sent. This statement is the foundational truth of Christianity. Salvation is through faith in Christ. The work of redemption from mankind's standpoint is accomplished by simple faith in Christ's finished work.

His hearers were not satisfied. They were not to be sidetracked from what was to be the most important matter of interest. Moses had given them bread from Heaven. Christ also had the power to feed them supernaturally, as He had proved the day before. Their question, they believed, was based on scriptural grounds. The pot of manna and the grape-clusters, incidentally, had been carved on the lintels of the very synagogue they were in at that moment. To have plenty of bread seemed to be to the Jews the most important thing in life.

They were willing to go along with Christ's interpretation that He was the true manna, but wasn't there something more? If He were the real Messiah, according to all traditions of the nation, He would enrich them, banquet them on the delicacies of Heaven, besides giving them the regular manna, just as Moses did. "Therefore they said to Him, 'What sign will You perform then, that we may see it and believe You? What work will You do? Our fathers ate the manna in the desert; as it is written, 'He gave them bread from heaven to eat'" (John 6:30, 31).

The people had quoted Nehemiah 9:15. But if they had only read a little further, they would have seen how little this great gift of earthly manna had spiritually done for the children of Israel. The text records that the people of that day dealt proudly, refused to obey, hardened their hearts, made a molten image, wrought great provocations, and slew the prophets (Nehemiah 9:16-26).

It was for that reason God had to deliver them over to their enemies. And because not only their fathers, but the generations who had come and gone since then, had done the same thing (Nehemiah 9:28), this was the reason the children of Israel were, at that time, under the yoke of the Romans. But like many others who read the Scriptures, they took the promise and overlooked the conditions.

Jesus would show them that faith must rest on a deeper foundation than just signs and wonders alone. They had to have other bread than the manna in the wilderness. They had to have the Bread of Life that the Father sent from Heaven. They responded by saying, "Lord evermore give us this bread,' but their minds were still focused on material things. They were asking for this bread as the man of Samaria looked for the water that quenched all thirst. "And Jesus said to them, 'I am the bread of life. He who comes to Me shall never hunger, and he who believes in Me shall never thirst'" (John 6:35).

This brought an angry response, not from the multitude, but from his opponents who were always lurking in the crowd to catch Him in some way. They began to exchange questions, directed not at Him personally, but to those who were close by: "Why was Jesus saying He came down from Heaven?" "Why does He call Himself the Bread of Life?" "Do we not know Joseph His father, and His mother Mary, and was not this man a mere carpenter?" (Mark 6:3; John 6:41, 42).

Jesus did not answer these questioners by explaining His supernatural birth. He did not argue the fact of His divinity. He simply pointed out that a heart filled with unbelief would not come to Him (John 6:44). But "All that the Father gives Me will come to Me, and the one who comes to Me I will by no means cast out" (John 6:37). He repeated what He had said before. Moses gave the children of Israel bread in the wilderness, but they all died. He was the true bread, and if any man ate of that bread, he would live forever.

"I am the living bread which came down from heaven. If anyone eats of this bread, he will live forever; and the bread that I shall give is My flesh, which I shall give for the life of the world" (John 6:51).

This concept became a stumbling block to their thinking. How could Jesus give His own flesh to them? They were so carnal-minded that they stumbled on the question, instead of seeking the true significance of the metaphor.

Some of these things were hard to understand. But they had seen enough to trust Him. The miracle they saw yesterday was enough to show them that this was the true Messiah. They had to agree that all those who ate manna in the wilderness died. This would mean that something more than manna was needed. However, it was just too difficult to understand. Slowly, the people began to go their own ways.

The excitement of the previous day was now gone. Several of His disciples said, "This is a hard saying; who can hear it?"

When most of the multitude had gone on, along with many of His followers, Jesus turned to the Twelve and said, "Will you also go away?" His own disciples looked sad. The great enthusiasm which existed only 24 hours ago was gone. Some of the disciples had also departed. But even though the Twelve did not understand all that was said, they did understand what He meant by eternal life. Peter, speaking out to the rest, told Him what was in their hearts:

"But Simon Peter answered Him, 'Lord, to whom shall we go? You have the words of eternal life. Also we have come to believe and know that You are the Christ, the Son of the living God'" (John 6:68, 69).

It was a rather faltering confession. For even the disciples had thought, just as the multitude had, that Jesus was soon to set up an outward kingdom of splendor. But understand it or not, the disciples still believed in Jesus, and that He had the words of eternal life.

There was one exception. The events of the day must have been a bitter disappointment to Judas. How thrilled he was the day before with the way the tide was moving. When the leaders of the multitude informed Jesus of their plans to make Him king, it seemed as if all his hopes and anticipations were to come true. He was shocked by the turn of events. He wanted time to think it over. Was this Jesus of Nazareth the Messiah after all—a man who did not know how to seize an opportunity when it was dropped in His lap? The seeds of doubt were there, but they were not yet fully germinated. Little did Judas realize how fearfully dangerous these seeds would be to him. He probably didn't understand any more than the other disciples did when Jesus said:

> "... 'Did I not choose you, the twelve, and one of you is a devil?' He spoke of Judas Iscariot, the son of Simon, for it was he who would betray Him, being one of the twelve" (John 6:70, 71).